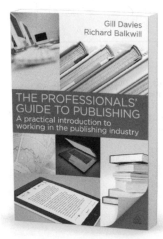

Gill Davies
Richard Balkwill

THE PROFESSIONALS'
GUIDE TO PUBLISHING
A practical introduction to
working in the publishing industry

The Professionals' Guide to Publishing

A practical introduction to working in the publishing industry

Gill Davies and
Richard Balkwill

Publisher's note

Every possible effort has been made to ensure that the information contained in this book is accurate at the time of going to press, and the publishers and authors cannot accept responsibility for any errors or omissions, however caused. No responsibility for loss or damage occasioned to any person acting, or refraining from action, as a result of the material in this publication can be accepted by the editor, the publisher or either of the authors.

First published in Great Britain and the United States in 2011 by Kogan Page Limited

120 Pentonville Road	1518 Walnut Street, Suite 1100	4737/23 Ansari Road
London N1 9JN	Philadelphia PA 19102	Daryaganj
United Kingdom	USA	New Delhi 110002
www.koganpage.com		India

© Gill Davies and Richard Balkwill, 2011

The right of Gill Davies and Richard Balkwill to be identified as the authors of this work has been asserted by them in accordance with the Copyright, Designs and Patents Act 1988.

ISBN   978 0 7494 5541 5
E-ISBN   978 0 7494 6258 1

British Library Cataloguing-in-Publication Data

A CIP record for this book is available from the British Library.

Library of Congress Cataloging-in-Publication Data

Davies, Gill, 1945-
  The professionals' guide to publishing : a practical introduction to working in the publishing industry / Gill Davies, Richard Balkwill.
      p. cm.
   ISBN 978-0-7494-5541-5 – ISBN 978-0-7494-6258-1
 1. Publishers and publishing. 2. Book industries and trade. I. Balkwill, Richard. II. Title.
 Z278.D38 2011
 070.5023–dc22

                                        2010043455

Typeset by Saxon Graphics Ltd, Derby
Printed and bound in India by Replika Press Pvt Ltd

CONTENTS

ACKNOWLEDGEMENTS

While working on such a wide-ranging book it has sometimes been necessary to step outside our own direct experience of being publishers and to ask for help and advice, both of which have been generously given by many friends and colleagues in the industry.

Gill Davies would like to thank all the people who have helped her, directly and indirectly, and they are (in alphabetical order): Will Atkinson (Faber & Faber), Jacki Heppard (Institute of Mechanical Engineers), Rachel Maund (Marketability), Claire Round (Random House), Jane Seaman (Sage Publications) and Elisabeth Tribe (Hodder Education). She gives her greatest thanks to Brad Scott, the digital publishing consultant (Brambletye Publishing), for the endless amounts of help he gave, and patience he showed, during an intense exploration of digital content creation! She would also like to thank her friends for their everlasting encouragement and her students (past and present) for the pleasure of teaching publishing to them.

Richard Balkwill consulted many people, both formally and informally, some of whom may not have realized they were being asked. Mark Bide and Hugh Look at Rightscom gave him the tough 'post-publishing' criticism he needed, while William Shepherd, an almost exact contemporary, gave him his views and experience from the top of both big and small companies. At Hachette UK, Philip Walters and Lis Tribe provided great help and wise counsel on what is and isn't different about publishing today, and Alyssum Ross generously helped to complete his production journey from paste-ups and double-page spreads to InDesign and XML. To the Publishing Training Centre and three universities – Oxford Brookes, City, and the London College of Communication – he gives his thanks for countless opportunities to teach and learn with so many delegates and students.

Publishing – art or science?

Introduction

In a world informed at the speed of a push on a digital button, and with an audit society ever keener to measure performance and get results, you may have bought this book expecting it to contain *The Answer* – how to publish a string of profitable best-sellers, build a formidable list of prestigious loyal authors, and manage your business and its employees with effortless skill, leaving you with enough time to spare to become a celebrity and share your secrets with others ….

Why is it not like that? Why is there no easy answer or instant solution that points the golden way to success in publishing? One reason is that publishing is a complex network of processes and people over which the publisher does not have complete control, and where the room for error, or sheer bad luck, is enormous. The risks are many and varied, and while we are not pleading a special case for publishing – other professions, such as insurance or the financial services industry, are equally prone to risk – the length of its product development phase, its reliance on amateurs as the main source of supply (few authors are professional in the sense that they make their living from writing), and the fickle part played by consumers with a huge choice, all contribute to what one publisher described as the 'blunderbuss' approach: spraying a target with a scattered range of shot in the hope that at least some will hit the target, and be successful.

'The good old days'

Nostalgia for publishing's literary past is just as strongly felt as it is by those who look back on the long summer afternoon of imperial success and calm that preceded World War I – and it is just as false. Yet the reputation that publishing still has as a gentlemanly and leisurely affair, devoid of crude commerce, and a refuge for creative and sensitive people lingers on. It is certainly not like that now, and there is much evidence to suggest that it never was, except in the delightful fantasies of the 1960s recreated by Jeremy Lewis in *Playing for Time* and *Kindred Spirits*.

Apart from the university presses that were, as the name suggests, principally printers with a remit to publish their scholars' research or other writing, publishers were men (sic) who might have been booksellers (Macmillan started with bookshops in Cambridge and London), and who had a strong ambition to build a literary heritage. In the 19th century, Macmillan was responsible for bringing us Thomas Hardy, Rudyard Kipling and Lewis Carroll, and it was the members of the family – Frederick, Daniel and later Harold – who built the list with single-mindedness and an autocratic hand on the tiller. They employed readers to advise them, for sure, but theirs was not the world of market research, focus groups and consensus publishing. In the 20th century, men (again) with a singularity of cultural as well as literary purpose contributed equally to a great heritage – people like Andre Deutsch, Victor Gollancz and Jonathan Cape, though benign despots like Sir William ('Billy') Collins funded their publishing through a successful printing business (Collins Cleartype Press, with factories in Glasgow).

Yet many of these publishers suffered from the modern day problems of embarrassing gaps in cash flow, long lead times between commissioning a book and being paid for its sales, and a shaky track record of overall commercial performance. If you read Diana Athill's sharp memoir *Stet,* in which she describes working for Andre Deutsch – both the man and the firm – you will find the company nearly folded when it decided to publish Norman Mailer's *The Naked and the Dead,* not so much because the work was liberally sprinkled with the then unacceptable f-word as because its huge success, once published, incurred enormous printers' bills they could ill-afford in their parlous cash-strapped existence. They simply were not paid quickly enough by bookshops to finance the next large reprint: a sobering example of how difficult cash flow can be in any publishing business.

Publishing companies in the old days were largely inefficient and, by modern management standards, poorly run. That is because they were run by individual proprietors accountable only to themselves who looked to employ people who agreed with their vision and were prepared to work for ludicrously small salaries with the dubious reward of being involved in and helping to create that literary or cultural heritage.

Yet for many the attractions remained, perhaps based on the mistaken belief that their own literary aspirations would benefit from rubbing shoulders with brilliant authors. At the beginning of William Styron's masterpiece, *Sophie's Choice,* we find the narrator Stingo (a would-be writer) fantasizing in this way as he dreams of rubbing shoulders at parties with John Cheever and Mary McCarthy. In fact, he has a dead-end job reading (and generally turning down) mostly hopeless submissions to McGraw-Hill. His fortunes take a turn for the worse when he rejects Thor Heyerdahl's *Kon-Tiki Expedition.*

One or two records from those times are more accurate, and give a few clues to what publishing was like. In Sir Stanley Unwin's 1926 classic, *The Truth about Publishing* (still both readable and surprisingly relevant), he describes publishers and publishing in this way:

> Publishers are not necessarily either philanthropists or rogues. Likewise they are usually neither lordly magnates nor cringing beggars. As a working hypothesis, regard them as ordinary human beings trying to earn their living at an unusually difficult occupation. It is easy to become a publisher, but difficult to remain one; the mortality in infancy is higher than in any other trade or profession.

In the same book, Joseph Conrad's *Notes on Life and Letters* adds a further level to an understanding of the indelible passion for books and publishing that is still so widespread, though he does so unwittingly:

> Of all the inanimate objects, of all men's creations, books are the nearest to us, for they contain our very thought, our ambitions, our indignations, our illusions, our fidelity to truth and our persistent leaning toward error.

Of course, Conrad was referring to the error of what we write and thus believe; yet, as a metaphor for publishing – 'a persistent leaning toward error' – it will do us very well in this initial search for what it is that distinguishes publishing – if anything does – from other businesses.

The hierarchy legacy

Publishing used to display all that was bad about the class system in Britain and, some would say, still is. Ironically, of course, publishing was perceived as a trade that was deemed unacceptable by those educated at public schools and Oxford or Cambridge, and for whom the professions, the armed services, or colonial and government administration beckoned. However, because 'real' publishers supported and sponsored the growth of literary endeavour, they were sometimes regarded as acceptable in polite society.

The same was not true of publishers who produced educational textbooks, and even as late as 1961 Alan Hill, the legendary founder of Heinemann Educational Books, found himself at loggerheads with the literary establishment at the Publishers Association who regarded schoolbooks as both marginal and rather grubby. That hierarchy conveniently ignored the uncomfortable truth that the educational wing of a publisher often produced the margins and the cash that the 'real' publishers so desperately needed. The legacy such battles left can still be found in the continuing enthusiasm among university students to become editors in publishers producing literary fiction, drama or poetry – some of the financial graveyards of modern publishing.

Yet the best-run companies usually managed to combine at least two kinds of publishing in their business. For a time, Macmillan funded its ambitious long-term reference publishing in the shape of *Grove's Dictionary of Music and Musicians* with a successful scientific and medical journals business, having been the publishers of *Nature* since its inception in 1869. Subscriptions for the journals were paid in advance and, almost literally, this part of the company became the banker with the cash for the 5 to 10 years of evolution that a major reference work required. Before John Murray sold his business to Hodder Headline and Hachette, the two distinct parts of the company co-existed successfully, with a strong range of school textbooks providing backlist sales at good margins to support the high quality literary publishing that had included Lord Byron in the 19th century and John Betjeman in the 20th.

Editorial and marketing

The same hierarchy that existed in types of publishing and that made literary fiction somehow 'better' or at least 'more important' than, say, an engineering textbook was until recently replicated in the companies themselves. Editors were seen as having the most creative and interesting jobs, partly perhaps because they were the ones who dealt directly with the authors. This seemed to give them status and seniority. Elsewhere, we try to qualify and define those editorial roles, separating them into the entrepreneurial commissioning editor, the painstaking author-companion, shaping and encouraging the evolution of a book, and those meticulous terriers of detail, the copy-editors who never mis-spell *supersede* or *Middlesbrough*, and upon whom authors often depend when avoiding blunders of fact, grammar or spelling.

To the outside world, the brilliant editor is someone who spots the new best-seller, discovers the next fabulous children's writer, or against all the odds champions the next John Grisham or Stieg Larsson. The reality is more chancy, and the way is littered with famous rejections of subsequent classics and the downright lottery effect of some publishing. *Watership Down* was rejected by half a dozen household names in publishing before Rex Collings (not Collins), both the man and his publishing company, took a punt and printed a modest 2,000 copies of the book. It would be good to think that the excitement of risk was what attracted so many people to the editorial role in a publishing company, but it's more often association with success and fame, and the hope that you will help create that celebrity that draws the moths to the flame.

Reading A Scott Berg's biography of the legendary US editor Max Perkins, who worked alongside Scott Fitzgerald and James Thurber, tends to reinforce this belief that the creative role of the editor is on a par with that of a writer. Some would wish there was a deliberate blurring of roles, and that many a masterpiece is really down to the brilliance of the editor. In William Styron's *Sophie's Choice*, Stingo is an editor, but he would much rather be a writer – and in our experience failed or would-be writers make poor editors. In fact, although Max Perkins never wrote, he was famously a slow reader and a poor speller; but his reputation as the greatest editor of his day lives on.

On what, really, is that reputation based? Flair? Luck? The ability to spot a best-seller? *(How can you tell in advance?)* A brilliant judge of quality? *(What exactly is 'quality'?)* When David Fickling, in front of an audience consisting mainly of publishers was asked a few years ago to explain what it was he brought to the creative process as editor of Philip Pullman's work, he self-deprecatingly struggled. 'I don't really do anything.' *(Laughter)*. The author helped him out: 'You have the courage to tell me when something I'm writing isn't working, and I trust your judgement.'

In this editorial hierarchy, it is not really surprising that other functions have come to be regarded as service wings or technical and clerical support, largely removed from the glamour at the editorial centre. Sales and marketing were merely adjuncts to the business, making sure that the brilliant best-sellers reached their intended audience. A good leaflet, calling on bookshops or visiting schools to ensure the new list was being inspected, ensuring there were enough stocks to meet demand – these were operational details that had to be got right, but they were surely not the main part of the business. You must also face the question, 'Can you sell a bad book?' While it is true that a much-hyped first novel from a young, pretty or famous person will probably make it into the best-seller charts, his or her second book – if bad – probably won't. There has to be some real quality in its own field, be 'good of its kind'.

The production department was often similarly regarded as another service wing of the company, responsible only for ensuring the books were typeset and printed efficiently, and to schedule – even when those schedules had often been changed or shortened by inefficiency or self-indulgence on the part of authors and editors. Until quite recently, several large publishers were also their own printers. Two notable Scottish examples were Thomas Nelson and William Collins. At Nelson's Parkside works in Edinburgh, there was a door connecting the publisher's offices directly to the works. It was sometimes said that all the editorial director had to do, once a book had been accepted and edited, was to take it through the door to the foreman in charge of the works (who wore, we must assume, a brown coat) and place the manuscript in his hands with the words: 'Thank you, Mr Rogers. We'd like this to be 192 pages, please, and as nice as possible.'

This possibly apocryphal story highlights the 'oily rag' status of people in production departments. Like salespeople, they did the jobs that were necessary: estimating costs, buying paper, organizing typesetting, finding good (or cheap) printers, and recovering from delays usually caused by people or factors outside their control. Publishing certainly suffered from more than its fair share of traditional enmities, even if the parties in the opposing camps were sometimes little more than crude stereotypes. Editors were often regarded as hopelessly impractical, unaware of the realities of cost control and schedule adherence, ignorant of the dire effect a late change to a colour illustration could have on the profit margin, blissfully unaware of the likely reaction from a wholesaler when a key new title is announced as arriving three months late.

Like all generalizations, these hostilities often contained more than a grain of truth. Only a few years ago, the production department of a publisher of literary fiction in the Chicago region sported a large poster by the door showing a full-face portrait of Clint Eastwood in one of his most violent 'Dirty Harry' movies, armed with two lethal weapons, one in each hand, unshaven, and with a hard mean look in his cold grey eyes. Someone in the department had appended a caption below the picture. It read, simply: 'Go ahead. Make one last change ....'

We shall argue that much of what makes publishing distinct from other businesses is that its main role is a marketing one. But many would say that that is what any business does – brings to market what its customers want. The difference is that publishing faces two 'markets' – the market of its readers, certainly; but also the market of its authors. You will still hear authors speak about 'my publisher', almost as if they were saying 'my hairdresser' or 'my wine merchant'. So, does the author serve the publisher (by providing good material to publish) or does the publisher serve the author by making a good job of *publishing* (making public) an author's work? In a well-run publishing company, the relationship is mutual, with neither party the servant of the other. But it is as well to remember that the readers of a publisher's books are not the only market it serves.

In some US companies, new book publishing decisions are taken by the marketing department, leaving editors to be mere shapers and finishers of the product. In Europe, the editor usually has a far greater entrepreneurial role in determining the way markets are evolving, and in discovering and promoting new talent in the form of unknown and unpublished authors. Yet aside from specific roles within companies, we must acknowledge the central importance that marketing plays in publishing – not in the sense of promoting publications to potential customers by advertising them, but in defining what markets are, determining their size, and deciding what share of that market a publisher can reach with a range of publications.

We tend to think of marketing as getting the maximum number of units to the largest number of potential customers, but it may prove to be better for a small or medium-sized publisher to concentrate on reaching a large part of a very small or 'niche' market, than climbing on to the bandwagon of a publishing area already over-populated with successful competitors. The main change to the world of publishing since those legacy days has been the end of the general publisher – the corner grocery store that sold a bit of everything to everyone. Instead, there has been a greater focus and more specialization.

Even as late as the 1970s, Thomas Nelson & Sons, by then based in London, was at one and the same time a general trade publisher, an educational publisher, an academic publisher, an ELT publisher and even (through its Young World division) a children's publisher. Such diversity soon proved unsustainable, in profit terms, and the same policy has seen an international publishing group like Elsevier divest itself of its consumer division (to Random House) and its educational companies (to Pearson), leaving it as predominantly a supplier of specialist or research material (much of it in digital format) to the legal and scientific professionals. Defining and quantifying the commercial potential of markets has become the main objective of modern publishers.

What about quality?

If the publishing industry of 50 years ago to some extent reflected the class structure in Britain, it also displayed a perverse kind of snobbery. This in turn made reading and books seem to some people an elite pastime, indulged in by the literary few. A recent statistic suggested that a third of the population had never set foot in a bookshop. It is easy to make generalizations about falling standards of literacy, the decline of reading as an activity enjoyed by children, and the end of the printed book – and all of them are false. Literacy standards are about the same as they were 50 years ago, children remain voracious consumers of books, and the printed book is alive and well. Indeed in 2008 we published over 200,000 of them, compared to a mere 49,500 in 1980.

Labels like pulp fiction, pot boilers, aga sagas and chick lit suggest shorthand is widely used to distinguish different genres of publishing, but the phrases 'literary fiction' and 'Mills & Boon-type romances' bring this uncomfortable issue of snobbery to the fore, the implication being that literary fiction is somehow of greater quality than a Mills & Boon romance. Who decides what is good enough for publication, and what criteria do they use? Does 'good' mean 'of literary merit'? How can we tell if a short story published in *Granta* (a literary magazine produced in Cambridge) is better that a short story in *Woman's Weekly*? Given that the circulation of popular women's magazines is around 10 times greater than that for a literary magazine, where does this leave our judgement on quality? And how exactly do we judge what is meant by 'better'?

We discussed with a number of senior publishers and editors how they (or their professional readers) judged quality when it came to making a decision to publish something. Was it 'gut feeling' or 'flair'? Both these popular labels were discounted. Certainly experience of what readers had liked was a powerful guide to what would work in the future, yet as they pointed out very little new fiction is produced by means of groups of readers being consulted. Besides, the creative genius of successful writers probably stems from a solitary and personal gift.

At a meeting in Oxford in 2006, the celebrated children's writer Philip Pullman was asked by someone in the audience if he consulted his readers about what they wanted before writing a new book. A look of irritation if not anger passed quickly over this normally peaceable author's face before he replied:

> Writing is something you do on your own. It's a totalitarian activity – despotic, tyrannical even. It's driven by what my imagination comes up with. I cannot even predict what may come up next. Writing is not some democratic activity undertaken with discussion panels and focus groups.

The word that many publishers used when referring to successful writing was 'original'. They meant that something good always had a new feel to it, rather than a well-worn sense of familiarity from having been seen many times before. It did not have to be cranky or way out, and it had to be believable – *authentic* was a word one publisher used. The book had to 'ring true'. The subject of authenticity is well illustrated in *Ghost*, a 2007 thriller written by Robert Harris. The 'Ghost' of the title refers to a ghost writer called in to take over the job of ghost-writing the autobiography of a recently retired head of state. The existing draft has been rejected: it is apparently terrible. The new ghost writer reads it and reaches the same conclusion. He then reflects as follows:

> All good books are different, but all bad books are exactly the same …. What they all have in common, these bad books, be they novels or memoirs, is this: *they don't ring true*. I'm not saying that a good book *is* true necessarily, just that it *feels* true for the time you're reading it. A publishing friend of mine calls it the Seaplane Test, after a movie he once saw about people in the City of London that opened with the hero arriving for work in a seaplane he landed on the Thames. From then on, my friend said, there was no point in watching.

Yet alongside these criteria of originality and authenticity we must set the consistent popularity of the Mills & Boon-type romance. This mass market romantic fiction is written to tight guidelines and strictly imposed formulae, and writers must abide by rules that govern both the extent of graphic detail that is allowed in the book and the style and simplicity required of the writing. This is true marketing – a close observation of what readers want, and careful adherence to what has proved popular in the past.

So, we might define 'quality' as something that most closely meets the needs of the audience it is aimed at – the market – even if meeting sales figures after publication is the measure of that quality and success, rather than consultation prior to publication. Besides, it has been shown that if focus groups are not properly managed and given professionally prepared questions, there is a real danger that respondents will sometimes give the answer they believe you want to hear, rather than their true belief or feeling. This is especially true in matters of what people like to read. Many will tend to exaggerate the serious or 'literary' nature of what they might choose to read.

Perhaps quality in educational and academic publishing is an easier concept. Here the opinion of consultant advisers and experts is crucial when assessing if something will meet the needs of the market, even down to the question of whether or not a student using it will be able to pass an exam. Keeping close to a curriculum, or matching the needs of an examination or professional qualification, is one measure of quality. Another is an ability on the part of the writer to communicate well with learners. Thus high-level academic excellence is often not such a valuable asset in an author as his or her ability to think and write at the level of a young learner, especially when that student is following a course of study in a language (English, perhaps) that is not his or her mother tongue.

Given that measures of quality are so subjective it is hard to see how publishers can make judgements that stand objective or independent scrutiny. Yet if you consider any books you have judged as brilliant or excellent, think for a moment if they do not all, in some way, match the criterion either of creative originality (rather than derivative imitation), or of 'ringing true', being authentic to their own standards, in whatever genre of publishing.

Money

If quality and originality used to be judged by a small band of owner-proprietors, or a revered inner sanctum of editors, where did *money* come into it? Was publishing ever highly profitable? Could a publisher make his fortune by setting up a publishing company? The answer to both questions is probably 'no'. Certainly the bookkeeping and accounting functions in publishers of 50 years ago were handled by people with little or no say in directing the company. Like the production staff, the accounts department was perceived as a boring necessity.

The conditions for making a lot of money in publishing are generally unfavourable. Most publishers publish far too many titles, the majority of which break even (if you're lucky) with very few becoming best-sellers. Even best-sellers may not make money, given the huge level of discount required to reach the customer, the inflated advances on royalty demanded by the agents of some authors, and the high number of returns from retailers.

For a long time, prescribed textbooks for the school and college markets were a good source of profit, with annual reprints being produced in sufficient quantities to recover easily the high initial costs, and regularly turning in excellent margins. Serials publishing made good money, especially scientific print journals. Here, annual subscriptions paid in advance, rates rising steadily more than the prevailing inflation figure, and generally low production values combined to make many successful businesses.

High-price reference works, too, particularly in the field of legal and regulatory standards and procedures, had similar financial attractions: selling by direct mail to a small group of known and easily reachable professionals allowed low or no discounts, while the market buying the reference works was often using someone else's money, meaning that price levels were rarely seen as 'sensitive'.

Now in the digital era, many of these gold mines have been worked out. One essential feature of successful print publishing was being able to spread any high initial expenses over many reprints by amortizing the plant cost. Another was to charge a high price for a one-off sale, either because the customer had to have the information contained in the publication, or did not mind what his or her firm would have to pay for it. New cohorts of pupils and students ensured the educational market had an endless supply of new customers, while changes to the law ensured customers of legal and regulatory information had to buy new versions of the book to keep up to date.

The digital environment relies on site licences or usage measures for its revenue, and the margin of price over cost has become harder to predict, as there are no unit sales to count any more. Publishers will tell you that the development cost of digital products – whether e-journals, website content, or supplements to print publications – always end up costing more than expected, planned or budgeted. Increasingly, publishers are being forced to add value without increasing the price they charge to recover the costs of those added-value items. Some are turning successfully to charging for complementary publishing, and outsiders like Google are already profitable through providing content free while charging for advertising associated with or attached to that content.

So far no mention has been made in this section about the main source of the raw material that publishers need for their business to operate: intellectual property that, initially at least, belongs to someone else – authors. Cynics might point to the wealth of publishers, such as they have any, and declare that it derives from a long history of being less than fair in terms of the money paid to their authors. In their defence, publishers are said to take all the financial risk from authors by investing in their book. Therefore, the argument runs, it is reasonable for publishers to determine what share of the margin and profits they generate can be shared with those authors.

The model that seems fairest is one that allows authors to retain copyright in what they have written, grant the publisher an exclusive licence to publish their work, and share in a portion of the proceeds in the form of royalties as and when the book sells. The position of the struggling writer paid a small one-off fee and being required to assign copyright to the publisher may, at first sight, seem less fair. Most academic researchers submitting articles for learned journals don't even get paid for their work, yet still have to assign their copyright.

However, relatively few writers are professional in the sense that they largely or exclusively write for a living. Realistically, the economics of much book publishing do not allow writers to gain a decent living wage, unless they are well established with a backlist of titles still selling well, plus income from some subsidiary rights deals. As a despairing publisher said to an author who was complaining about the terms of the contract: 'If you don't like the terms, you don't have to sign the contract!'

Until recently, alternative routes to market for authors were a lot worse, financially. So-called vanity publishers sometimes charged as much as £6,000 to an author desperate to see his or her autobiography in print, and then delivered low-quality finished books, lacking any professional layout or design and riddled with editorial solecisms, such as 'King Edward 8' or 'the local registry office'. Now competent and affordable processes of self-publishing are becoming available, and the likes of Author House, Lulu and even Flickr provide a genuine service.

Back in the accounts department of most publishers, the headaches of cash flow are never far away. A relatively modest advance of £5,000 paid to an author, even if split 25 per cent on signature, 25 per cent on receipt of an acceptable typescript, and 50 per cent on publication still requires cash to fund these payments, as well as cash to pay for the pre-press costs, and settle most of the printer's bill before any wholesaler or retail bookseller has managed to pay for copies sold, leaving aside the additional headache of returns.

Those publishers that have succeeded, especially small and medium-sized enterprises, tend to be extremely conservative (in the literal sense) of cash, modest in the way they run their business, and thrifty (if not mean) when it comes to staff salaries. An owner-proprietor publisher once said: 'I have been successful because at all stages I always treated the money as if it was my own. That's because for most of my early days, it was my own.' Another small publisher who owns her own business bemoaned the problems she faced in growing the company:

> A wonderful opportunity comes up to publish a good author who is offering us (and our competitors) an excellent new proposal. The project goes to auction, and we do not have the resources to bid for it. Rather, we do have the resources – but only if we do not pay the staff any wages that month.

Publishing has acquired a reputation for paying well below what could be earned in other professions like accountancy or law. Nevertheless, the half dozen universities in the UK that offer a publishing MA degree course are never short of students eager to get started in the business. There are many stories of even quite modest job advertisements promising low salaries and (recently) only short-term appointments, receiving 60 to 100 applications, often from people seriously over-qualified for the post.

What *is* it that draws so many people to the publishing industry? If it's not well paid, often not very well run, is it just that making books is more enjoyable or rewarding (in the non-financial sense) than making steel girders or selling insurance policies or managing investment and savings accounts? It may be that the last two sections of this chapter will give you a clue.

Risk and luck

Are successful publishers, or editors with good reputations, skilled at taking risks, or just plain lucky? The publishers we spoke to acknowledged that their success was often down to both these things – assessing risk and taking a chance, and being lucky. The luck was often a matter of timing, not of the brilliant masterpiece dropping on to the editor's desk. Sometimes a one-off opportunity might crop up, or good research might produce knowledge of a change to curriculum or exam syllabuses before anyone else got wind of it.

In February 1971, the UK changed its currency from the old familiar (but complicated) pounds, shillings, and pence to a decimal currency, whereby 100 new pennies make a pound. An educational publisher at the time saw this event coming, and published a 32-page consumable workbook entitled, simply, *New Pence Workbook*. It sold and reprinted hundreds of thousands of copies, as every primary school pupil in the country needed to grasp the way the new money worked. In 2005 a plethora of publications appeared to mark the 200th anniversary of the great sea battle at Trafalgar, and the death of Admiral Lord Nelson.

To some degree, then, it is possible to manufacture luck, or to prepare for events and turn good fortune in your direction, by anticipating opportunities. What about risk assessment? An intangible skill in publishing is most definitely the weighing up of risks and the commitment to a plan, once that risk has been analysed and the decision taken. We also need to distinguish between uncertainty and calculable or manageable risk. Much of good publishing can result from the discovery or resolution of unknown or uncertain facts, and the consequent reduction of high risk. Yet this risk is rarely if ever along the lines of choosing a set of random lottery numbers, going for black 35 on the roulette wheel, or backing the outsider in the Grand National that comes in first (or more often doesn't) at odds of 100 to 1.

Some of the management skills that have been developed in big business have been incorporated into some bigger publishers. Scenario planning is a technique that identifies a range of possible long-term opportunities, then analyses and tries to quantify the fixed or known data, the main uncertainties, the riskiest moments in a project's evolution, the key drivers for change, and the choice of likely or probable outcomes. These are often carried out against a cost risk – what would need to be spent, and what would be the scale of loss, if a certain outcome was not achieved? How much would be lost if the project was abandoned at certain points? From this last assessment of when to abandon a project that is not going to be successful, we assume the phrase 'cutting your losses' owes its origins.

Evaluation of data will reduce risk but it will never remove it, and for those who like to be in possession of all the facts before making any decision, publishing will prove a disappointing and frustrating career. Some of the most meticulously researched and analysed opportunities still fail to deliver the windfall successes that are expected, or – worse – have been promised to the main board directors and shareholders. Yet unlikely or marginal publishing proposals can sometimes hit the jackpot.

In 2003, Lynne Truss wrote (and Profile Books published) a book about punctuation and grammar entitled *Eats Shoots and Leaves*. Although there were several good, even better, books on the subject already on the market, this book was a phenomenal success, hitting the best-seller lists that Christmas to the point where everyone was getting or being given a copy. Why was it such a success? Perhaps it was that the author was already an established writer and broadcaster. Possibly the clever title helped. As it stands, the words of the title define the habits of a panda. With the addition of commas (*'Eats, Shoots, and Leaves'*) it could refer to a bank robber at a service station restaurant ordering a hamburger, being challenged by police, firing a gun and making a hasty escape.

The truth is that in trade and consumer publishing, success and popularity can be the result of a sudden but overwhelming trend or fashion. The characteristics of these mega successes are that they are more often than not one-offs. Like shooting stars, they rise dazzlingly into the sky and then almost as quickly fall back and disappear. Sustaining these successes is part of the challenge in managing risk and luck, and the outstanding international success of J K Rowling's *Harry Potter* books, although greatly enhanced by the spectacular films, is to some extent based on the fact that the books form a sequence, thus raising expectations and creating demand by the prospect of the next book and the continuation of the story.

As with the runaway success enjoyed by Lynne Truss's book, humour and originality also play a part. Consider the eccentric genius of Roddy

Bloomfield, an editor at Stanley Paul (part of Random House), who decided to publish a book called *Fly Fishing by J R Hartley*, having seen (as we all had) the television advertisement for 'Yellow Pages' in which a tweed-jacketed author holding the Yellow Pages telephone directory in the comfort of his sitting-room is apparently phoning his local bookshop to enquire if they have a copy of *Fly Fishing by J R Hartley* – clearly the book he himself has written. In the fickle world of consumer publishing, such a charming oddball publishing 'policy' certainly has its place.

Relationships

As we suggested at the beginning of this chapter, the relationship between author and publisher, between Thomas Hardy and Frederick Macmillan, was at the heart of success in publishing when proprietors were also men (sic) of letters. How important are relationships in multinational companies publishing editions simultaneously in several parts of the world? It is likely that the authors will be in one country (Spain, let's say), the pre-press typesetters producing finished pages as digital files in another (India, perhaps), and the printers in yet another (China probably, if colour is involved). Despite this international (or 'intranational') process, which we explore later in the book, all publishers will emphasize the importance of strong personal relationships within a company. Why?

It has been said that publishing is a complex and lengthy process in which many of the participants and stakeholders are remote from the publisher's office, and not controlled or answerable to that publisher. If you ask someone who knows nothing about the publishing business to explain what it is that a publisher actually does, he or she may well struggle. After all, publishers are neither authors nor printers. In most cases they aren't booksellers either. To say they add value by investing in someone else's ideas and distribute the end result into ultimate consumption sounds very weak, worse than the generalizations to be found in a *Ten Minute Manager* guide. They are certainly investors and bankers, as well as risk takers. But they are also highly skilled managers, directing a process with many stages and levels, and over which they do not exercise direct control.

A lot of professional relationships in publishing have to be based on respect and trust. Publishing is probably the antithesis of the armed services, where seniority of rank and direct reporting via line managers is the norm. On the other hand, friendly and informal requests for help, or appealing to someone's good nature, will not do as management techniques either. An editor trying to persuade a production manager to keep to a schedule while delivering a typescript three weeks late, or begging a marketing director to postpone an advertising campaign because the book's running late, requires a special kind of personal and persuasive negotiating skill if he or she is to succeed.

Where authors are concerned, a lot of the skills an editor needs are what might be called *social skills*. Having the confidence to approach an eminent but unknown author at a conference, being clear-headed enough to make a pitch for your company with only the briefest of opportunities, and remaining polite and realistic with your promises – these require a personality that does not flinch from chatting up strangers, and can keep figures and contract details in your head (or at your fingertips). An editor once described his success at finding new projects and commissioning new authors as very similar to his ability to hitchhike:

> You need to know where the best sites are for getting a lift. Both editing and hitchhiking need patience and determination. You need to make close eye contact with your lift. You have to be able to talk to all kinds of people, and appear interested or objective when they talk about themselves or a pet interest.

These social, or relationship, skills are important in all parts of a publishing company. Tasks and responsibilities are fragmented and distributed over a wide range of different people and, often, a variety of locations. In Chapter 3 we look at the concept of the editor as the hub of a wheel, centrally involved if not responsible for liaison with the author, publishing services, production, sales and marketing, even the finance department. Responsibility for decisions across groups is hard to achieve in a formal or structural way – the promotions assistant does not work for or report to the editors, yet what is needed in terms of a publicity leaflet may need to be agreed with editors, and they may want to use their influence (if not their authority) in determining where the assistant fits the job into his or her timetable and workload. Once again, personal persuasion is crucial.

The old 'corner-shop' publisher tended to be more flexible about who did what jobs, and in small companies a lot of doubling up was done – an editor might help to sort out addressograph plates[1] for a school mailing, while being taught later in the afternoon how to do a cast-off[2] or learn what an imposition scheme[3] looked like. In big companies today, there are sometimes 'silos' of job function in which people stick closely to the part of the process for which they are responsible, making it hard for them sometimes to relate to other departments, or have any real knowledge or appreciation of what exactly their colleagues are doing.

Such working relationships and professional collaborations are important when the pressure is on to complete a job in a short time-frame – the so-called 'fast track' route. A trend in recent years has been to outsource functions in a publishing company, especially production, pre-press or development phases. Some academic and professional publishers have transferred the pre-press stage of all their projects to a big facilities company, such as HCL Industries in India. Although there are clear cost benefits, the companies contracted to do this work are not some kind of third world sweatshop: on the contrary, those undertaking this work are highly professional operators working in air-conditioned modern offices.

The challenge that outsourcing faces is how to manage a large number of complex projects at a distance. The process works best when projects or publications are all produced to a small number of standards and formats. This allows common briefings, and yields benefits in speed and efficiency once those undertaking the work have been trained and have grown proficient at managing the various stages for which they are responsible.

Outsourcing sales and distribution to a dedicated logistics operation is another common method of handling standard or repetitive processes. Besides, most small and medium-sized publishers can no longer afford to handle all the stages of fulfilment – storage, order processing, packing and dispatch, invoicing and collection, and credit control. For international sales, remote or shared facilities are often the most practical way of earning extra sales, so long as the cost per unit does not exceed the commission charged by the distribution company.

The word 'relationship' implies that people working together in publishing companies remain on good terms. Certainly, most people have enjoyed working with publishers because the atmosphere is friendly, and the environment perhaps less cut-throat than the world of financial services or stocks and shares. Historically, this attitude has sometimes led to dangerous assumptions, the most frequent of which was so-called company loyalty.

Under this dubious banner, people were so grateful to be working in the hallowed halls of publishing, as often as not working with if not for the eponymous proprietor of the firm, that they gratefully accepted what were sometimes derisory salaries, and never thought of asking for a review or an increase (this would, it was assumed, be in very poor taste). The result was unfair, and led to a pattern in which salary levels fell and stayed well below what a first-class graduate could expect to be paid in other professions. A consequence of this was sometimes that a newcomer, once he or she had learnt the ropes and gained on-the-job training, would soon apply for (and get) a job at another company. This was sometimes the only way to increase your salary. The cost to the company through the rapid turnover of good recruits was usually dismissed with the argument that 'there are always plenty of new recruits eager to join'.

This *laissez-faire* attitude to building up people as assets of a successful publishing company has perpetuated the overall low level of training opportunities, as well as a lack of common work standards, still less qualifications. The publishing industry has come near to celebrating its amateur status, and in some quarters an absence of professionalism can be shown to have lost companies money. A few years ago an initiative was set up to formalize standards for certain key jobs in publishing. The Publishing Qualifications Board offered a process whereby people could work towards gaining an NVQ (a National Vocational Qualification) in their job, whether commissioning editor or rights executive.

Managers in publishing generally welcomed the standards – the formal description of what an editor actually does, for example – but begrudged the time it took for candidates to amass the evidence needed to show that they were indeed competent in the job, and eligible to gain the qualification. The process was not widely adopted, and has since disappeared. It was as if publishing managers were saying:

> We have never had to struggle for new recruits. We would rather train them up when they join in the way our company does things. If we gave them time out to get a professional qualification, it would probably make them more attractive to one of our competitors. If they leave after a short time, there are always plenty of others we can appoint.

In other words, most publishers regard formal qualifications as more of a risk than a way of improving standards or the quality of work within the company. A less charitable view might be that the old snobbery had reappeared. A senior manager at the time dismissed the whole idea of NVQs with the words, 'Isn't that what shelf-stackers in supermarkets have to get?'

Conclusion

We have tried in this chapter to capture the way that working in a publishing company is distinctive by highlighting some of the qualities that seem to make a good publisher. Some of the attributes we have identified are to do with personal and social skills. Publishing is indeed reliant on good working relationships, and not just between editor and author. We have tried to stress that publishing is, above all, a marketing job. But we have also been at pains to underline the risky nature of the business, partly because a large segment of it – trade and consumer publishing for adults and children – is linked to an economy where fashion, taste and personal whim play an important part.

Finally, we asked a group of senior managers in publishing for their views of what makes a 'good' publisher. Below, you will find a non-attributed range of the most common and most strongly felt responses. In the acknowledgements on page viii you will see some of the names of those who made them. We are grateful for their views.

> Luck, of course, plays a part. We're not so sure about 'flair' or 'nous', unless these are shorthand for intelligence, talent and common sense, or code words for market knowledge and awareness, and long-term experience. A despairing marketing director once asked why we didn't just publish the best-sellers, and not bother with the rest. Today, some sectors in publishing have established the principles of market research, focus groups, customer analysis and reams of data to support every publishing proposal.
>
> Yet, frustratingly, if you analyse the way best-sellers were developed and published, many appear to contradict the rules for success. Some were of course famously rejected by dozens of publishers before hesitantly or grudgingly being allowed to see the light of day. Others were late, over-length, over-budget, involved copious author rows and legal near-misses, yet still went on to join that hall of fame.
>
> So, what do you think? What skills and qualities does the successful publisher (person or company) need in order to find and secure the winners, the steady best-sellers, the valuable long-term assets, and the cash cows? Please send us your thoughts: a single word, 10 bullet points, a page of credo, even reflections on what publishing isn't – we don't mind.

Some of the key conclusions were:

- Knowledge of markets, immersion in them, empathy for them – yet an ability to judge them objectively.

- Commercial ability, and a knowledge of the financial consequences of your decisions.
- Having the courage to be original without necessarily being cranky or eccentric.
- Strong analytical skills: using the past for information, but not depending on it.
- Recruiting the right authors, communicating well with them, and persuading them of the value the publisher's role brings to the process.
- Open to creative ideas and arguments from colleagues.
- Having more than one thing on your side – a definite element of (managed) luck.
- Capacity for enjoyment, and in finding reward from making a difference (eg, to children's learning).
- Willingness to take and see through manageable risks.
- Persistence in the belief that a project should proceed and finish, once the case for it has been successfully argued.
- Understanding the need to satisfy two markets – customers and authors.
- Clear strategic goals that are not just financial.
- Developing and managing interpersonal skills to creative ends.
- Realizing that customers are often not end-users.

Further reading

Athill, D (2000) *Stet*, Granta Books, Cambridge
Lewis, J (1995) *Kindred Spirits*, HarperCollins, London
Styron, W (1967) *Sophie's Choice*, Penguin Books, London
Unwin, S (1926/1990) *The Truth about Publishing*, Lyons & Burford, New York

Notes

1 Playing-card-sized metal plates with names and addresses embossed onto them; selected plates are placed in a grid, inked, and the impression printed on to pre-positioned envelopes for promotional mailings.

2 Estimating how the number of sheets of a manuscript or typescript will translate into a (different) number of pages in a printed book.

3 In sheet-fed printing, 32 or 64 pages are printed on a single large sheet of paper (both front and back) known as a signature. The imposition scheme is a key that shows how each of the pages must be positioned in advance – which way up, which way round, and on which side of the sheet. This is done before each signature is printed so that, when the sheet is folded and trimmed, the pages all read in the correct sequence.

Publishing as a business

02

Introduction

In less than 100 years publishing has changed from a craft industry led by individuals who owned their publishing houses and followed their interests and enthusiasms, to one now dominated by giant international publishing corporations. Yes, small publishers still exist, and often snap around the heels of the giant corporations proving that lashings of money do not necessarily produce the most interesting or successful books. By and large, however, only the corporations are able to have access to the kind of resources that can fund big advances for big authors, flashy and extensive marketing to sell their books, and teeth-grindingly high discounts for book retailers. Publishing is just another example of an industry with polar extremes. There is one significant difference: Rolls Royce can charge premium prices for its cars, unlike the Ford Motor Company. In publishing, the equivalents of RR and Ford have to charge roughly the same prices for their books. In that sense, there is very little exclusivity in publishing: books are books as far as the average buyer is concerned. A common sense necessity to follow business principles and practices, therefore, tends to unite all independent publishers apart from the truly eccentric, and the very rich. The big corporations appear to think only in terms of business principles.

Ownership

There are still publishing houses owned by individuals, and by families or friends. In a few cases, such as Faber & Faber and W W Norton, part-ownership is also in the hands of staff. Private owners will be as concerned as investors that their publishing house does not make a loss, has sufficient resources to employ good-quality staff and to be able to attract and reward good authors. However, they have far more freedom than a house that is owned by an investment company or shareholders, or whose existence is dependent on loans from a bank. The difference concerns accountability. In a private company one can make quick decisions, provide rapid, often informal, feedback, usually in face-to-face settings. The owners are either a comparatively small team, or just one person. If you are short of money, as many independent publishers are, you might wonder if this really is freedom.

Once ownership moves up from that fairly basic but recognizably human level to something larger and more complex, you will find that systems of accountability need to be put in place. Without systems, it is harder to keep track of what individuals are up to in larger companies. Not only does your company need to be transparently correct and honest in its financial accounting, but it has to become accomplished in explaining the way it does business, and why, to people who may have never worked in publishing and have very little knowledge of it. Explaining your company and its results is one consequence that flows from broader ownership. Accepting that the owners need to know and understand how the business is working is another necessary demand on you. It's quite understandable that publishers might not like people who know nothing or little about publishing 'sticking their noses in' or being critical, but if you ask or want people to invest in you and your publishing judgements, then you must accept their needs too. It is their money that you are using, after all.

Ownership, and its consequences, takes one of the following forms. Private ownership is classically a publishing house *set up and, usually, run by the founder,* although it could mean ownership by a small group of people. This person has had sufficient private funds to cover the running costs, including during the early period of the house's life when there are still no books to publish. Authors have been found and contracted but they have yet to finish writing, and then the books have to go through the production cycle. This can be a long, drawn-out period with nothing but costs and no income coming in. Either this person is genuinely rich and has no financial worries, or he or she has been lent money by a friend or relative. In the latter circumstances, the owner and the lender need to be quite open and honest about the status of this loan. Is it a gift for ever? Does it have to be returned within a specified time period? Is interest going to be paid on it? You can well imagine how misunderstandings, indeed arguments, can arise if this has not been made absolutely clear from the start. Quite often these beginnings can be spontaneous and enthusiastic and little attention is given to anything quite as coarse as money. Publishing interesting books is all that matters.

Private ownership can also have created its financial underpinnings by persuading *a bank to provide it with a loan.* Here the bank will make absolutely sure what the status of this loan is. A period for repayment will be specified, as indeed will the interest to be paid on it and when. Banks usually require some sort of collateral against a substantial loan, that is, something of value in the possession of the owner of the publishing house, which the bank can sell should the publishing house fail and be unable to pay back the loan. A surprising number of private owners have taken the risk of placing their own homes as collateral, thereby rendering themselves and their families homeless should the company fail. Would you consider doing something this risky? If so, you would need to ask yourself if you are, a) reckless, b) driven by an idea you know will succeed, or c) reckless and driven. Whichever way you look at this, it is very risky.

Private ownership can also be *funded by private equity companies,* which are investment companies providing sufficient money to fund the running costs of enterprises. The private equity companies have access to large amounts of cash, supplied by individuals who like to invest in entrepreneurship. This sounds an ideal situation. A publishing house can get access to money provided by people who understand business, unlike the banks! The substantial drawback here is that the private equity company will set a time limit on its investment, which is commonly about five years. Everyone knows that at the end of five years the company will be put on the market and sold. The difference between the sale price that is realized and what the private equity company first invested is the profit, and the raison d'être of the existence of these investment companies. They don't do this for love. Of course the original owners will share in that profit, but anyone entering into such a bargain needs to understand that the company will belong to someone else five years later, unless you can find money from somewhere else to pay off the investment company. You may be richer, but perhaps your heart will be a little broken.

Private ownership can convert to *public ownership* some years after a house has been founded. If a publishing house has traded very successfully for sufficient years for everyone to believe that it is now properly embedded and developed (anywhere between 5 and 10 years), then it can 'go to the market'. Here the company goes to the stock market and invites potential shareholders to invest in it, thereby creating many more owners of the company. A share is literally a share in the ownership of the business. This is a wonderful way of taking in potentially huge amounts of cash from the sale of shares to the shareholders, and also persuading the business market to take one's publishing house very seriously. But it does have downsides. The first is that it creates a whole class of owners of your house who are probably not familiar with publishing but like the idea of investing in books. The second is that these people will require accountability from you, meaning that you are in all respects answerable to them for your results and therefore your publishing decisions. The third is that your results are publicized far more than they would ever be if the company were in private ownership, leading to criticism or speculation even when the results are good. Think of how the results of Bloomsbury were picked over during the *Harry Potter* period: when they were outstanding, the company was constantly put under pressure to reveal how it would invest its profits, and then later, how it would cope when *Harry Potter* was no more.

The reason we've spent time considering ownership is because publishing, although a business, is unlike many mainstream businesses. You need to understand the nature of ownership and its consequences, because the business of publishing is based on a series of quite small-scale investment decisions. These investment decisions concern the choice of books to be published. Publishing houses can be making anything between tens and hundreds of such investment decisions during the course of the year, depending on their size. This makes publishing very different from other mainstream businesses, because they simply do not invest in so many products.

Publishers in practice require a large degree of freedom to make these decisions. Imagine trying to consult your shareholders over every book you want to contract. Surely there are enough professional publishers involved already in the process of deciding what books to publish. The requirement for this freedom, therefore, is reasonable, but when shareholders, or a bank, or a private equity company back you by providing you with this freedom, think how upset all these people will be when your results are poor! Of course, this does not in itself make publishing different from other businesses but there is an inherent potential for conflict here in that publishers still demand freedom to choose what they publish. This independence of thought and choice is still inseparably associated with publishing in a way that is absent in, for example, the business of supermarkets or car makers. In a sense, publishing is 'loaded' with ethical, social, cultural and intellectual connotations. What publishing wants is owners that understand that special position, and it does not always get them.

Ownership defines what you have and what you can get. Let's look first at a small, independent publishing house. The average owner (or small group of owners) has limited resources for everything. This would include buying or renting property for the company, paying salaries and government employment taxes, furniture and furnishings, computers and broadband, telephones (land lines and mobiles), heating and lighting, facility overheads, and expenses (travel and publishers' lunches, for example). Until you have set up a company, you have no idea just how much 'stuff' an office needs. It also has limited resources for paying advances and royalties to authors and marketing campaigns. The cost of selling and distribution is usually based on payment by results (this is covered later in Chapter 5, on sales) but a small publisher must make sure it is not paying one penny more than it should for any transaction. Furthermore, it must produce its books as efficiently as possible to try to save money, and sometimes it will need to calculate what bills it can afford to pay on time and what might be a little late, for which it will apologize profusely to the supplier. In short, the speed with which cash moves in and out of the small publishing business is as real and as pressing as it might be with your own bank account. However, no one is telling the small publisher what to publish. It has freedom of choice but, sadly, very little resources to help it exercise it fully.

Classically, small independent publishers constantly live on their wits and in the hope that there are authors out there who would like to publish in a small publishing home where they might feel comfortable, instead of in the comparative loneliness of a vast corporation. Lynne Truss's extraordinarily successful book *Eats Shoots and Leaves* is a very good example of an author opting to join forces with a small publisher that had the wit to realize that a book on the apostrophe might strike a chord with readers and then bring originality and vigour to its sales and marketing campaign. Likewise, *Harry Potter* also did not start life in a huge publishing corporation. Both houses chose to publish books for which they did not have massive expectations and were nicely taken by surprise. A publishing corporation would have demanded those massive expectations before proceeding – and lost out because of this.

The corporation is in the reverse situation. It has, by comparison, access to very large amounts of resources, whether it is a private corporation (they do exist) or is owned by shareholders. Whereas the small house is hoping to grab a few winners, which others have overlooked, the corporations are able to smash their way to the 'Big Books' by offering lucrative deals to successful authors and rather large discounts to the retail sector. They are in a better position to throw this kind of money at a product than the small houses, although this should not excuse a careless or cavalier attitude towards the company's money. A company that has become big wishes to remain big, and in that sense its investment decisions will reflect that position. A big corporation is not interested in 'good enough' books, or 'useful' books, or books that challenge convention. The greatest numbers of readers for books do not lie at the periphery of the market: they occupy the centre ground. To remain big, therefore, one is going to invest in books that happily meet the needs of most people, and you find them mostly in the middle ground.

Being big or small does not automatically determine whether you are in a better position to publish 'good' books or not. Examples of good books lie in either camp, as do bad books. All we can say here, without going into deep philosophical waters about whether size has an impact on excellence, is that in publishing, size will determine many of your investment decisions because of the inevitable connection between size and availability of resources, ie money!

Risk

It is perhaps in the attitude to risk that observers have seen some of the greatest changes in investment decisions in publishing. For much of the latter half of the 20th century, those who worked in publishing were influenced by the editor's enthusiasm and commitment shown towards a book that he or she wished to contract. The prime position of the editor contrasted with the relative unimportance of marketing. An editor who was determined to contract a particular book would, therefore, succeed in getting agreement from colleagues. The period of the 1970s and 80s was a time of growing general affluence and expanding budgets in the public sector. For publishers this meant that there was money around for buying books for libraries, universities and schools. It also meant that editors could be a little experimental occasionally in their choice of books, and management could afford to let them support less-than-obvious money spinners. Some of these 'sleepers' enjoyed great success. The ones that failed pushed their editors further up the learning curve. As they say, one learns most from one's mistakes.

Towards the end of the 20th century two things of major importance happened to publishing. The first was that public-sector budgets came under pressure and books were bought far more sparingly by libraries and educational institutions. This first issue was connected to the general health of the country's economy. The second was the growth of globalization as a business movement. We are all very familiar with the growth of international brands to achieve predominance, but for publishers there was another issue involved and that related to the fullest possible exploitation of copyrights. Copyrights are valuable. They do not reside just within books, but offer the possibility of even greater revenue to be gained by the selling of rights in those books for transformation into films, television and non-terrestrial media, as well as translations. Later, rights began to be exploited in digital forms. With this vision of even greater income, large publishers decided that they would like to control the publication of their books on a worldwide level. They decided not to sell rights to local publishers around the world but to exploit their books themselves. Many began the process of setting up their own overseas offices.

To gain an even bigger share of the market, and driven by that decision to keep control of exploitation, the larger houses started to buy up small houses. They got bigger and bigger and it is quite difficult now to try to remember who bought what and when! Their behaviour, however, had one aim in mind: to grow and to dominate, internationally.

What has this to do with risk? When a company is enormous, its size begins to influence not just its determination to remain big, which we mentioned earlier, but also the way in which it functions. Big companies inevitably become bureaucratic. No more living for the moment and by the seat of one's pants. They have strict divisions of function. Unlike a small house where the editorial director may be examining manuscripts in the morning but then being begged to come and help out stuff leaflets into envelopes in the afternoon, everyone in a big organization knows exactly what his or her job is supposed to be and is not encouraged to deviate from that. You can understand why. On that organizational scale, things would quickly degenerate into chaos.

Every large department within that company will have its own plans and management. There is nothing inherently wrong with this level of good organization, but it can lead to a tendency to demand that everything fits into the mould, and that can include books. In the larger companies far more time will be spent on issues such as:

- Does this book fit in closely with our lists and our future plans?
- Will it generate sufficient income and profit?
- Will this book help increase our share of the market?

Again, there is nothing whatsoever inherently wrong in any of these questions, but they can lead to the exclusion of books that, with everyone prepared to live with a bit of uncertainty and take a risk, could prove money makers. *Harry Potter, Eat Shoots and Leaves* and earlier, *The Diary of Adrian Mole* all fall into this category. However, *The Da Vinci Code* does not. In this case, a particularly experienced editor with a fantastic 'nose' for a commercial book could see its potential and, given his record, the company could back him. One could also perhaps say in respect of that book is that it is transparently 'commercial'!

There are always exceptions to the rule, and until recently the rule has been that the bigger houses will be more cautious. In a small house it is possible, and likely, that those involved will be more prepared to back a hunch. Each has its place as a way of publishing, but it is interesting that, for example, Random House has decided to let all its imprints function as though they are completely independent houses in order to ensure that independent thinking and vigour guide its investment decisions.

What we can say of risk and its relation to size is that the latter inevitably will influence the former. Yet publishing cannot live without risk. We never know until a book has finally hit the marketplace whether it will succeed because we can never quite second-guess what our market really wants, however much we have submitted every potential new book to detailed examination. 'Does it tick all the boxes?' Sadly, too many publishers try to copy success, thinking that the market will want more of the same, thereby eliminating risk, so they believe, in their investment decisions. Think of the succession of celebrity biographies and celebrity novels that have been rolled out. Eventually, book buyers get bored with the same old thing. Even in specialist publishing the same attitude exists. This approach leads to endless publishing of textbooks.

There is definitely a need for textbooks, but believing that if you publish textbooks you will be 'safe' is also a mistake: this is an exceptionally competitive area where many textbooks will remain unadopted. Textbook publishing is very expensive both in book production and marketing terms.

Risk is part of life and therefore of publishing. We are neither recommending nor celebrating risk but pointing out that you will need to live with it, and that the way you will live with it will be a reflection of the kind of publishing house you work in. This book, after all, is intended to address the acquisition of professionalism in publishing. Being professional means eliminating unacceptable risk. There is a simple rule of thumb when assessing the degree of risk. Once you know how, in an ideal world, you *should* proceed, the further you move away from that, the greater the risk. Modern, corporate publishing prefers to avoid risk. There is very little to recommend risk-averse publishing if we still like to believe that books are the source of knowledge, inspiration and originality, but the CEO of a large corporation would rightly say that it is giving the public what it wants and therefore growing the readership base. Those celeb offerings are providing valuable income that helps fund more speculative works, and there is some truth in that. Perhaps some parts of the industry need now to be seen as closer to the entertainment industry than traditional publishing.

Planning and management in publishing

There is scarcely a publishing house that does not have some element of planning and management when conducting its business these days. Even tiny houses whose existence seems to proceed on a day-to-day basis, and may have next to no staff to manage, will have some notion of how many books they can afford to publish in the year and the associated costs, and whether they have, literally, the time to get the work done. Yet again, size will be one of the main determinants of the degree of planning and the extent of management. Planning for the future is encapsulated in the business plan.

The business plan

The plan sets out the aims and objectives of the publishing house, and how to achieve them, usually over a period of three years. In the past, this period was often five years, but as change seems to take place more quickly these days, three years is a more sensible timeframe. This business plan will be updated and revised on a yearly basis, again reflecting changes that have taken place. Mostly, therefore, the business plan will be a rolling plan, with the exception of a new start-up, which will set a plan to cover the business from its beginnings.

The directors are responsible for the business plan. They will meet, look at how the company is performing, and begin to draw up aims and objectives for the house in the following years. These are likely to include:

- An increase in sales income (a target figure will be proposed).
- Profitability rising (this will again include a target figure).
- The start up of new lists (new areas will be proposed).
- Withdrawing from certain current lists (to be stated, and with financial performance figures provided to justify the withdrawal).
- Improvements in marketing and sales and distribution (this might include efficiency issues or quality issues).
- Cutting costs and overhead (the areas will be targeted).
- Increasing market share and attaining greater dominance in the market (figures for market share will be proposed).

There may be more, but these will certainly be the areas that they will want the business plan to address. Note that, sometimes, sales income can improve, but not profitability. The two things are not necessarily linked. If you improve your sales, but do not hold back costs sufficiently, your profit will not always rise. Only efficiency, allied with increased sales, is likely to improve your profit line.

Having stated the aims and objectives, the directors will share these with the management levels below them for feedback and discussion. As a result, some top-line aims might be revised. Once general agreement is reached, those aims and objectives will be translated into action plans. Each action plan will be the responsibility of the departmental area to which it relates. The result is that each department – editorial, production, sales and marketing, administration – will know what is expected of them. In a well run company, one would expect that the departmental managers will also share the draft company plan with the rest of the department and encourage feedback, which in its turn will be fed back up the management chain.

The benefit of this sharing and discussion is that everyone has a hand in it. Everyone knows what is expected of him or her and why. This is a huge advantage when one is requiring staff to work hard and purposefully, and also efficiently. Everyone 'owns' the plan. By contrast, companies that simply impose their plans on staff, plans that may be rather ambitious and hard to achieve, are likely to breed resentment.

The end point of this plan is that the company is able to set figures against every income and cost line, which translates into the company's profit and loss account (P & L) for the year. As the year goes on, and the directors meet, usually once a month, the results can be looked at in conjunction with the P & L, and they can judge how well the company is doing. There is a year-end P & L for a publishing house in the case study at the end of this chapter.

The springboard for the plan is encapsulated in the mission statement, which appears at the beginning of the plan. Mission statements are often lacklustre, with every aim and objective crammed into one long paragraph, or are so general that they have no meaning. They are meant to be a defining 'call to action' that galvanizes the staff and gives them a sense of identity. In practice, publishing houses seem to find it as difficult as any other company to provide a mission statement that really sets the world on fire.

Management style

If it is just you, publishing a few books a year from a desk in your spare bedroom, then you only have yourself to manage. This may not be easy, of course, because the presence of colleagues can provide some sense of control over any tendencies you might have to waste time, be distracted, or just stay in bed for the day. Once you employ people, even if just a few, you have a responsibility to ensure that they are getting work done to schedule and to your desired quality, but also that their working conditions are, at the very least, reasonable. It is in your interests to make life for your employees comfortable and efficient, and above all, involving and enjoyable. They will work better as a result.

Management in publishing is 'collegial' in style. This means that there is a recognition of individuals' rights and qualities and that strict hierarchies are not always the best way to manage organizations that are full of people who are highly intelligent, motivated, possess initiative and are often asked to take on heavy responsibilities. This is the type of person publishing needs to employ. Much of the work is going to require good judgement, accuracy and attention to detail, as well as commitment and hard work. Publishing employees are usually highly educated and able to think for themselves. They are more often than not sociable too, which is an advantage as the work often involves meeting and getting on with people whom they do not know well, such as authors, designers, retailers and agents. Employees with characteristics of this sort do not like strict formality or carrying out orders. They like to understand what they are doing and why they are doing it. Many of them, particularly at entry level, will not be as well paid as they might be if they had entered another profession. As financial rewards at that stage are not great, rewards must come in other ways, and one of them is certainly a high degree of satisfaction.

Do not make the mistake, however, of thinking that because the managing director is friendly and open that he or she is just the same as you, and it is perfectly in order for you to say what you like. There is an underlying understanding of the differences between roles, responsibilities and power even in publishing houses. Ultimately it is the MD who has to take responsibility for the performance of a publishing house and therefore it is appropriate that the power lies with that individual.

Management problems

At one end of the spectrum, with an individual running a house alone or with just a few colleagues, any bad judgement, mistake, or chaos is going to be immediately apparent. At the other end, in a huge corporation, the chief executive is going to have to rely on the management below him or her to spot problems, sort them out, and report up anything that is potentially serious. This makes CEOs vulnerable to the quality of the management beneath them, and we have to rely on the CEO and directors to appoint high-quality staff. Publishing is just like any other industry in this respect; however, there are differences. We mentioned earlier that publishing makes a huge number of investment decisions (the choice of books to be published) compared with most other industries. The design, construction and launch of a new car are going to dominate the lives of the CEO and directors of a car company. The ability to focus on a comparatively small number of issues is therefore possible. In publishing, this is simply not practical. In a large corporation, the top-line directors are only likely to get involved if someone is proposing an exceptionally large advance to an author.

While we can accept that the CEO and his or her fellow directors are unable to get involved in a level of detail that would require their approval of book contracts, or of marketing campaigns, for example, the danger that arises from this is that the top management can quite quickly distance itself from the everyday life of publishing. This is still, to a large extent, a craft industry, if you can accept that meanings of 'craft' (as cited in the *Oxford English Dictionary*) include skill, art, strength and courage. Art and skill are most certainly required in modern publishing, and many would like to see more displays of strength and courage amongst its practitioners. The point is that to be a good publisher, one has to do it, whereas to be a good car manufacturer, one does not need to work on the assembly line. There are two signs of senior management becoming remote. The first is an unequivocal approval for *anything* digital, often driven by a fear of appearing behind the times. The second is a fairly rapid loss of recollection of the process of doing publishing, normally demonstrated by higher-than-average demands for increases in turnover and profit. Anything greater than a 10 per cent increase in profit or turnover from one year to the next is ambitious, especially at times of low inflation, when it is more difficult to justify putting your prices up. Here the CEO is losing sight of just how long the lead-in times are for a book to get to market. The author has to be found, to be accepted for contract, to be given time to write the book, and then we have to publish it.

To a large extent, the forward programmes of publishing houses are conveyor belts. It is very difficult to increase the forward programmes dramatically. If your CEO is asking you to do just that, then we have a very hands-off CEO. Your hands-off CEO not only can make life difficult for the publishing staff by either ignoring, or forgetting, realistic publishing practice, he or she can make some powerful mistakes in the area of recruitment. A hands-on CEO can spot signs of competence and experience when getting involved in staff recruitment. A hands-off CEO is more likely to be duped by a plausible individual offering 'solutions'. In recent years there have been too many examples of less-than-adequate management, often by individuals with not enough publishing experience, but who have attained important and influential positions in large corporations. This could turn out to be a worrying trend, to which we can add the arrival of more 'generalists' coming into the industry from other sectors.

Recruiting a high-level individual from outside the publishing industry would in the past have been unthinkable. It happens now because modern corporations begin to see themselves as *businesses*, comparable in attitude and approach to many other industries. This is a distinct cultural shift away from the traditional view of publishing as a craft industry, combining distinct skills, long-term experience, and cultural capital with manufacture. Whether publishing is a mass-market sector (a frequent indicator of big business) is open to debate. There is no mass-market industry that produces, as the UK publishing industry does, 130,000 new product lines a year (the figure for 2009). The sheer size and variation of the output defies the usual dynamics of a true mass-market industry, which, by comparison, is infinitely more streamlined and can obtain true economies of scale. Nevertheless, many have become convinced of the value of what they call transferable skills, which can be imported from other industries to the benefit of publishing.

Brands

The kind of business thinking that has just been referred to is nowhere more evident than in the use of the word 'brand'. It is a comparative newcomer in the publishing scene but is being used with enthusiasm. Its use, however, is far more limited than it is in other sectors. When we say, 'Mercedes' or 'Ford', or 'Ralph Lauren' or 'Tesco', we need say no more than that. We have quite a firm grasp of what these names mean to us. But if you say 'Random House', 'Hachette', or 'Elsevier', this may mean something to you, as someone who works in publishing, but will it mean anything at all to the customer? It is very unlikely, unless you are talking to one of their authors. Publishing houses, with the great exception in the UK of Penguin, mean nothing at all to the people who buy books. They do not buy them because the books are published by Company X, whereas they might very well buy a BMW because of its brand strength. People who buy books are by and large publisher-blind.

The only true brands in publishing are the authors. Yet there are relatively few for whom the customer gives strong allegiance, and usually it is based on the purchase and rewarding reading of many books produced by an author over a number of years. These authors are 'stayers'. They are the core of the backlist of publishers, books that can be reprinted many times, bringing in extra profit. Dan Brown's output is tiny by comparison but he did write a book that has been commercially so strong that, in this instance, just like a car, we just have to say his name and we all know what we mean and think. You could argue that a series such as 'Dummies' is also a brand. Yes, it is thoroughly recognizable. That is its strength, but we must acknowledge that not every 'Dummy' reader will buy every new book just because it is a

'Dummy'. The series is too wide-ranging for that. There is a subtle difference here.

Author brands do not just exist in consumer publishing. There are many authors in more specialist publishing whose names have equal resonance with book buyers, especially in textbook and reference publishing. The publication of a new dictionary from Collins or Oxford University Press, or a new edition of *Grey's Anatomy* is a major event in publishing terms. However, we have seen the progressively sloppy use of the word 'brand', with authors who may have only published two or three books. Such use is disquieting because if you have convinced yourself that an author *is* a brand, there is an awful temptation to assume that there is a great deal of loyalty out there and that the next book from this author is a guaranteed winner. If you think you have already won, will you really try that hard to beguile readers to buy it?

Marketing

The enthusiasm for a word such as 'brand' reflects the growing power and influence of marketing in publishing. In the large corporations, that power is not growing: it has arrived. Marketing's current position is not just a reflection of publishing's realization that it is now a business, but also society's own familiarity with marketing output and techniques. We are very used to being sold products, often in a rather sophisticated way. Books have to compete with many other products for our attention and our spending power.

Interestingly, the average marketing spend for a new book is not much higher than it ever was, which is a reflection of the efficiency and focus that marketing departments bring to what they do. 'Nice ideas' that do not work, lavish and inappropriate expenditure, often driven by author demands, are fairly rare now. No longer do editors insist that their marketing colleagues conduct expensive campaigns that will make the editor and the author feel that the book is being given lots of attention. Attention, yes, but not inappropriate attention. The marketing chapter in this book covers how marketing departments work, and how they think about expenditure in relation to sales income.

But does marketing really determine what gets published? Another truism that needs to be questioned is whether the accountants determine what gets published. Again, much depends on the size of the publishing operation: the bigger the publisher the more likely that both parties have real power. Even so, one of the challenges that a CEO has to deal with is bringing some balance overall to how power is dispensed. There is more about accountants below.

The marketing, and sales, departments are responsible for ensuring that books sell. In that respect alone, they deserve and should be required to play a large part in deciding what books are contracted. In a large corporation, the marketing department will be very big indeed and its practitioners need to be outgoing and often creative in their plans because, after all, what they do faces outwards, in the direction of the marketplace. Editors, who deal with authors and text, tend to be quieter and more reflective (there are exceptions of course) and young editors in particular, still learning their trade, can sometimes feel oppressed by the presence of the big personalities of the marketing department. They will have to learn to compete when faced with a battery of questions grounded absolutely in 'provable' terms: 'Why?', 'How many?', 'To whom?', 'Can't we change the title? It's too vague' and so on. It is still not unknown for editors to talk about their titles in the most general terms when it comes to nailing the market for them. Frankly, it is the duty of the marketing department to ask for specifics and the duty of the editor to know them.

As yet, marketing does not make the publishing decisions, but it does influence them. The one exception is in textbook or reference publishing where what the marketing department knows by way of sales, customer profiles and the competition will be central to how the content of such publications should be constructed. These products are planned from the outset using input about the market; the marketing department will also be deeply involved in testing projected products with focus groups. Even so, this is fairly limited in terms of influencing what gets published. The commissioning editor essentially retains the power of selection, because it is he or she who makes the initial choice, from the many projects offered by authors, of what might be forwarded for the consideration of other colleagues. The editor is the gatekeeper.

The influence of accountants

'Bottom line' publishing is a much-favoured expression amongst those who do not like corporate publishing, either for what it publishes or how it conducts itself. Accountants are not necessarily the culprits. By and large, accountants who work in publishing are of the gentler variety, with a real interest in the books that are published and are often quite supportive in explaining to editors in particular the financial side of the business. The function of a publishing accountant is rather like a car mechanic. The mechanic can tell you when the brakes need renewing, the clutch adjusting, and so on, but cannot tell you how to drive the car. His or her analysis might give you some clues about your driving, but only you can sit behind the driving wheel. Similarly, the accountant can tell you when your expenditure is too high, when your profit levels are lower than required and this should all be explained to you in terms of how you are not meeting the necessary ratios for expenditure and costs that the company requires of any book. However, the same accountant cannot tell an editor how to acquire books. An accountant's guidance can rarely go beyond, 'Sign up books that make X amount of turnover and Y amount of profit.' You probably would want to do that anyway, but as advice, this is not very helpful in a practical way.

Bottom-line publishing is a phrase whose real meaning is the assessment of books only in relation to the income and profit they generate. Everyone can collude in this if they are only interested in the figures. Examining the figures is absolutely necessary but they need to be looked at in conjunction with other factors in assessing potential. Sadly, there is anecdotal evidence that books are turned down in the larger publishing houses solely on the basis of the figures. If this is true, then we are looking at another manifestation of risk aversion.

Takeovers and mergers

These were fairly rare until the late 1980s when the forces that began to emerge in publishing, referred to earlier (globalization in particular), began to exert their influence. What began as essentially a US invasion of British publishing gradually turned into a worldwide phenomenon in which European publishing has also played a large part. Mergers are quite rare. Takeovers still play an active part in publishing although what tends to happen more often these days is that one part of a publisher's list will be taken over, rather than the whole house. The big players have now become so big that massive funding would be required for one to take over another. Small houses that are still independent but growing in influence will be of interest to the corporates, and if the time and price is right, they will buy. Much of what we might regard as takeover 'foreplay' takes place secretly. A corporate might approach the

MD of an independent, and subsequently conversations will take place over drinks or dinner, where the question is popped. Perhaps the MD of the independent will be the one to make the approach. In either case, both parties know what they want. In some situations a publishing broker might get involved. The publisher will talk to a broker and state that it wants to buy or sell, and ask the broker to look for something suitable. The job of the broker then is to bring both sides together and help them come to an amicable agreement. If the company is owned by shareholders, then the situation is more complex because the shareholders have to agree to the takeover. They will if the price is right because it will enhance the value of their shares.

The main reasons for wanting to take over a publishing house will be to:

- increase the publisher's share of a sector of the market;
- enter a sector of the market in which the publisher does not yet have a presence;
- gain ownership of valuable copyrights;
- extend publishing into another geographic area through the purchase of a foreign publishing house.

Of course greed, egotism, or satisfying the shareholders can also play their part. For sellers, being taken over can mark:

- the retirement of the owner who now wants to maximize earnings, having devoted perhaps a lifetime to setting up and running the business;
- the conclusion of a tough time, trying to make the business more successful but, sadly, realizing that it cannot reach its potential while financial resources are limited;
- simply being overwhelmed by an incredibly good offer to sell which the owner cannot resist.

All takeovers are accompanied by reports in the media in which the buyers and sellers glowingly approve of the deal and cite the advantages that will now flow from it. High on the approval ratings will be 'list fit', which is another way of saying that the publishing list of the company that has just been bought is going to dovetail perfectly with the buyer's lists.

Another favoured word is 'synergies'. In other words, the directors are thinking, 'We can merge administration, HR, warehousing and distribution and immediately get economies, and perhaps further down the line we can also do some merging of editorial, marketing and sales and make further savings there.' The objective of takeovers, in addition to what we have said above, is to buy for the best possible price and make savings that will help balance the expenditure laid out buying the publishing house.

The business of merging functions can be tricky, especially when it comes to editorial, marketing and sales. This is where the pain lies in takeovers. Jobs will certainly be lost in all the main functions. Publishing, being a 'people industry', does not shed staff easily or comfortably. Further pain can be felt by the authors, who do not like their books being taken over by another company. After all, they chose by whom they wished to be published, and they do not like being 'sold on'.

Author contracts can be another source of difficulty. Imagine you are an author at publisher A. Publisher B buys A, but publisher B gives its authors lower royalties than publisher A. Publisher B will inevitably try to persuade the author to accept the lower royalty and the justification for this will be, 'We have a better marketing and sales operation. We will sell more copies of your book, and in fact, you will end up better off.' Authors will be sceptical, and if they have agents, they will be even more sceptical.

Finally, while the directors of the company that has made the purchase will be delighted, the effect on the staff can be rather different. Stability is important to publishing. The business of finding authors, nurturing them, publishing them and then keeping them, takes time. For that to be done well, one needs everyone involved to be able to concentrate on what they are doing. Takeovers are a huge distraction and can intrude on the everyday business of publishing.

Are there benefits? Frankly, we do not really know. There is very little research done on the long-term consequences of takeovers, either in publishing or in any other industry. In truth, the financial statements of the corporations are so complex that it would be quite difficult to track whether the takeover was of benefit to the buyer or not. Aspects of the house that was taken over will certainly be lost, most commonly the house's name. So will staff, and not just the ones who were made redundant but staff who simply do not like life under the new owners. We have to accept takeovers as part of life and a reflection of the modern business world. We should also emphasize that for many small houses, struggling to compete, yet offering excellence, being taken over by a larger house can offer a comparatively safe haven that allows them to prosper. They can prosper if there is enlightened and intelligent management in the larger house, and often there is.

A new business model?

Earlier we mentioned that publishing requires stability. That stability is now going to be severely challenged (if the pundits are correct) by the arrival of digital publishing. For as long as the oldest inhabitants of publishing can remember, we have been able to rely on a fairly stable business model. Our product has remained roughly the same, even if some current content is now questionable. A book is a book: we can price it according to the 'going rate' – what people appear to be happy to pay for it – and raise those prices in line with inflation. We have a rough idea of what the cost of making that book is going to be. We search constantly, of course, for cheaper ways of making it, usually by sending a proportion of book production overseas to countries where labour costs are lower. We have fairly well-defined methods of selling our books too, although our relationship with the retail market has changed drastically since the abolition of the Net Book Agreement, and rising discounts have had a profound effect on publishing's profitability.

But, fundamentally, we know where we stand. It seems that our understanding is about to be tested. Throughout this book we will make reference to digital publishing and its consequences for content creation, marketing and sales, distribution, copyright, contracts and rights. We are recording what is already happening. However, if the book as an object disappears, or only remains on the wish-list of people who really do prefer to read their content within the covers of a book, then we are looking at the emergence of its successor, currently called a 'hand-held device' (this could also include 'tablets' and mobile phones). This device is able to download content. Downloaded content is infinitely flexible, as you will read in the digital publishing section of Chapter 3. This has implications not only for publishers but for authors. These authors could not only find themselves continually writing (and how will you pay them for that?), but they may be part of a writing team. Our relationship with this content and its teams will bear little resemblance to that for book writing. However, many of our skills will remain – choosing what to create, finding authors, advising and managing them, nurturing them.

For hand-held devices, what may we be looking at:

- Content you can only get by agreeing also to buy multiple titles or will we be able to buy just one title?

- From where will we buy our content: direct from the publisher, or from bookshops that are happy to sell pre-loaded devices, or from Amazon, which only wants you to buy titles pre-loaded onto its Kindle?
- What kind of discounts are we going to give retailers? The retailers will want more, because they know that by avoiding book manufacture, our costs will be reduced.
- We shall be dependent, of course, on readers wishing to invest a sizeable amount of money upfront before they can read a word! If you want to have it both ways and produce some titles as books before then making them digitally available, how will you spread your costs?
- What will be your timing for these releases?

It will take years of experimentation to find out what works. We shall be living in a period of constant flux before the future business model emerges. We can guarantee that this will be an expensive business until then!

Let us end this chapter by looking at a P & L. It is a reflection of the current business model.

CASE STUDY A profit and loss account for a publishing house

Gradually, in the course of your publishing career, you will be introduced to financial figures: profit and loss accounts and budgets being the most common. Almost every activity a house undertakes will have a budget attached to it, showing the people involved the amount of money they have to spend. The profit and loss accounts present a more complex picture, revealing what income has been made and what money has been spent. We expect that a well-run publishing house will make a profit; if it makes losses, it will find it difficult to remain in business.

To make a profit is surely a good thing? Much depends on the size of your profit, of course. Your ability to make a profit, and the size of your profit, will depend on two things: the success of your books in the marketplace, and costs. Are you selling as many as you predicted? What are the costs of making these sales? We are referring here to what is known as 'the overhead', which is the cost of running the business. We are also referring to the cost of manufacturing your books. Your books may be selling well, but have you managed to hold your costs at an efficient level?

Let us look at the P & L for a house that publishes some specialist books and some consumer books. It is part of a large publishing group, and that will be reflected in some of its income and costs.

	This Year Sums of money (000s)	%	**Last Year** Sums of money (000s)	%
Sales figures				
Home	12,388	77.7	13,456	81.1
Book club	4	0	4	0
Group special sales	156	1	119	0.7
Export	3,400	21.3	3,010	18.1
Export intra group	0	0	13	0.1
Remainders	1	0	0	0
Total net sales	*15,949*	*100*	*16,602*	*100*
Cost of sales				
Cost of sales	(4,209)	26.4	(4,103)	24.7
Stock destroyed	(42)	0.3	(281)	1.7

continued

	This Year Sums of money (000s)	%	Last Year Sums of money (000s)	%
Gratis	(196)	1.2	(134)	0.8
Royalties	(1,626)	10.2	(1,713)	10.3
Total cost of sales	*(6,073)*	*38.1*	*(6,231)*	*37.5*
Gross Margin	**9,876**	**61.9**	**10,371**	**62.5**

Other Costs and Sources of Income

Costs

Stock write-down	(240)	1.5	(143)	0.9
Royalty advances	(24)	0.2	(84)	0.5
Returns	(51)	0.3	(72)	0.4
Total	*(315)*	*2.0*	*(299)*	*1.8*

Income

Subrights income	428	2.7	483	2.9
Sales commission	39	0.2	70	0.4
Other	6	0	(17)	0.1
Total	*473*	*3.0*	*536*	*3.2*
Total contribution	**10,034**	**62.9**	**10,608**	**63.9**

Overheads

Publicity and marketing	(532)	3.3	(491)	3.0
Customer promotion	(30)	0.2	0	0
Sales commission	(106)	0.7	(69)	0.4
Distribution	(1,189)	7.5	(1,349)	8.1
Staff costs	(3,552)	22.3	(3,715)	22.4
Administration	(463)	2.9	(575)	3.5
Group property charges	(480)	3.0	(479)	2.9
Other Group charges	(600)	3.8	(949)	5.7
Group IT charges	(300)	1.9	(278)	1.7
Total overheads	*(7,252)*	*45.5*	*(7,905)*	*47.6*
NET PROFIT	**2,782**	**17.4**	**2,703**	**16.3**

As we go through the table, you will see figures expressed both as absolute sums of money (in thousands) and as percentages. We have to look at the sums of money in percentage terms as this is the best way to make sense of them. We calculate the percentage by taking the absolute sum and measuring it as a percentage of the sales income. So, for example, the royalty sum this year of 1,626 is divided by the total net sales sum of 15,949 and multiplied by 100. This produces the percentage of 10.2. As we said earlier, we have to find out how these costs look in relation to the sales made. For royalties, our percentage is down on last year's, but that is because we have paid less in royalties. However, that percentage of 10.2 indicates that our royalty bill looks to be falling within the norm – royalties can range from 5 to 15 per cent. We can also measure income in the same way. This is a far better way of measuring success or failure than by just looking at absolute sums.

Sales income

The first thing we notice is that home sales have gone down by about 4 per cent on last year. That is not a huge drop, but it should concern us. Either our new books are not good enough for the market, or the market itself might be in decline. If the latter is the case, then we and our competitors will all be experiencing trouble. Our export sales, and sales to other companies in our group (our overseas companies), have gone up, but not sufficiently to compensate for our home sales. Overall, we are over half a million down in income.

Cost of sales

These are costs associated with stock and its disposal. Our first line in these figures shows the cost of making the books and the cost has gone up compared to last year. Are we paying our suppliers too much, or are our books unnecessarily high in physical quality? Not all books need Rolls Royce finishing.

We have also destroyed some of our stock. We have too many copies of certain titles in the warehouse, and we are of the opinion that we will never sell them, so we have decided to dispose of them. There is a cost associated with this. We paid to make them, so we cannot just forget about that bill. We look at the production value of those books and we subtract it from our income. Note, however, that we destroyed far more stock last year. So perhaps this year's figures reveal a decision to have a further clear out, or slightly more efficient stock handling. We have given away more books this year (gratis). As it is definitely part of the marketing plan for any book to give free copies to influential people whose recommendations will help create sales, perhaps we were too mean last year.

Our royalties have, of course, gone down slightly because we have sold fewer books, so we cannot congratulate ourselves on that. However, the overall royalty paid is 10.2 per cent, which comes well within the royalty norm.

As you can see, our total cost of sales as a percentage is up slightly on last year. When we have subtracted the cost of sales from our sales income, we find that our gross margin (another name in common use for 'profit') in money and as a percentage is down on last year. As for the gross margin itself, well, it is still a healthy one and would be considered acceptable by a publishing house working in this area. Different sectors of publishing have different levels of acceptability when it comes to profit. A specialist house sells its stock more slowly than a consumer house, because it is a more time-consuming business to get books known within specialist markets. Consumer books sell far more quickly, because they are mostly sold through the shops or through Amazon, and for this reason, consumer publishers can live on lower profit levels, because they get cash back from the customers more quickly. Every house sets itself acceptable profit levels, and if you are working in publishing already, you will probably know what your desirable profit levels are.

Other costs and sources of income

There are additional areas for making money apart from selling copies of books, as indeed there are other costs that a company must bear, and these fall into this section. We start with stock write-down. Unlike the stocks that have been destroyed, these are books for which we have some hope of making sales. But we must not assume that we will sell them all. We therefore begin to write down the value of them. Imagine you have a new car. It was worth £10,000 on the day you bought it. It is worth a third of that once you have driven it, and the longer you own it, the less it is worth. This is of concern to you when you decide to sell it. The same principle operates with books. We have to ask ourselves, how many of these books will we sell, and are therefore still holding their sales value? This is a kind of educated guess. We know that in sales terms, they are worth X thousand, but we need to estimate how many of those books will actually convert into sales. For those copies we think we might not convert, we calculate their lost value and we subtract this from our income, because it is a cost to us. We had to pay to make these books.

When we look at our figures, we can see that we decided to write down far more of our books this year than last. Someone has made the bold decision that more books will be ultimately unsaleable. Again, this indicates that either our books are not as attractive to the market as we thought, or that the market is going through a tough time. Our competitors might also be writing down more stock.

Next we have written in our royalty advances as a cost. This is money paid to the authors, but will their royalties ever exceed the advances we paid? The problem of unearned advances is an issue of concern in consumer publishing, but less of a problem, normally, in specialist publishing. We have also made a provision for returns as a cost. Here, however, we are feeling more confident about returns because our cost is down on last year. Perhaps, although we are selling fewer books, the ones we are selling to booksellers are more likely to sell through to the book-buying public.

Having been through the additional costs, we now look at additional income. Rights would be the main source. Unhappily, our Rights department has not done as well as last year, but only fractionally so. Similarly, the sales commission we earn by selling other companies' books, usually in export territories where we have sales forces, has also gone down. It would appear that both the Rights department and the commission reps are trying to sell books that are not so attractive to their markets. There is another line called 'other' income. We can only guess where this has come from (it will not be from conventional book sales), and there is not a great deal of it, but this is a better performance on last year, when we actually made losses.

Having deducted our extra costs and added our additional income, we come to our total contribution (that is, all the money we have finally made) and we find that it is 1 per cent down on last year's. But we are still half a million adrift.

Overheads

We now come to the cost of running the company; until we have accounted for that, we cannot arrive at a net profit. If we add together publicity and marketing, promotion and sales commission, we see that we have spent 4.2 per cent of our total sales on this, compared to 3.4 per cent last year. This is not good news because we have spent more money trying to get customers to buy our books than last year and yet our sales are down. Again, what can we conclude: that our selling side is not very good, or that what they are trying to sell is not so attractive to the customers, or that the market is collapsing? This is an issue that the directors of the company will have to think long and hard about.

The cost of distribution is slightly down on last year's, but that is because we are not selling so many books! This figure looks good, but it is good for all the wrong reasons. Staff costs are almost the same, so we are not overpaying anyone this year! It is the next set of figures that are interesting. While the group property charges (accommodation) are roughly the same, and the cost of IT has gone up (probably because this company like all companies is spending more on IT), the 'other' charges made on this company by the group have gone down quite significantly. We can only guess here that the managing director has successfully negotiated a lower cost for some of the overhead charges.

The net result, therefore, is that our overall performance is up on last year's. Let us be thankful for that, but also remember that to an extent we have been rescued by some cost savings, which are divorced from the top line, ie the sales of our books. We cannot hope that we can effect the same group savings next year, and we therefore need to concentrate on signing up more robust books that translate into increased sales. Of course, if our specialist market is not holding up well, the same challenge will have to be faced not just by us but also by our competitors.

Conclusion

Publishing today *is* a business. That needs to be repeated, because too often young people, still, enter the industry with a romantic view of publishing, believing they will spend a lot of their time in enjoyable conversations with authors, working together with them on their texts, nurturing great writing, engaging the media in the excitement of the books they will publish, conceptualizing great design, and overall contributing to the cultural life of the country. While we depend on that kind of great enthusiasm and idealism, they will have to be tempered by the demands that are imposed on publishing in the modern business world.

Publishing has emerged from a privileged and amiable backwater serving the reading needs of, mostly, the educated and financially comfortable. It needs, and is trying, to serve much broader audiences.

This inevitably means that a much greater variety of publications will be on offer to an increasingly diverse society. Included in those publications will be books of no great merit or interest to the habitual and long-term book buyer and reader. The true publisher is open minded, practical and opportunistic. When all is said and done, a good and successful book from Mills & Boon is as worthy of our respect, as publishers, as a good and successful book from Faber & Faber. The publishers have served their readers: they have given them what they wanted. What is not worthy of our respect is short-changing the readers by giving them bad examples of what they wanted. It is those publishers who need to question their policies, practices and management.

Trying to extend the audiences for books lies at the heart and purpose of modern publishing and accounts for its gradual movement towards business principles. The demands on publishing staff have shifted away from their own interests to an added requirement to justify what they publish in terms of the market. Today's publishing has to balance the need for individualism, commitment and enthusiasm on the part of its staff with the requirement to test whether their output will have readers. This inevitably means reference to sales figures, discounts, marketing plans, turnover and profit. Without that process, the risk is too high. It is when either indulgence or risk-averse attitudes take the high ground that publishing houses and their output suffer. Publishing is like any other industry: it must find customers, it must trade successfully and it must make money. A publishing house that goes bust is ultimately abandoning its authors, without whom we are nothing.

Further reading

de Bellaigue, E (2004) *British Book Publishing as a Business Since the 1960s*, British Library Publishing, London

Bradley, S (2008) *The British Book Trade: An oral history*, British Library Publishing, London

Clark, G and Phillips, A (2008) *Inside Book Publishing*, 4th edn, Routledge, Abingdon

Davis, C (2009) *Eye Witness: The rise and fall of Dorling Kindersley*, Harriman House, Petersfield

Epstein, J (2002) *Book Business*, W W Norton, New York

Schiffrin, A (2001) *The Business of Books*, Verso, London

Thompson, J (2005) *Books in the Digital Age*, Polity, Cambridge

Woll, T (1999) *Publishing for Profit*, Kogan Page, London

Inside Book Publishing (listed above) is strongly recommended for anyone wanting a comprehensive view of publishing in its broadest sense. It is an excellent introduction to publishing and contains much valuable information on many things, including professional bodies and associations, training institutions, and useful websites.

The work of the commissioning editor

03

Introduction

So, you think you want to be an editor. Perhaps you have put your foot on the first rung, in which case you are probably an editorial assistant. This is the classic position, working alongside an editor, where you can learn about and observe how editors do the job. Equally important, you begin to learn something about authors – how they work and our relationships with them. If you work hard and display competence and initiative, you will become an assistant editor. Here too you are learning, but responsibility increases. You may be 'looking after' authors, supporting them and keeping track of their writing progress, under the management of the editor to whom you report. Make no mistake: you are not contracting books at this level. That is the editor's job. But unlike the editorial assistant, who is working almost entirely under the direct supervision of the editor, you do have some scope for independence of action and judgement.

Both these positions prepare for the job of editor. This job is often prized and longed for, until you get it. Then it is a different story, as the newcomer realizes that he or she is now occupying what most people still consider to be the most demanding job in publishing. It is demanding for four reasons:

1 The editor is the gatekeeper who chooses which publishing projects will go forward for consideration by colleagues in the publishing house. That is a lot of power.

2 Having exercised that power, it is the editor who will organize all resources – financial, commercial, practical and possibly intellectual – to persuade colleagues to back a particular project. That is a lot of persuasion to find.

3 This exercise in persuasion has to be informed by a true understanding of the market for the project; the market not just now, but the market in a couple of years' time, or more. That has to be a really very good guess.

4 If these projects succeed, the editor must be ready to share credit for them with colleagues; if they fail, the editor will suffer alone. That seems very unfair, but ultimately, responsibility does lie with the editor.

The first points above imply the truth of the editor's role: it is one of huge power. You can pick and choose what the house will give serious consideration to, and it is your powers of persuasion that will probably have the greatest influence on what gets published. Therefore, you will have to take greatest responsibility for the outcome.

It is fairly common for a newly promoted editor to experience regret that his or her dream has come true. The sheer anxiety that can surround living with the reality of the four points listed above can seem overwhelming at times. However, like most things in life, practice and exposure can partially conquer anxiety, allowing you to harness it as a source of energy. It is true – fear can be the spur to the achievement of the best things you will do in publishing.

A different challenge: working with authors

It is time to state here something that is so simple and so obvious that it often gets overlooked in discussions about publishing, and yet it bears down precisely on the work of the editor.

Publishing is one of the few industries where the content/artefact/product is not produced by company staff but by people who are not employed, and are unlikely ever to be employed, by the publishing house. Just think about most of the things you are likely to buy in life. Everything from cars to clothes, beds, carpets and so much more will have been produced and sold to you by a company whose products have been invented or designed by their employees. Not so authors, who in this respect resemble musicians who perform for recording companies. Like the recording companies, publishers choose what will be made commercially available and then attempt to sell it. This choice entails risk.

The relationship between the author and the house, therefore, is by far and away the most important one of all, because you are central to that relationship – its success and its continuation. (We will be looking in more detail at working with authors later in this chapter.) It is the editor's responsibility to take care of that relationship, and one of the greatest challenges of the job. How for example, will you manage to deal with a very human and common challenge of being an editor – keeping your balance and judgement when dealing with one author, whom you dislike, and another whom you like very much indeed? As a professional, you will learn to treat them even-handedly. You will have your favourites, but you will keep quiet about that, especially when talking to other authors!

An editor's main responsibilities

Choosing what gets published

There is a misconception that the editor works alone – reading and assessing synopses and manuscripts and making the decision about what should be published. One of the main changes in editorial work that has taken place since the late 20th century is the move away from editorial 'freedom' to choose towards a kind of collective agreement arrived at within a team that is likely to consist of editorial, marketing, sales and financial staff. This agreement will be reached in team meetings where projects are examined, assessed and often argued over. It is the editor's job to present all the information that the team needs to help it make a decision.

So, if you are an editor, what is this information you need to assemble for your colleagues?

The project

Projects usually arrive on an editor's desk in one of two forms: most commonly a synopsis, but sometimes a manuscript. The latter is fairly rare. Most authors would prefer to write and present a synopsis and find out whether the publisher is going to be interested or not. They would prefer not to have to go to the trouble of writing a whole book, only to have it rejected. A synopsis should consist of the following:

- A rationale for the book – the author's assessment of the need or demand for or attraction of the book. Here the author is justifying why this work should be published.

- A detailed description, chapter by chapter, of the book.

- The author's assessment of the market for this book – who will read it, and why.

- Contextual information such as examples of what are called 'competitive texts' – what is wrong with them and why this proposed project will be superior. Similar information can be presented showing that this particular genre of book is enjoying success with the reading public. In sum, the author is using his or her powers of persuasion, harnessed with information gleaned about who is buying what books, and why, to convince the editor that there is a demand for this type of book.

- The author's assessment of how long the book will be (usually expressed in number of words), and how much time he or she needs to write it. As we shall see later in the chapter, this assessment can often go badly wrong.

This is usually enough information for editors to set to work on a series of procedures that might lead them to the point where they can recommend to their colleagues that publishing this book is an acceptable commercial risk. Remember, when recommending a book to your colleagues, you are asking the company to invest in it. Investment means money and a lot of effort, so editors must get this recommendation right.

Occasionally, you will find yourself dealing with an author who does not want to put the effort into writing up a proper synopsis. The solution here is a simple one: turn him or her down. Writing a synopsis is the most effective way for authors to think through properly what they want to write. An idea is not enough: execution is everything. So, if they are not prepared to put themselves through the disciplined process of working out how their ideas can turn into a viable, structured text, then they are probably not up to writing a book or going through the entire publication process.

Do not be surprised either if, perhaps a week or two after receiving a proposal from a hopeful author, you get an e-mail or a phone call asking if you have reached a decision. The tone of voice often suggests that the callers assume that they are dealing with a laggard who needs to be reminded that they have not got all the time in the world to be waiting for you! Politely explain that they are, effectively, in a queue; that each day e-mails and the post bring in dozens of book proposals that have to be treated fairly – first come first served – and give them a rough estimate of when you *hope* to be able to turn your attention to theirs. Our experience is that this sort of author has not written the kind of book you are likely to publish. Confident authors seldom need to resort to bullying. We can also safely assume they have not been published before, because if they had ever seen the inside of an editor's office, they would have seen that this person is drowning in proposals!

Assessment

As well as the information provided by the author, the editor will have his or her views on the commercial viability of a project. The editor is more likely to be influenced in the first place by the proposed content. As with the paradox mentioned in earlier chapters – business versus creativity – here the editor might wrestle with liking or admiring a project in the face of evidence that the project might not work. Alternatively, a particular genre of book could be popular at the moment, and the editor needs to be careful that he or she is not being carried away by fashion, when the book under consideration is not a very strong candidate in that genre. One thing we can be sure of: no editor should be proposing to colleagues projects about which they feel unenthusiastic. Neither should you be proposing books to try to reach your commissioning targets. This is not appropriate to the editorial role and arena. You will only achieve excellence if you aim for it.

So how does this assessment proceed? Simply reading and discovering if you are drawn into and interested in what you are reading. If neither applies, you are likely to reject the proposal. You will also be doing a mental checklist of whether the proposal hangs together. Does the structure have a logic to it that allows the work to develop? Is anything missing? This kind of macro editorial assessment is something all of us do without thinking when we are reading anything. You may be reading a novel and suddenly thoughts emerge: 'What happened there? I don't understand. Who is this character? I need to know more. I am beginning to be confused by the plot.' And so on. Most inexperienced editors need simply to be reassured that they should let their intuitive powers of judgement come into play, which they exercise every day in their 'ordinary reading'.

If you are an editor of specialist books, in whose subjects you can only really aspire to be a well-informed amateur, you can turn to people outside the house who will help you. These are called advisers and they are experts in their field. You can send your proposals to them and ask for advice. You pay them a fee for this, of course, as their recommendations are vitally important. If you are a consumer publisher, you can also use experts. They are often called 'publishers' readers', and they are very experienced in reading and making judgements on material sent to them. These people are vital in helping you with the workflow, as it is difficult to read everything properly.

Of equal importance is making sure you have a good understanding of the market for any book. You cannot simply launch a book into the outside world and hope someone will buy it. To a large extent you can turn to the sales records of books in a similar genre and see what the demand is. This will allow you to make a reasonably accurate guess of what your print run should be.

Finally, you will be thinking about the competition. Can this book take on your competitors? Will it help enhance the publishing house's reputation? Will it, at the very least, maintain your reputation? For distinguished houses, whose brand value is that of excellence, this is a serious consideration. University presses are married to this notion, as are literary publishers such as Faber & Faber or Jonathan Cape.

During your assessment you can also consult colleagues in sales and marketing to ensure that they feel comfortable about it commercially – they know they can sell it – or production, if the book is going to make demands that are outside normal production procedures. Examples would be highly illustrated books, or children's books that come with add-ons such as soft toys (known as a 'plush').

Finally, you will want to take a view on the timing of publication, given how long the author says he or she needs to write the book. There are various dangers involved here. An author who wants to take five years can only be allowed to do this if it is a major work on a subject that is fundamentally unchanging (for example, ancient history). Most subjects are time-sensitive and you will have to bear that in mind. Even the content of academic books can be influenced or affected by the passage of time: no one should be allowed to take five years over a book about media or cultural studies, both of which are defined by their changeable nature. Similarly, you will have to think carefully about a book in a genre that is currently fashionable. Will the fashion be over by the time the book is out?

You are hoping, obviously, for a straightforward conclusion to all this. Your advisers are behind the book. There is good evidence of market demand. Your print run should allow you to manufacture the book at a cost that means each copy sold will make sufficient profit. Quite often, however, the situation is more complicated. For example, the advisers' reports may have thrown up issues that the author must tackle. Can you get the author to agree to make changes? You might be surprised at the number of authors who genuinely believe that their books are exactly right. This means the editor has to handle the discussion with some diplomacy, but should never avoid the difficulty that will be involved. The point that always must be made to the authors is that this is all part of the process of turning the book into the strongest possible candidate for publication, to ensure that when it hits the marketplace it has muscle. They should see the good sense of this, and if they cannot then you probably cannot work with them, so let them go.

Every now and then (but it is genuinely rare), you might find yourself in possession of an idea (it might even be your own) for a book or books that are genuinely breaking new ground. How on earth do you assess this when you have no evidence from the market? Here's an example. Many years ago, a young editor in academic publishing thought that there was a need for a series of books about the position of women in society. Feminism was building up a head of steam, yet apart from Virago re-issuing 'lost' novels written by women, there was nothing much else around. So, she constructed a list of titles around certain themes and spoke to a number of women doing research and writing in the field. The editorial staff were strongly supportive, but the marketing and sales departments (mostly male) did not like this idea at all. One even went to the trouble of finding out how many Women's Studies courses there were in the UK. He found just five: hardly enough in his opinion. But, she won the day by pointing out that these books would be 'must' reading on undergraduate courses in the social sciences, and furthermore she had done her homework and discovered that 50 per cent of undergraduates on such courses were women. The potential, then, was impressive. The books were published and sold very successfully, and reprinted many times.

The lesson to learn from this is that there is always data and information out there if you take the trouble to go and find it.

Commissioning

We call our editors 'commissioning editors', yet most of the time they acquire books. When you commission a book, not only do you have the idea for a book but you also know who you want to write it. So, in these circumstances, you purposefully set out to persuade someone. Unless this author is a well-known, true, writing star, it is best that you seek some discreet advice about the person you have in mind. If you ask one person (a colleague or adviser) and they say, 'Yes, this would be the right person', you are encouraged. If you ask a second one and they say, 'Yes', then you can begin to assume you are working along the right lines. If a third says 'Yes', this is the time to pop the question to that author.

It is a fatal mistake just to rush in and ask the first author who comes to mind, especially if you do not know him or her. Imagine, you take this person to lunch. You have to explain that there is something you want to discuss over lunch. Then during the course of the meal, you realize you would be making a big mistake. What do you say? 'Sorry. I thought you might like to write a book I had in mind, but now that we've talked, I realize you would not be the right person.' Take your time over this in your early days as an editor, because you do not want to find yourself covered with this kind of embarrassment. It has happened! As you get more experienced, you will learn more about authors (who is out there, who is writing what, who is interested in what) and you will get far more decisive and more confident about popping the question.

Finances

So, now we come to the money. Not so very long ago, editors said, 'We have to publish this book and we will worry about the money later', or 'This book is so marvellous that I simply know it will make lots of money for us.' Those days have gone, although it has to be said that in small, independent houses, owned by one or two individuals, that privilege of choosing what to publish, 'because this is what we want to publish' can still exist. We have to hope that their bank balances are robust. For most of us, we have to examine the financial side of every book we publish and demonstrate to our colleagues that the book will make sufficient revenue and profit.

So, what is involved here? Knowing the size of a book and the number of illustrations, drawings, photographs (in fact everything that the book will physically comprise) allows us to make calculations about the cost of manufacturing it. Chapter 6, on production, explains how these costs are calculated. The costs vary according to the format (hardback or paperback) and how many copies you wish to print.

With this information to hand, you can begin to experiment with the figures, but within the boundaries of reality. The information allows you to calculate what the turnover (or revenue) and the profit will be according to the print run and price you choose. If you choose a large print run, the unit cost for each copy printed will be smaller than if you choose a modest one. You will therefore achieve a higher profit on every copy sold, but the challenge for you is to decide whether or not you can sell all those copies; and do not forget, the overall production cost for printing more books will be higher. So, if you do not sell them, then not only has the company had to pay a bigger bill for production, but you will have lots of unsold copies stacked high in the warehouse.

So, experimenting involves looking at different print runs and deciding how many copies you can realistically sell and reach an acceptable level of turnover and profit. Most publishing houses will have targets for both, and every editor will be firmly told what they are. Editors who recommend a book for publication that does not appear likely to reach those targets will be told to look at their figures again.

How are the figures chosen? The print run should be based on sales for similar books. While every book is different, most conform to the characteristics of all books within a particular genre. So, you and your colleagues can look at the sales performance of similar books in cookery, or adult popular fiction, or school textbooks, or whatever subjects you specialize in. You need to look at the performance of books during the past year or so, not books that were published years ago. The market changes and so does demand. To the print run you now factor in the price. Multiplying the number of books to be sold by the price – less discounts to the retail trade – gives you the turnover. (Discounts are covered in Chapter 4 on marketing and Chapter 5 on sales.) From this you subtract the cost of making the book and the royalties to be paid to the author. This gives you what is known as the gross profit. To find out the net profit, you now factor in the overheads, which consist of the cost of marketing and distributing books, and all other costs involved in paying for you and your colleagues.

What you will have constructed by now is a profit and loss account for a book, known as a P & L. This is your 'best guess' at the book's financial performance if you do sell all the copies you want to print, and this is what you will take to the publications committee. There is an example of a P & L in the case study later in this chapter.

The publications committee

Different publishing houses give different names to this team meeting, but whatever it is called in your house, its function is to discuss books that have been presented as candidates for publication, and to jointly agree on whether they should be published or not. It is the editor's job to do the presentation as it is the editor who is responsible for bringing the book to the attention of the committee. The process will involve a verbal presentation (and possibly a written submission), plus all the paperwork that is involved – the P & L, the synopsis, the advisers' reports. Clearly, the editor is expected to be persuasive: to articulate the strengths of the book, the author and the market. This is no time to be shy or tongue-tied. Fundamentally, the editor has to raise interest in and excitement about the book. Again, doing this well is something that comes with experience, and the inexperienced editor who attends these committee meetings should listen carefully to how expert editors do it.

However, this is not a performance listened to by a passive audience. Audience participation is the method of the committee, with colleagues representing all the other main functions – sales, marketing, production and finance – joining in and giving their opinions. This can be very tough, even for experienced editors, so if you are new to it, be prepared to find it rather nerve-wracking. Even with experience editors can still be nervous, which is no bad thing as it keeps you on your toes and makes you determined that you will only propose books with real potential.

In large corporations it is not unusual for there to be two stages in the publication committee. For books that might require a very large advance royalty for the author, the book will go through the committee as described above, and if it is agreed, go through another committee made up of the publishing house's directors. Large advances drain very large amounts of money out of the company's bank account, which is why they need approval at the highest level.

Commitment

If you emerge with a book that has been agreed to be contracted for publication, it is now the editor's job to negotiate a contract with the author or the author's agent if he or she has one. Your P & L will contain assumptions about the rate of royalty to be paid, and the committee will have agreed the advance. You now make the proposal and hope to get agreement. Many authors will be happy with what you propose and some will ask for more. It is your job to convince the author or agent that your offer is a good one, but should you be prepared to offer a little more, you need to refer this to the editorial director. Never make an offer that you know the company cannot afford or is out of line with what you know is a typical offer for a certain kind of book. There is always a lot of informal information going around publishing circles about the kind of offers most publishers are making to their authors. You are not working in the dark here.

At this stage you will need to confirm absolutely with the author the length of the book and the delivery date, as they will form part of the contract. There is more about contracts in Chapter 7, and later in this chapter we cover difficulties that can arise with authors who deliver late or write more words than were contracted.

There is a breed of author who likes 'playing the field'. You make your offer. Out of the blue, he or she tells you that another publishing house has also made an offer. You did not know the author was sending the book out for multiple submission. He or she makes it clear that there are better terms on offer. You consider increasing the advance and the royalty. You do your sums and discover that you could still make the required profit on the book. But what if this person is lying? You have to consider the possibility. Well, perhaps after much reflection, you increase your offer. That really must be your final offer because, no doubt, Publisher X (if it really has made an offer) has also had pressure put on it, and your author then comes back with a further demand. This could go on and on! If you finally give way, you will probably comfort yourself with the thought that the author will really appreciate your 'interest' and have warm feelings towards you. He or she will be loyal. Not so. For his or her next book, he or she will be off again, chasing the rainbow of much increased terms.

List building and management

We've looked at one book, but that book you have committed to is just one of many you will be responsible for; this is known as a 'list'. A list is a collection of published books in a particular subject area, written at a particular level, and produced for a particular market. Let us look at popular fiction. You may be an editor for books in romantic fiction. We therefore have the subject, but 'romance' can take many forms. In this case, the level is 'popular'; in practice this means books that are highly 'accessible' – easy, page-turning books, unlikely to be submitted for literary prizes, but as the word 'popular' implies, having many readers. We now have the level, which means we have a notion of the market.

The word 'notion' is a deliberate choice, because no publisher can ever know *exactly* who reads their books. With millions of books sold every year, how could anyone have that kind of precise information?

Book publishing is just like many other forms of commercial activity. For example, a car manufacturer, a clothes designer and producer, a holiday company also have broad notions of who their typical purchaser is. Design, pricing and marketing are all built around what that typical purchaser will find attractive. With books, the interest of the typical purchaser gets translated into format and price. So, for popular fiction, we can fully expect a paperback with fairly basic production values but an eye-catching jacket, published at a price that will not cause the purchaser to think twice about buying it. In addition, the marketing department should have developed some well-worn routes to this market. They will have priority places to advertise the book and to attempt to get it reviewed or featured. Using our popular romance book again, we will expect the book to be advertised in mass circulation magazines and on websites, and to be sent to middle (or even low) brow newspapers for review. The question we will be asking ourselves is, 'How do we get to our typical reader to notice this book?', and all our marketing strategies will be built around that. There will be more on this in Chapter 4 on marketing.

So, it is the editor's job to take care of this list. Imagine it as a kind of family. All these books are in some way or other related to each other. Like families, there will be the occasional one that will be 'odd', but in many ways these books resemble each other. There are advantages to this. It will help you as an editor to be more selective in what you choose to publish: you will be looking for a certain kind of book that fits the list. It also has huge marketing advantages. Your marketing colleagues will have tried and tested routes to the market. The net effect is efficiency in process and in resources because of that cumulative experience.

List management means more than just preserving the coherence of your list. It means *reprinting* books that still have potential for future sales; *repricing* them so that you can make as much profit as possible out of every sale. It might mean *re-jacketing* them too if the jacket has now dated. You might even convince the marketing department (or they might convince you) that it is time to do a promotion of your list as a whole. All this is designed to keep that list alive and well. Sometimes, an editor is so over-stretched signing up new books that he or she forgets about the ones that are already in print and which, with a bit of care and attention, could carry on selling for many years. The academic house,

Routledge, has many distinguished books on its backlist – the work of Foucault and Jung, for example. Some years ago it made the decision to put many of these books in a series called 'Routledge Classics'. This created a kind of brand that would help give a renewed push to these titles, and would also allow it to repackage the books.

We must also consider *list building* here. You could find yourself in the position of being asked to start a brand new list, or suggesting this yourself. To do this, everyone needs to be convinced that the subject and the market are strong. Starting a new list is very hard work because you do not have an existing list to support you. You will be investing in something that will not make money for a few years. For a start, all the books have to be written, and by the time you add the period taken for production, you are looking at a lead-in time of at least two or three years. Until those books come on stream, all you are doing is spending money, with no backlist revenue coming in. In practice this means you have to be convinced, and to convince your colleagues, that the subject will have a strong market demand. More often than not, you have to make a shrewd judgement that this demand will still exist next year, or the year after, and so on, because of the long lead-in times. Depending on what publishing sector you work in, you might consider doing some market research amongst potential book buyers. Most certainly, you will want to consult the data compiled by a collector and analyser of book sales, such as Nielsen Bookscan. You will need to convince yourself also that you can do better than your competitors in this field – better content, better marketing. Above all, you will need to be convinced that there is *author availability* – that there are authors out there capable and willing to write these books. Some of them will have literary agents, who you will need on your side. You want their books to come to you, not your competitors.

Your list is your calling card. This collection of books represents what you, an editor, and your publishing house, are all about. It is a reflection of your strength in an area and is what brings authors to you. You neglect its care and management at your peril.

Digital publishing

Increasingly editors now have to take digital publishing into their portfolio of responsibilities. This is a quite different challenge from those that come through publishing books. To begin with, let us make clear what we mean here. In this section we are not covering books that are made available online as simple PDFs, or for use on an e-reader. These are essentially exact copies of the books, though additionally being delivered via a digital platform.

We are referring here to books that are generically developed into a different, digital form. That form is interactive and often multi-dimensional. By contrast, a book is a linear platform. You begin at the beginning and you move through it until you come to the end. You can, if you wish, skip some sections, or you can recap and go back to an earlier section. The linear form of the book, as we proceed through it, allows us to pursue a train of thought, absorbing what is essentially a narrative. We are following the author's train of thought and the way the author wants us to work through the book, bit by bit, in a logical fashion, as he or she wrote it. We tend to think of narrative as applying solely to novels, but the author of any book is trying to gain our attention through the gradual unfolding of a kind of story.

There are huge advantages to this traditional form. Progress through reading is comparatively slow, allowing the mind to absorb, reflect and remember. This is why many people get alarmed at the idea of the printed book disappearing because they fear that people will lose the ability to focus and remember, and their concentration will become fragmented. They also do not wish to see the demise of what is one of the most successful artefacts ever invented. It has survived because it is extraordinarily effective at conveying thoughts, ideas, information, reflection and entertainment and is very easy to use!

Publishers, however, have to be pragmatic and also have to reflect cultural changes, opportunities and demands, which is why digital content creation has to figure in their activities and their plans. Some content is ideally suited for digital development. The digital format allows readers to interact with the product, using it to follow their particular needs or interests. A book cannot, by the touch of a button, have one of its sections expanded, or be linked to a video, or to the sound of music, or to a series of photographs. A book has a certain number of pages, bound in a linear order, and therefore has a comparatively 'concrete' structure.

So, what do you publish, and what do you think could be turned into an interactive product? At this point, we need to caution readers not to go into imaginative freefall, but to focus on what is practical, especially from the point of view of the user. Think of this book, for example. Theoretically, there is no reason why, if a digital version were developed, you could not, at the click of a button, see a video of a Booker Prize presentation, or see the progression of roughs from the designer who worked on a jacket, or listen to a disgruntled author talking, or watch a video of a sales conference, or the inside of a warehouse, or books being printed. It would be such fun but would it be financially viable? After all, the market for introductions to publishing is very, very niche. Would the revenues justify the development costs?

This leads us to first principles, which apply as much to a digital product as they do to a conventional book:

- Is there a market for this product and can I define that market?
- Do I know how to reach this market; that is, can I outline the routes I would take to the market to make sales?
- Do I know exactly why this market would find it beneficial to buy this product?
- Can I produce the product in a form that the market would find attractive?
- Can I produce it to a price that the market will find acceptable and that will ensure I will make the required profit?

You must satisfy yourself that you have the answers to these questions. Furthermore, you must be able to define what you wish to achieve with this product, which means evaluating its aims and how they will add value to what the buyer could get by simply purchasing the book. Being able to access a video, or music, for example, must really enhance the viewers' understanding or perception of something that has been stated in a book. Your product will not be powerful if it is not strongly linked to learning values.

Remember that you are not entirely on strange territory here. As an editor who has come to grips with your books and their markets, you already have a good knowledge base of what the reader is interested in, and how that interest might be developed. If you have any uncertainties, you might choose to test your assumptions about the product by working with a focus group, composed of readers, advisers, teachers, librarians and authors, depending on the precise nature of the content and the market.

Our relationship with costs for these products differs from those for books. A book is by comparison a simple thing. It is written, prepared for press, printed and bound. Its progress is also linear. The development of a digital product is more complex and will often involve an outside party, called a developer, although some publishers may have their own in-house software development team serving the same role. It will be the developer's job to take the book, listen to your briefing – what you want to achieve – and then in a structured way, play with and explore the book, creating something different, but generic, in the sense that it grows out of the book. This involves not just expertise and imagination, but also time. The cost of that time is likely to be your greatest overhead. Costs can vary quite considerably, but you may need to give your developer some freedom to explore properly what might be achieved.

What comes first – the book or the e-package?

Currently, most publishers will see the book as their core product but will have ambitions to develop a more complex, interactive package out of that book. However, such a book-centred approach may not be the most appropriate when considering digital development; in the electronic publishing world, it makes more sense to think of all the products equally (for example, website, e-books, mobile version, iPhone app and book), and the printed book may therefore be just one product that is spun out of the project as a whole, and may not be the biggest earner for the publisher.

The starting point for our hypothetical project (training book in publishing?) may be you and the author sitting down to plan the development of a strong book, just as you always do. But this time, there will be far more planning involved because you have to look beyond the book. Imagine that your book has a flexible outline: you can expand it in different directions. The questions that you and your author will want to explore may be along the following lines:

- If I can imagine my book content not being bound – literally – by static pages and printed words, which bits of content would I like to expand, which I could not contain in a book anyway?
- Of these areas of 'expansion', which will the reader-viewer find interesting, useful, compelling?
- Are there any additional features that could usefully accompany the text that would help the user/reader?
- Which pieces of content lend themselves to updating?

Such questions will also be asked of colleagues in the publishing house, especially the digital team, and of any special advisers you may have. In this case, we could imagine that we want to add many extra case studies, plus a multiple-choice assessment package that sits alongside the main text. This may already create a challenge for you; perhaps your author does not have the time or skills to create all the questions and answers for the multiple-choice tool. If this is the case, you will need to commission someone else to provide that content in the correct form. He or she will need to liaise very closely with the author of the text so that the questions are closely integrated with the main text.

Your small team of authors will eventually deliver the work in an agreed digital format, which will be converted into structured XML format either by your production department or by an outsourced agency. From this XML, the core book content (without the extra case studies and the multiple-choice questions) will be made into a PDF and can be sent to the printer. The XML will also be used to generate a number of e-book formats; as your content is in XML it can become something more ambitious than just a traditional book, or a book that can be read digitally on the screen or a hand-held device. It can now be seen as a database from which one can develop richer ways of interacting with the content.

A good approach in the development stage would be to plan the complete package, containing all the added-value, multi-media content that you and the author believe will be attractive to your market. At the core of this may be the printed book, which can be extracted from the XML database and printed. However, it is entirely possible that, by the time the author team has delivered the content, the market may have changed and you decide only to publish online or as e-books and not to include a printed artefact at all. Planning it this way around, instead of just constructing the content for the book and from there thinking about where you might go digitally, has great advantages. It allows you from the beginning to think of this product as a large, flexible collection of resources, which you might use in different ways.

The digital content will present you with additional editorial decisions to be made:

- Which of the possible content resources will you actually use? If you have included them in your development plan they probably have merit, so do not discard these ideas. They might be put to good use later when you have the budget to use them.

- If you are going to use multi-media in your e-product, such as video, audio, pictures or artwork, you will need permission to include them, and there might be substantial fees to be paid.

- You need to ask yourself which of these resources really are useful, or would including them just be 'a nice idea'.

- Some material might be judged 'background material'. This would not be essential to the flow of presentation but could, perhaps, include something about the author. Again, you need to make a judgement about its value.

- How much do you wish to include links to other resources – websites, for example, including your own website and other digital materials? You will need to think about how to monitor if the links go dead, and what the editorial process would be for updating them or adding new ones.

- Would it be preferable to have these links in a separate section if they are not essential to the narrative flow of your e-product? Some reader-viewers might be irritated by them, although it is possible to provide a device allowing the links to be temporarily suspended.

- How do you envisage the narrative flow in operation? Remember that this is not a linear flow, like a book. Your reader-viewer is now capable of entering one section and then switching to another. Yet, as a whole, it has got to hang together and make sense. It is possible now to have several versions of the same content within this package. The versions could be pitched at different levels, for example, of difficulty, or with different focuses. The reader-viewer chooses the version he or she wishes to start at, and then progresses to another.

- If you are planning to update the text content, for example by adding new case studies, up-to-date references in the bibliography, or new questions, you will need to agree the terms for such provision with the author, and plan how often those updates will occur and what the workflow will be to add them to the live content.

You will need to make these editorial decisions in conjunction with the author team, your digital colleagues and with the marketing department. These kinds of e-packages require group-based development work far more than most books ever would. For very large complex projects comprising hundreds or thousands of aggregated works, the authorial vision may well owe much more to you and your digital publishing colleagues than to any of the creators of the individual texts or other items of content. For these electronic products, you will also need to think about them in one fundamentally different way. Whereas a book would be published and reprinted, and perhaps be eventually developed into a second edition or more, your digital package has the potential to last far longer because it can be constantly updated. Do not assume that all these packages will be with you forever. Just like books, some will be in greater demand than others, but you can improve all of them with relative ease.

How will the development work progress?

These days it would be very unusual for a publishing house not to employ someone with the specific objective of e-publishing development, unless the house has made a decision to keep out of it and stick to books at least for the time being. Your knowledge of the subject field for which you publish is, clearly, very important, but your e-publishing development manager has knowledge of the technology, how it works, and how it can be designed to suit users. Depending on his or her experience, this person can be a major contributor to the development of an over-arching vision of the product, as well as having the skills to manage and oversee its day-to-day production.

The digital packages you are devising force you to think about your customers – their needs, their interests, how they will use the resources you are putting together – in an acute way. This is a kind of bespoke publishing on a large scale. You will need the input of your e-publishing development colleagues, but also those in the marketing department. This is without question a group effort, and in fact your part may be a relatively minor one by comparison to that of book publishing. The team is likely to include you, the editor, the digital development manager, the marketing manager and two or more production colleagues, one of whom might be responsible for the book version. But let us not forget about the author! There may be more than one for such a large project, although in such cases their role may amount to little more than assigning you the digital publishing rights. Alternatively, an author could be a graduate student on a short-term contract with the publisher specifically to create content for the online product.

The relationship with the authors is not unlike that for books in many respects. The author or authors will write the material, and since they understand the market for their material very well, you rely on them hugely. But, as with books, it is the publisher's job to bring discipline to decisions about what is actually to be included. An author might want a tremendous amount of freedom to choose content, but it will be the job of you and your team to rein in any unrealistic 'wish lists', as indeed you would with a book. It will be you and your team's responsibility to persuade the author to concentrate on the book itself but to join you in discussions on what digital enhancements you wish to provide. Finally, although all slippage is bad, the impact of late delivery on digital projects will be much worse than for most books. Much greater revenue is likely to be dependent on the content, and schedules with the developer may need to be renegotiated at your expense. The timely provision of data is always the biggest significant risk for any digital project.

The team is likely to start with an outline for a project to which a fairly rudimentary budget has been allocated. Such a project will have to be approved, of course, before any work can begin. The next task is to refine the outline and add detail before it goes out to tender with developers. Within this process, anticipated costs now need to become far more accurate. Once the plan and the costs have been refined, you turn to the developer who will (ideally) ask you detailed questions, then provide a response and a cost estimate. If you have approached several developers, you now decide with which you will work. Once you have made your selection, and if that is approved, the project goes into the design phase. The aim of the design phase is to produce, with the developer, a document of detailed requirements that will focus on content, scope and specification. Once that is finally approved, along with costs, the work begins.

This approach, where the publisher and developer work out everything in fine detail before any software is written, is only one possible way of working, although it is the method used by many publishers. You may want to work with your developer in a more flexible manner, without a detailed specification. In this way, the developer would produce many iterations for critical comment, and devise the resource in a more collaborative way. This can achieve results much more quickly, but certainly requires a considerable amount of trust in the developer.

Community and community benefits

You will often read the word 'community' in connection with digital publishing. 'Community' can apply not just to the reader-viewers and their particular interests, but is reflected in the way in which publishers work together to develop these projects and bring them to market. These projects allow authors to write collaboratively, and some have become quite accustomed to working this way either on the web or by contributing to blogs or wikis. Because of this prior activity, a groundswell of author-led interest and involvement can develop, which will be of great commercial value when your project is eventually launched. It will also provide great benefits for your marketing colleagues as this same community can be reached through the ever-growing number of social networking tools. Your development team can use members of the reader-viewer community to test out ideas as the product is being written and developed, and after the launch. There is the potential for a depth of involvement that could never be achieved when publishing a book.

Income and profitability

Here we are working on different dimensions than those for books, where there is a relatively simple set of relationships between cost, print runs and pricing. The cost of digital development is often very high compared to most books. The income from the printed book should not be seen as supporting digital costs. The book can stand alone, but so must the e-package. You will have various options available to you when you launch it, which can include:

- Selling it outright for a price that reflects that of the book but also the benefits of the digital enhancements. It should, therefore, be higher. However, if it is online, you may still need to charge an annual hosting and maintenance fee, since you will have ongoing costs simply to keep it live on the internet.

- Selling it via a subscription model that allows the buyer to have full access to the package for a certain length of time, with the option to renew the subscription.

- Encouraging and accepting advertising for your e-package site, which will require your marketing department to engage with the online advertising market.

- Taking payment from authors who would like to write commentary on aspects of the site.

As with books, you have to make educated guesses about the sales income you will make, based on your assumptions of user take-up and traffic. Books have provided us with much hard sales evidence over long periods. It will be some time before you are able to work with relatively secure business models for these digital packages, although the large publishers who have been publishing digitally for some time now have very good data. What is more, new digital products provide a great opportunity for your marketing colleagues to conduct some effective market research and analysis to help make the strategic case for publishing your project in the first place. Although you may be breaking new ground, you need to hold fast to those questions posed at the very beginning of this section on digital publishing. You are still a publisher. The potential of digital technology provides the ability to publish material in a different way. The questions remain the same.

Working with other departments

You are part of a team. Some work will be done just by you and your assistant – project assessment and contracting authors being the main ones. But as has been implied, even that is not strictly done alone. At various crucial points you will combine with colleagues to reach collaborative decisions. Your responsibilities in relation to your colleagues are wide ranging and ongoing and it is undesirable that you see your job as being separate from theirs.

Marketing

Your responsibilities here are two-fold. The first is to provide the marketing department with all the relevant information needed to construct marketing strategies for your new books. The marketing department will be experienced in this respect, but in a general way. They have a good grasp of broad approaches to marketing your genre of books, but you must supply them with the vital detail that helps them tailor-make a good marketing campaign. Each individual book and author will have some interesting difference that provides the hook, or hooks, on which to hang a successful campaign.

The author knows more about the book than anyone else, and you are the person who knows most about it after the author. You examined it in detail in the first place and you know the arguments in favour of publishing it, which included good information on the market and demand. This must be transferred to the marketing department in your briefings to them – on paper and verbally. This information will include:

- readership and level;
- competitive titles, with differences and strengths between your title and the others clearly stated;
- author track record (if this is an established author), and/or anything notable about the author that could help sell the book; in this respect, notoriety could be as helpful as distinction;
- sales information about comparative titles you (or your competitors) have published so that the sales representatives have

good evidence to present to the bookshops to endorse the book's potential;

- any topicality about the book that will help with the timing of the launch;
- publications likely to review the book and other media opportunities.

In addition to this, it will be your job to ensure that the author fills in the authors' questionnaire (AQ) properly. Most authors do not like filling in forms, although the more entrepreneurial ones will take the opportunity to fling as much information onto the form as possible to ensure the book is marketed properly, some of which will not necessarily be relevant. The AQ gives the author the opportunity to provide as much information as possible about the book and its readership. It also asks the author to describe the book, usually in about 200 words or so, which will be used (once polished by the editor) as the basis of the book's blurb, catalogue copy and advertisements.

In practice, the information that the editor gives the marketing department mirrors to a great extent what the author has provided, supplemented with the editor's own market knowledge, which is why it is important that the editor ensures that the author takes the AQ seriously. There are authors who have been known to answer questions with: 'I'm sure you know more about that than I do, so I'll leave it to you.'

Most authors will try to influence how a book is marketed, and some will genuinely have good ideas and be good self-publicists too. But, bearing in mind that most authors have never worked in publishing (and often do not fully understand how it functions), or in marketing, you need to exercise some control here, keeping in mind what is most realistic. What authors are likely to hear about in respect of book marketing are the big deals and the big campaigns, and many want a similar hard sell for their book. A surprising number of authors tick the box that asks, 'Would you be prepared to go on television?'

There is one thing you must never do and that is to allow the author to drive the marketing campaign. In practice this means not agreeing with the author that he or she can definitely have an author tour, or a book signing session, or will appear on radio or television, for example. It is the marketing department's responsibility to draw up the marketing plan and decide on the most effective way of spending its resources to achieve maximum sales. Undoubtedly, there will be some authors whom the marketing department will want to make very good use of, as part of the publicity drive behind a book, but that is for marketing to decide.

This section has dwelt entirely on the editor's role in working with marketing on new books, and that is appropriate because it is with new books that the greatest marketing spend and effort is made, and where you can make your biggest contribution. There is, of course, much more for you to consider in the next chapter, on marketing. One aspect of marketing new books, and your role in that, deserves special mention, and that is the sales conference.

The sales conference

Editors are still (mostly) the people who present new books to the sales reps. In high-profile consumer publishing, you now find colleagues from the marketing department carrying out that function, but generally speaking, it is the editor's responsibility. Frankly, there are many editors who would prefer someone else to do this, because this is a difficult, demanding responsibility. Many editors find the process daunting or frightening.

What you have to bear in mind is that the reps will be the first people to go out into the marketplace (in this case, the book retail sector) to persuade the bookshops to buy the books. They need good evidence of a book's potential. They want to be shown very attractive book covers. They want to hear about the first-class marketing plans for the books. At least the latter is someone else's job – the marketing department – but the core challenge of exciting their interest and enthusiasm is down to you.

So, you have to stand there and 'sell' the books to the reps. This will not entail giving them the full detail of the content. Editors have been known to outline the entire plot of a novel to the reps – a brilliant way of turning them off. What they want to know is:

- Just a little about the book. They will have time to read catalogue copy and blurbs on jacket proofs during the course of their work so they have a better understanding of its content. So do not waste time on this at the sales conference.

- Who is going to read it? Who will have to read it (because they need to)? Who will want to read it (because they will find it interesting). In a perfect world, of course, it is good to be able to combine 'need' with 'want'. By and large, 'need' books tend to be specialist books, and 'want' will be consumer books.

- Evidence of market demand – your sales figures for similar books, or maybe the success of similar books from other publishers.
- Finally, there are the classic 'three bullet points'. You will be expected to sum up the strengths of the book in three points. These points are always expressed in terms of the 'benefits' to the reader in buying the book. This means you have to turn your relationship with the book around. This is not about how you rate the book, but how you think the book-buying public will rate it. This is a small but significant twist, and many inexperienced editors find this very difficult at the beginning of their careers.

This information should be presented to the reps in an interesting and preferably entertaining way. You want them to listen to you; you want them on your side; you want them to remember your presentation. Reps have heard it all, including too many misconceived, false hopes about new books. The reps are more likely to take notice if you are completely honest when you say something like, 'This book is in no way original. It's a kind of "cookbook". The author has compiled a textbook in exactly the way he knows the students will find most useful, and let me tell you why.' You have shown confidence by being honest (confidence in yourself and in your book) and you are also showing a full understanding of market needs.

Production

It is the editor's job to hand his or her manuscripts/disks over to production in a state of readiness for preparing for and manufacturing the books. For pre-press work, this means:

- Ensuring the manuscript is complete and that the disk version is identical to the hard copy version. 'Complete' means you have everything that appears in the contents list. Occasionally, a publishing house will accept a less-than-complete manuscript if the book has a high priority. In this case, the author will be feeding bits through to the editor as soon as they are written. This, however, is an ideal recipe for confusion, so is best avoided.
- Checking to make sure that all illustrations (if they are to be used) are also there.
- Asking the author to verify that permission to quote someone else's work in this book has been cleared.

- Checking that the work is the length stated in the contract. (This is a frequent issue that is covered below in the section on problems when dealing with authors.)

- Letting the production department know if there are any dates when the author is not available for answering copy-editing queries or checking their proofs.

- Informing the production department about anything unusual in the work – spelling, typefaces, foreign languages, for example – that they need to be aware of.

- Providing a rough brief, at this stage, of the type of jacket that will be suitable/desirable for the book.

Once everything has been checked, you will pass the manuscript and its disk to production and, in theory, there will be less involvement for you. (The next stages in the life of a new book will be covered in Chapter 6, on book production.) Your job, however, has not finished. You remain clearly visible in the background. You may have passed on the project, but your responsibility for it has definitely not ended. You keep an eye on progress, to ensure there are no delays in production, and you must make it clear to your colleagues that you are there to intervene if the author is difficult in any way. This author is still *your* author.

Contracts

You may have a contracts department, or you may have model contracts that you adjust according to your needs. You may also find yourself dealing with literary agents who insist that their client be provided for not through *your* contract but *their* contract. This agent will draw up their contract for your and the author's signature. In the past, publishers resisted this, but agents are now very powerful. The issuing of the contract has symbolic value: it shows who is in charge!

Contracts departments are commonly found within the large publishing corporations, especially those with consumer publishing programmes. Such consumer books need expertly drawn-up contracts adapted to individual commercial needs. Model contracts, on the other hand, are quite common in specialist publishing where mammoth advances, escalating royalties and special deals are less likely to be found. Remember, any contract is a reflection of the commercial potential of a book.

We will be going into further detail on contracts later, in Chapter 7, but for the moment, let us look at the editor's prime responsibilities:

- Negotiating with authors over advances and royalties, and the territories that the author is prepared to license to the publishing house.

- Further negotiation over particular rights such as electronic, translation, TV and film tie-ins, which you might want to include in the contract.

- Being prepared to fight or haggle occasionally. Even academic authors have been known to ask for advances or royalties that are above the norm for their kind of book. It will be your job to offer what is realistic, and above all, not to get so caught up with negotiations that you end up paying too much.

Rights

Although books can achieve good revenue and profits in their original formats, there is often additional income to be made in the valuable extras, called 'rights'. Most commonly, rights are sold in the form of translations, television and film versions, serialization and digital formats. All these represent a change to the book in its original format, but nevertheless, they are generic developments of an original work of intellectual property. We shall be looking at the work of the rights department in Chapter 8, but for the moment, what are the editor's responsibilities in that respect?

The relationship with rights is similar in some respects to the relationship with the marketing department. Even if your rights department is run by very experienced and expert colleagues, they will need you to give them the kind of detail that should help them sell rights. Rights colleagues will want to know about the:

- subject;
- readership;
- level;
- overseas potential;
- different media potential.

If your author, with your encouragement, has filled in the authors' questionnaire properly, you might find that he or she has been able to provide some relevant information that will help in selling translation rights. This information could be about similar books that have been translated into, for example, Italian, French or Chinese. It could be information about the interest in a subject in a particular part of the world.

Added to this are your insights and hunches about any other, different, form of a book that could have commercial interest and which a skilled rights executive can sell. This would include digital platforms and film and television formats. As ever, one is thinking about what projects have succeeded before, and if that success can be replicated with a new project.

It will be the rights executives' jobs to sell these 'spin-offs' of your books, and many of them are both imaginative and assiduous in their work, but they will be even more effective if you give them all the relevant help they need. Experience will eventually teach you what is 'relevant' and what is simply unfocused enthusiasm. You cannot sell all books into translated editions, or to television or film executives, or to digital publishers. So, forget about trying to help the rights department take over the world, and give them information on projects that they can realistically expect to sell.

Working with authors

Working with authors is one of the greatest pleasures but also one of the most difficult aspects of the job. Earlier we pointed out that publishing is almost unique in that the creators of the company's products do not work for it. They have a kind of freelance relationship, which in turn involves a set of processes and responses that are different from those between employer and employee. The freelance offers his or her skills to a publishing company, which then decides if they are needed or wanted, and pays the freelance accordingly. If these freelances (your authors) turn out to be writers of successful books, you will want to keep them – by which time you might find yourself in competition to keep them!

Your authors certainly will not stay if they think you did a poor or half-hearted job of publishing their books, or if they think they can get better paid elsewhere. A 'poor job' could mean second-rate production values, or second-rate marketing. In a way, that is a more difficult problem to fix than one of raising their earnings (ie royalties), because it suggests that the skills resources in your publishing house are inferior.

A fertile area for difficulties between publisher and author is one where expectations differ. Your author has one thing in his or her mind's eye regarding the publication of a book, and you have something rather different. There really ought not to be such differing views, but there sometimes are because you are working on the inside of a publishing house, and your author is working outside it. Those outside the business see the reviews, the review articles, the adverts, the media appearances for books and authors who are able easily to garner attention. Sadly, this kind of treatment is not destined for the vast majority of books that get published, but it does not preclude some authors from thinking they will, or ought, to get that treatment. This is where grief lies.

What authors want to be reassured about is that they are not being given a lesser treatment than a similar author or book, and that all plans and resources really do fit the needs of the book and its market. If the authors have agents, you will most certainly be going through a justificatory exercise with them, if you want to keep these authors. The second thing that authors want is not to be told that they are lucky to get the publishing treatment they have been given. If you allow that message to get across to your authors, eventually they will leave to offer their next book to another publisher.

Next we discuss some of the classic problems that can arise in dealing with authors.

Late delivery of the contracted work

This is so common that in a way it is unremarkable. It is called 'slippage' and every publishing house suffers from it. Its effect, however, is not unremarkable. Succinctly put, here we have a situation where a product is not available for sale at a time when the market was expecting it. Imagine how the buying public would feel if other sorts of products simply did not turn up when expected. Think of the media coverage if a new car did not hit the forecourts of the car dealers. While there are greater sums of money at stake when it comes to selling cars, each individual book that does not make it to the marketplace on time represents income that is delayed. That is serious.

This situation illustrates the difference in relationship between the creator and the producer in publishing a book and how it is unlike most other products. The author has been contracted but, since writing a book is considered not to be a mechanical exercise but one involving deep and critical thought processes, books cannot be churned out. This is the common attitude and one that many authors subscribe to. Although conscious of the contracted delivery date, they believe it is reasonable for them to have extra time if they need it. In principle, one should be able to allow for that, but publishing is a business, and the author is in a business relationship with you. In turn, you are in a business relationship with the market, and that means that a book must be available to the marketplace at the time announced. If it is not available, then you cannot sell it and you and the author have become responsible for a minor hole in the company's finances. If this just happened to one book, the problem would not be serious, but sadly, this is what happens to many books. Imagine the cumulative effect in a very large house with dozens of editors with a large proportion of the titles they are handling arriving late.

Books whose length is greater than contracted

Again, here is an area where the authors feel they are entitled to some latitude. 'A few more words will not make much difference, and they might improve the book.' Rarely is the issue about a few more words; quite commonly the book is 10 or 20 per cent over length. Remember when you proposed your book to the publication committee? You also provided them with a profit and loss account that showed the projected cost of making that book. If your author exceeds that length, then the cost will go up and the company's bills will be bigger. What do you do? Do you ignore the problem and hope nobody notices that your projected 250-page book is in fact 300 pages long? Do you consider putting the price up to compensate for those extra costs? What if the market thinks that price is too high and resists purchase? Or do you negotiate with an author to make cuts?

Your immediate problem is that any author who has struggled through the immensely demanding process of writing a book will not be in the mood to cut it now. You might be lucky: perhaps there is some obvious replication that can be removed. Mostly, if you pursue making cuts, you will be involved in some difficult negotiations with authors.

Occasionally, you will decide you cannot cut. An editor once commissioned an author to write a book on psychiatry, at a length of 80,000 words. She was so pleased when it was delivered that she did not look at its length but immediately began to read it. She was very pleased indeed with it, and even happier when the adviser to whom she sent it wrote back that it was the best book on the subject he had read in 20 years. Off into production, with cheers and hurrahs, it went. This was followed by a stunned silence when production reported that the book was, literally, twice the length. After much discomfort and internal debate, she decided to go ahead with the book as it was, since it was truly exceptional, and to price it about £2 above the norm. She knew this was a risk. However, on publication date, when full-page and very flattering reviews appeared in the quality dailies, she knew she had made the right decision. That same book went on to appear in four editions.

This is a nice story. But do not fool yourself that many of your over-length books will fall into that category. Mostly, they are not better for being too long.

Inappropriate author behaviour

This is the arena where the core of the problem of different expectations is played out. Imagine being an author. Would you not think it reasonable to have some involvement in, say, the jacket design, or the marketing plans? We are confident that you would have some expectation in respect of both, quite rightly so, but there is a difference between being involved and expecting to drive either of these areas. It is sometimes difficult for authors to stand back from their work. Self-evidently, so great has been their control over creating the content, they cannot let go. Yet very few authors are either jacket designers or marketers.

Publishers must and should be allowed to exercise their expertise. After all, marketing plans are drawn up and jackets designed every day of the working week in publishing offices. We should, and do, know what works. This is why the majority of author contracts state that control over the production and marketing of a book resides with the publisher, but exercising that right can sometimes be complicated. As with any industry, the marketplace and the product look rather different from the inside than they do from the outside. The outsider can be prone to 'good ideas'; the insider has learnt from experience what works and what does not.

Authors have been known to leave a publishing house and take their next books elsewhere because they have been infuriated by their publisher refusing to use their favourite picture on the jacket, or ignoring their suggestions for widespread advertising, for example. One author abandoned an editor when she published a book with a picture of a man on it. He was adamant that people would think this was him. No persuasion in the world could convince him that if there is a picture of an author on the jacket, it is usually either on an inside flap or on the back.

Striking a deal with authors

The deal is not just about the money and the contract. It is also about creating and maintaining a professional relationship with your authors. What both parties should be prepared to develop is a partnership, which acknowledges that the interests of authors and publishers coincide almost completely. It is not a partnership of identical rights and obligations but one that recognizes that each party has different strengths and weaknesses. The author must be prepared to recognize that the publisher has professional strengths in the processes of publishing. Why else does the author need a publisher! Similarly, the publisher must acknowledge that the author, whose writing is his or her creation, must be encouraged, supported and sometimes guided during the act of creation. The publisher should no more attempt to write the book than the author should attempt to publish it.

There should not be a high wall between these two areas of expertise but a reasonable dividing line over which each can hop. The editor, in some ways, is in the more advantageous position. Editors develop knowledge and experience in the subject areas or genres that they publish, and their markets. They are often helped and guided by other experts – those advisers referred to earlier – who can provide very good content and marketing information. The author is by comparison left in ignorance about how editors and publishing work.

Quite often all the author will know about how we publishers actually work is through stories: stories in the media, stories from other authors he or she might know, including stories from angry authors who felt they were not treated properly, and stories from happy, satisfied authors.

At the beginning of your relationship you can take the opportunity to begin constructing a partnership that stands a good chance of becoming a good story. Let us imagine being an author and knowing next to nothing about how publishing works. If you know nothing, your imagination begins to fill in the empty spaces. That authorial imagination can range from one where authors are asked for their choice of paper that the book will be printed on, can include as many illustrations as they like, can choose the jacket design, will be invited and paid to go on author tours and will see their books reviewed in every single national newspaper, to the other end of the continuum (sadly sometimes in real life) where they had absolutely no say in anything, and worse, the publisher completely neglected them and their modest requests. In sum, they felt excluded from the publication of the very books they wrote.

All good relationships are founded on reality, with a little bit of fantasy included to lift the spirits. Publishing these days is definitely grounded in reality, but if you are an editor you also need a bit of fantasy (about success) to push you through all that work. So perhaps the way forward with authors is to combine both. Spell out the reality, but enjoy working together to attain your dream of success. How might this work?

Reserve some time with your authors to help build a picture for them about how publishing works. We do not mean how all of publishing works, but how your publishing house and your colleagues will work on their books, and what their part in this will be.

Explain the planning and financial consequences for the house if the book is delivered late. Also spell out the consequences of much higher costs, and therefore higher book prices, if the book is delivered at a length that is not the one stipulated in the contract and agreed by the author.

Give them a reasonably accurate estimation of when they can expect to be asked to answer the queries that will arise from the copy-editing of their book. Depending on your house's scheduling practices, you could say something like, 'Queries will come to you about a month after you have delivered the manuscript', and then a similar kind of estimate for proofreading. At this point make it absolutely clear that the dates they will be given for their part in either of these activities really do have to be kept.

The role of the marketing department and how it works needs to be clarified here too. You can explain how the marketing department never takes a 'blue skies' approach but uses tried and tested routes to the market. Depending on the subject area of your list, you could be talking about campaigns involving mailings to known book buyers, viral marketing, in-store campaigns, targeted advertising, school visits, bookshop signings – the list is potentially very long, and there is more on this in the next chapter on marketing. What you are aiming to explain to the author is the choice of route to the market and why you are taking it. If the author asks for a treatment that you know will not work, say so, and explain why. In all seriousness, an author of a social work book should not be expecting you to send lots of review copies to national newspapers or magazines. But you can console them with your alternative view of success: a campaign to the main professional journals and magazines, to the training bodies for social work, and a book launch at a social work conference. Your main message to all authors is that every book gets a marketing budget and that the money in that budget will only be used for activity that is likely to lead to sales. You will not spend it on what might seem like a 'nice idea'. One final tip about marketing is that if the author comes up with an idea and you are really not sure whether it would work or not, talk to your colleagues in marketing before you make any promises. If you are really stuck with an author who does not believe you are going to do a good marketing job on his or her book, show them one of your successful titles. He or she will probably recognize it. Tell your author that you will be applying the same treatment to his or her book that you did for that one. Now your author knows you are not underselling him or her, and it will be up to the content of the book to make its way to success.

A fertile area for author concerns will be the jacket or cover of his or her book. If you are very lucky, you will find yourself dealing with authors who recognize that design is not their expertise and will leave it to you. Or you can equally be struggling to explain to authors, hell bent on having their favourite Rembrandt picture, or a photograph by Man Ray, or their daughter's watercolour of the Thames at sunset featured on the jacket, why you cannot use those visuals. The first two will be very expensive to use – they will command high permission fees. The third could just be quite bad art. All three might, in any case, be highly unsuitable for the book.

This is not something from which you can entirely exclude the author. Having written, perhaps, 75,000 words or more, the author has a perfect right to want to feel happy about the outside appearance of his or her book. During the course of this relationship you are building with the author, you need to address directly the question of how the book will look and be prepared to discuss his or her ideas, and if any of them are suitable, to pass on the ideas to the design department. If his or her ideas are not useful, you must explain why you will not use them. You cannot simply say, 'No, I don't like that.' If an author persists with an idea that you know will be too expensive, or too complicated (the best design is usually simple design), or will misrepresent the book, say you will run it past the sales department. Sales will inevitably agree with you, and experience shows that most authors, when faced with the opinion of a sales force, tend to accept the opinion of the experts.

In relation to jackets, the best way forward is to include authors by asking for their views. Many, once given the opportunity to get involved, will quickly defer to you and your design department. They most certainly will want to get directly involved if you tell them that their opinions are neither sought nor valued!

These are the main problems that tend to arise, and they should feature heavily in the 'deal' you make with the author. By explaining how things work, and directly addressing problematic areas, you are being honest and you are being helpful. Authors will have a far better idea of the publishing process and what they can expect for themselves and for their book. They also begin to have a proper understanding of their part in the process. They are no longer excluded. No one likes being excluded, and if you try to push the author to one side, you are asking for trouble. You are instead beginning to deconstruct that cooperative and professional relationship you hope for.

When should this conversation with authors take place? Ideally, roughly at the time when the contract is signed, so they can begin their writing work with a context to think about. Obviously, you should only need to do this with new authors. Yes, the publishing process is some way off. It will not begin until their books are delivered, but at least they will come to it prepared. For editors dealing with authors of consumer books, you will inevitably be dealing with an agent, who will certainly want to get the best for his or her author but who should have some understanding, indeed experience, of the publishing process and, in turn, will be able to guide the author too. Agents can sometimes be good allies of editors, but they will be quick to complain and ask for redress should you be less than professional in dealing with their authors.

Making life difficult for everyone else

Your responsibilities and your challenges do not lie solely with authors. They also lie with your colleagues. The publishing team is the sum of many abilities, talent, experience and hard work and one weak member of the team can undo all the good things provided and achieved by the others. Here's where editors can do most damage:

- Believing they can work in semi-isolation and being resistant to team work.
- Behaving as though they are the most important people in the publishing house and expecting everyone to defer to them and to their opinions.
- Expecting that everyone else in the team will always agree with them over a book's potential, because they have got too close to the book or the author and have suspended objective judgement.

These are character or attitude weaknesses and a good line manager will or should put them straight. Eventually, editors might do this themselves, as they begin to sense their unpopularity. However, we must also not overlook carelessness or laziness. Attention to detail is vital in publishing. Let us look at some examples.

Getting the contract right. Once a contract is written and signed by the author, you cannot change it without great persuasion. Mistakes can be very expensive, so the deal you make must entail advances and royalties that are appropriate for the book, and you must know exactly what rights you have bought. *Harry Potter's* publishers famously turned down the film rights, which would have been a very expensive mistake indeed if they had not done rather well with book sales! Another publisher sold 3,000 copies of a book to a US publisher, without realizing they did not have US rights to sell. This was both illegal and very expensive because the books had to be destroyed.

It is usually the editor's job to call up the ISBN for a new book. An International Standard Book Number is the key identifier for any book. There are dozens of books called *An Introduction to Psychology* in print. The only way to pin down exactly which book we are dealing with is through its ISBN. If you put an incorrect number for the book through the publishing house's system, you can cause mayhem. The retail trade will become very angry if it is trying to order a book and no one recognizes its number.

Next, you cannot get by with inadequate briefings. It is the editor's duty to give a full briefing on a book to the production and marketing departments. In practice this means that you make detailed submissions containing all the information that those departments really need to know. Sloppy and incomplete briefs soon become incorporated in the system, leading to mistakes, inefficiencies, further expense and delays.

At proof stage, many authors will try to take the opportunity to rewrite their books. They will have been briefed by the production department that changes should be kept to a minimum. If they do rewrite, it is your job to back production completely. You should have raised this in that 'educational' conversation we covered earlier. If the proof stage results in a hefty bill for rewriting, you must inform the author and require payment from him or her. All authors are allowed, within the terms of their contract, some latitude for making changes to the proofs, and this will be clearly stated. Anything that goes over that allowance must be paid for, and not by your publishing company.

For marketing you must pass on briefing documents and have face-to-face meetings to tell them everything you know about the market for the book. You must not leave the marketing department to make 'educated guesses', resulting in a misjudged marketing strategy. Of course, if you do not understand or know little about the market for a book, you are in no position to advise anybody. Remember that being an editor does not entail just receiving authors' ideas for books and publishing them. It is equally important that you get to grips with commercial realities and that means being able to describe exactly the market for any book, and why people will want or need to buy it. If you fail to do that, the marketing department has very little to work with.

The authors' questionnaire was referred to earlier and it is really your duty to send it to the author and make it clear that he or she will need to fill it in as fully as possible. If you do not, many authors will excuse themselves from the detail and pass it back to you to fill in. But you cannot supply that detail, because you are not the author. There is really no point in passing on a half-filled AQ. You need to explain to the author that this probably the only opportunity he or she will get to influence (through his or her knowledge of the market) the marketing plan.

What if your author moves house and gives you the new address? If you do not pass this on to the royalties department they will, through no fault of their own, send royalty statements and payments to the wrong address.

Copy that appears on the jacket or cover originates from the AQ, where the author is asked to describe the book in around 200 words. That copy is then polished by the editor until it is in a fit state to help sell the book. Some editors pass this work to their assistants and fail to check it properly. The editor must check that the copy is strong enough and that there are no grammatical or spelling mistakes. The former, if it is inadequate, will not help sell the book, and the latter gives an unforgivably bad impression.

Although editors do have holidays, and should be encouraged to take a break, walking off the job for a week or more, leaving crucial issues unresolved and no one covering one's desk is a recipe for disaster. Your colleagues should be briefed about any issues that are likely to arise, with arrangements made for actions to be taken.

Finally, we turn to forecasting. In the first chapter we learnt about how publishing functions financially. One of the main roles that the editor performs in this area is to produce the budgets for each new title. This entails forecasting the number of copies a book will sell, and the likely price of a book. The editor must exercise extreme care in making these forecasts, because together they combine to show the sales target for the publishing house. If the target is not met because editors have been too ambitious, that is, unrealistic, in their forecasts the house will be in trouble with the owners, the shareholders or the bank manager.

Many of the issues raised in Chapter 2 on publishing as a business directly relate to you and your ability to forecast.

These are some of the areas where you can go wrong. To get things right, the fundamental message is: *attention to detail is everything.* Detail is hard work because it means concentrating, caring about what you do, and understanding that many people in the publishing house depend on your getting things right, and the reputation of the house depends on that too.

Your work load

Editors can perhaps rightly claim to have the heaviest workload in the house. While marketing and production will spend most of their time working on books going through the publication process, editors not only have to maintain their responsibilities in respect of those books, even if they are not working on the detail that is involved, they are also assessing the mountain of material that gets submitted to them. During your working week you can be:

- Assessing new material.
- Writing rejection letters.
- Having material examined by outside experts, some of which might involve active discussion about the strengths and weaknesses of the material.
- Negotiating with the authors whose proposals are likely to be forwarded to the publications committee. You might be negotiating with their agents.
- Instructing your contracts department about the detail of new contracts or drawing up model contracts yourself.
- Putting together packages for the publications committee, including profit and loss accounts for individual books.
- Compiling financial information for annual budgets.
- Providing copy for marketing purposes, including the jacket blurbs.
- Compiling information about books for production and for marketing that will help them process these books.
- Briefing the design department about jackets or page layouts.

- Providing detailed information for the rights people that will help them to operate successfully with sub-licensees.
- Attending meetings – editorial, interdepartmental, with authors.
- Preparing for and presenting at the sales conference.
- Travelling to meet authors or perhaps to your overseas offices.
- Researching your publishing subject area in order to come up with new ideas.

That is a lot of work, even if you have an editorial assistant to help you. It is continuous and seamless. Within this mêlée, you need to find considerable amounts of time for reading material, whether you are looking at new proposals or a contracted manuscript that has arrived and which you need to assess before it goes into production. For reading, you may find it easier to read at home. As long as you get clearance from your line manager, you could get through far more material if you read it, undisturbed, at home. But you need to tell everyone where you are, and that you will only be at home for a limited time.

Clearly, with this weight of work, you need to prioritize. You also have to determine how you deal with e-mails. Choose times in the day when you will deal with e-mail and stick to them. Answer immediately e-mails that you can deal with quickly, reserving time later for those that need more serious deliberation. This advice should apply to anyone working in any department of a publishing house. Everyone is likely to be suffering from e-mail overload!

The art of prioritizing entails judgement – what *must* you do now; what can wait until tomorrow; what can wait until later in the week. Compiling lists can often be a successful way of sorting out the order in which you do things. What you must not do is start the week by diving in and hoping that you will get as much done as possible. You will end up confused and, probably, dismayed at how little you have achieved.

CASE STUDY   A profit and loss account for a book

We now turn to the P & L for an individual book. This time we are looking at an academic book published by a company that has offices overseas. It publishes for highly specialized markets, and this is reflected in the high prices it can charge for its books. These are 'must have' publications.

The main elements shown in this P & L are the sales income, the cost of making the books and paying the royalties, the cost of marketing the books, and the company overhead. The P & L is drawn up at the point of printing the book. By then, the production department will know what the cost of manufacture is. So, what we need to do is decide how many copies we want to print and what the price of the book will be. In this example, the book is being printed jointly in hardback and paperback, typically how academic publishers proceed. The hardbacks are for the university and college library market and the paperbacks are for individual sale. Remember that while the P & L for the company is based on actual performance, this book P & L is predicting sales and costs. It might look rather different once the book has been published and real sales kick in. We can reasonably assume that the predicted costs will not change significantly.

Academic publishers by and large do not juggle with figures. They have fairly accurate perceptions of how many copies they will sell into their markets, based on past sales figures. Unlike a consumer publisher, which expects to sell copies quickly, our academic publisher is printing for a period of about 18 months, and can bring a reprint on stream fast if stock sells out before then. As we mentioned earlier, specialist books sell more slowly: it simply takes longer to get the books known by their buyers. These are not impulse buys. A specialist book needs to build a reputation (often through journal reviews) and that takes time. On the positive side, returns are consequently much lower than in consumer publishing.

What do we know about this book?

We will be printing 200 copies in hardback and 1,600 in paperback. The price of the hardback is £65 and the paperback is £22.99.

We will give away 75 hardbacks (gratis) and 150 paperbacks. This appears to be a very high number, but review copies and inspection copies will mostly account for frees. The cost to the publisher is the production cost of making those frees. It is not a high cost relative to everything else, and it will be essential for building the book's reputation. However, these frees will be deducted from the total print run when calculating sales, because we will not get any income from them.

The average discount for these books is 35 per cent. This looks very low compared to the kind of discounts that consumer publishers have to give to retailers. The general position on this is that specialist books are less of a risk to the retailer because they are less speculative than consumer books, but also, and this is crucial, the prices of these books are far higher than consumer books, so the retailer is getting 35 per cent of a higher price, and therefore is making just as much money.

The company trades books with its overseas companies, which will then sell them on into their own territories. It is common practice to trade with your affiliated companies at a far higher discount, usually at rates of 75 per cent and higher. The aim here is for the overseas companies to pay as close to the cost of manufacture as possible for the books so that they do not, in turn, have to price them too high for their own markets. They will, of course, have to pay for their own overheads – marketing, staff and distribution costs. The author will receive a royalty as a percentage of the sum of money paid by the affiliated company to the main company. This is far lower than the royalty paid on home sales, but most authors are happy to accept this in academic publishing because they are very pleased to have their books sold overseas.

Let us now look at the figures in this P & L. The sales to the affiliated companies are referred to as 'aff'. The figures represent sums of money made, or spent, not the number of copies sold, and then expressed as percentages.

	Sums of money	%
Sales income		
Home hb sales	3,169	15
Home pb sales	16,438	75
Aff hb sales	650	3
Aff pb sales	1,609	7
Total sales	**21,866**	**100**
Cost of sales		
Typesetting and design	274	1.3
Editorial fees	2,437	11.1
Paper, printing and binding	2,426	11.1
Royalty	1,550	7.1
Total cost of sales	6,686	30.6
Gross profit	**15,180**	**69.4**
Marketing and distribution	3,505	16.0
Trading profit	11,675	53.4
Company overhead	8,467	38.7
Net profit	**3,208**	**14.7**

The sales figures show the high reliance on the home market for sales. But, the sales to the affiliated companies come to 10 per cent of the total sales, which is roughly the average export sales achieved by British companies. So the figures seem to be on track, if the overseas companies can sell them; otherwise, they will come back as returns.

The company spends just over 25 per cent of its sales revenue on making its books, which for this kind of specialist publishing is fairly typical. Note that the cost of typesetting and design is low. This is because academic publishers require that their authors deliver not just a manuscript but a digital file. The typesetting has essentially been done by the author, although a professional typesetter will make adjustments to provide pleasing layouts. The anticipated royalty statements also come within the usual range.

Our gross profit is over 69 per cent. This is very good but not untypical of academic publishing. It is noticeably higher as a percentage than that for our publisher in the case study in Chapter 2. That publisher has spent more on manufacture, but as a likely textbook publisher, it will have to deal with more than just printed pages of words. Layouts will be vital. Our education publisher also spends more on royalties, but with textbook authors to look after, the royalty rates will need to be higher.

Our company spends 16 per cent on marketing and distribution. Assuming that its distribution costs will be about 10–11 per cent, its marketing spend is between 5 and 6 per cent, again fairly typical for this kind of publishing. This is more than our textbook publisher spends – perhaps it should be spending more!

We come to our trading profit, which comprises sales less manufacture and royalties and the cost of marketing the books. The ratios look healthy here. Finally, we must deduct our overheads: the cost of running the company, including salaries. The publisher imposes a fixed overhead on every book it publishes, as it would be almost impossible to calculate every cost associated with a single book. How would you attribute, for example, an HR or an admin cost to a single book? To impose a fixed overhead in this way is typical of the way a publisher would calculate what the net profit is going to be.

Our company overhead here is 38.7 per cent of sales. This is considerably higher than the overheads for our textbook publisher. Is this a company that pays higher salaries and generally spends more on everything, or do the directors impose a very conservative (high) percentage, in an effort to ensure that provision is made for everything? We can only speculate.

Our net profit is a respectable 14.7 per cent – again within the traditional range of net profits for academic books. But the sum of money it represents is only £3,208. A lot of effort has been made, and money spent, to end up with a modest sum. One would have to publish a lot of books in the course of the year to build up a decent overall income for the company. Indeed, academic publishers do have very high output. Perhaps this academic publisher, in common with many others, balances the income act by publishing academic journals, which are known to enjoy very high profits indeed.

Conclusion

So let us look again at those four issues raised right at the beginning of the chapter: the editor's power, the editor's persuasion, the editor's 'guess', and the editor's responsibilities.

1. Power

You have the power. You see all the submissions that come to the house. What happens to them will depend on you. You cannot rejoice in that power because you quickly realize that you have the power to make mistakes as well as the power to spot potential successes. It is important, however, that you remember that you are not alone. As well as your own critical analysis which you will bring to bear when inspecting proposals, you have colleagues and advisers to help you make that choice. Your editorial line manager can give you guidance, but you can also ask for the opinions of colleagues in marketing (especially) and in production. Your outside advisers are people chosen for their experience in the subject and in the market for those books. You should use them as often as you need until you reach a position of greater confidence and, therefore, greater decisiveness.

2. Persuasion

Even first-class books will not make it to publication and the marketplace if you are an inadequate spokesperson for them. But even if you are a first-class spokesperson, these books will not make publication unless and until you understand and can explain exactly why the book has commercial potential. This means not just understanding the content but equally important, knowing the market. Nothing is more persuasive than an editor who can grasp the content and then place it in the market – the readers, the level and the competition, backed with facts, which are inevitably centred on sales records of similar books. An editor who cannot do this, really ought not to be an editor. This is another area where experience will make a difference, because as you gain experience, so you will gradually learn about presentation.

3. The 'guess'

It is a guess. Some books succeed wonderfully and others fall by the wayside, and often we do not know exactly why. Books are full of surprises, which is why publishing is essentially a risky business. Do not comfort yourself when facing a failure with that old, familiar expression, 'That's life': you could be in danger of becoming complacent. If you are doing your job thoroughly, your risks will always be acceptable ones. Remember all the processes you went through in assessing a project: if you did that thoroughly and had the full support of your colleagues, then you can be forgiven that kind of failure – as long as it is occasional. One can see some accidents waiting to happen, such as selling a serialization of a book just before publication, and then wondering why the book sales were not made. Or going back to the market with a copycat book of an earlier success and discovering that readers have now lost interest. The market is just like individuals: it develops sudden interests, it can become bored after a while, or it can be fickle. The successful, and consistently successful, editor learns to anticipate that kind of movement.

4. The responsibilities

By now you know they are many and varied, and early in your editorial career can seem overwhelming. Remember that most inexperienced editors feel like that to begin with. We would like to say that your greatest responsibility is to your authors, but it lies, in fact and in practice, with the owners of your company. The owners provide the capital that allows the company to publish. If you do not make sufficient revenue and profit, the company goes bust. So, your first responsibility lies with making sure the company remains solvent, because you will then remain employed, and authors can be published. After that, yes, the authors enter centre ground. We pointed out earlier that authors have a kind of freelance relationship with publishers, which is why finding them, helping and supporting them and accompanying them to success can be both demanding and rewarding. Accomplishing all that requires that you also exercise your responsibilities in relation to your colleagues. The success or failure of your books will ultimately reside with you, but whilst you might taste failure if you attempt to drive the entire publishing process, you will certainly not enjoy success if you do not involve yourself properly within the full publishing team.

Further reading

Gill Davies's *Book Commissioning and Acquisition* is essential reading for anyone who wants to pursue in greater depth any of the issues raised in this chapter.

For a very different, personal, view of the work of the editor, Diana Athill's *Stet* is a rewarding read, portraying an editor of great flair who worked at a time when some of the current preoccupations of publishing were absent. Yet publishing has always needed to make money, and Diana Athill was doing her work in a small publishing house, on which there are always great financial pressures. What is inspiring is her commitment and her ability to take well-judged risks. Jeremy Lewis's book *Kindred Spirits* is a portrait of an earlier time but is one of the funniest books on publishing you will ever read.

Athill, D (2000), *Stet*, Granta, London

Davies, G (2005) *Book Commissioning and Acquisition*, 2nd edn, Routledge, Abingdon

Horn, B (2006) *Editorial Project Management*, Horn Editorial Books, London

Lewis, J (2008) *Kindred Spirits: Adrift in literary London*, Faber & Faber, London

Marketing

04

Introduction

So you have a book that needs to be launched into the marketplace and you are wondering how you should go about this to maximize sales. Contrary to the notion that you now dream up some ideas, or snatch them from the blue skies, in fact what you need to devise is a strategy. With over 130,000 new titles published each year in the UK alone, tactics are likely to be more important than ideas. You are going to need tactics to cut your way through all that competition! Once you have them, then you can start to think of some original ideas to put some zest into your marketing plan.

Whichever way marketing is dressed up, essentially what you need to think about is:

- Who is going to want to read this book?
- How will I get to these readers?
- What messages must I send out to persuade them to buy it?

There are of course other marketing issues too, such as the price and the book's format or appearance, but these are likely to have been developed as the book has progressed as a product. The book has been designed to appeal to its market. It has been priced similarly. The combined expertise of editorial, marketing and production has already worked on that process. Now, perfectly formed, your book is ready to be introduced to the world.

Not so long ago, we had only one main vehicle for sending messages out to the market, and that was the printed word. No one working in marketing these days is going to stick just to that, because digital technology provides so many options and possibilities for promotion. Other platforms, of course, present themselves as powerful, indirect, marketing tools, such as serialization in the newspapers or on the radio, or film versions of books, but they will not be part of your strategy. Makers of films or radio programmes are unlikely to be influenced by the marketing you do for a new book, so marketing to them cannot be part of your plan. They will simply be drawn to the content of the book, however and whenever they discover it, and they will develop their own ideas on how they can work with it. Few best-sellers make it to another medium. Interestingly, often these books are old or out-of-print. Of course, if you strike lucky and one of your books does hit the small or big screen, the effect on sales will be wonderful. Don't forget, however, that a serialization could also kill off the sales of a book!

One qualification here: selling serializations or adaptations to other media is the job of the rights department, who themselves are marketers and sellers. The rights department never works in isolation from editorial and marketing, and both departments are likely to have a strong hand in the direction in which a rights department will move on a title.

The main tools of marketing

All books get a basic marketing treatment. 'Basic' here means a common or unifying treatment that all books are subjected to. For each book, there are various routes and platforms that publishers use to reach out to the market, and each of them is likely to serve a different purpose, bearing in mind the kind of audience we are trying to connect with. The messages for a bookseller, for example, can be different to the messages for the book buyer. Next we discuss the main elements of a basic treatment.

Catalogues are usually produced twice a year in the spring and early autumn. Structurally, they tend to be organized around the publishing house's subject areas or genres – fiction, non-fiction, cookery, travel, and so on. Specialist publishers will produce a catalogue just for one subject or maybe a combination of two or three subjects. In consumer publishing, the main recipients of these will be booksellers and wholesalers. For specialist publishing the recipients will include key individuals in universities, schools or other institutions, as well as the bookshops. The catalogue is the equivalent of your shop or stall where you set out your new goods. Some catalogues will contain successful backlist titles, to remind the customer just how good this list is and to keep sales rolling in. These days catalogues are available in print and digital formats.

Leaflets or flyers are quite common in specialist publishing. They can be tailor-made to focus on a particular section of the potential market. This same flyer or leaflet could also be used at conferences and to accompany a mail shot – quite common in specialist publishing where it's possible to accumulate names of known buyers or subject specialists. You would not use this piece as a press release, which requires a particular kind of copywriting skill.

Advertising is something that most publishers would prefer to avoid, because it is difficult to prove that it helps to sell books and most publishers are convinced that what does help sell books is word-of-mouth recommendations (both literally or digitally) and good reviews. It is also expensive. Let us accept that all publishers will do some advertising but will be sparing in the amount they do. The most cost-effective use of advertising is to cover two or three titles within the same ad, although a consumer publisher would not do that with a title where maximum impact is needed. Remember that one of the most effective ways of reaching many people is not through classic advertisements at all but through the links between your digital messages (on your own website) and the search engines. By writing good, focused copy you are more likely to be picked up by the search engines and placed high on their lists. If the search engines pick you up, it is vital that there are clear links through to microsites for your books.

Advance information sheets are essential for the book retailing sector. This is your book reps' key piece of paper for when they are selling in stock to a bookshop. Both shops and reps will use them. AIs contain basic factual information such as page length, format, price, illustrations, and the International Standard Book Number (the ISBN). All information must be absolutely correct, including the title, subtitle and author's name. It is sometimes in these utterly fundamental areas that mistakes are made, so you must check yours for accuracy. The AI will also contain a short blurb about the book, setting out the 'key selling points' – a ubiquitous expression implying the absolute necessity of writing copy that is convincing (more about writing copy later). You can include testimonials (endorsements) for the book written by famous people, and excerpts from reviews of the author's previous books, if appropriate. The bookseller will also want to know about any marketing and PR campaigns being organized for this book. Quite subconsciously, any bookseller reading about a special campaign will think, 'Ah, the publisher is trying hard with this book. It must be good!' And that assumption will help you generate sales.

Book covers and jackets are sent to bookshops. It is often forgotten that when the jacket and cover are designed, the first audience we are trying to influence is not the book buyer but the retailer. Retailers will be influenced by the book's appearance and may even display the book face out in their stores if they really like it.

Review copies will be sent to publications recommended by the authors, although you must make sure that the author is being realistic. It's one thing to want *The Times* to review your book on medicine for the elderly, and another to see it reviewed there. Someone in the marketing department will be asked to draw up a list of where reviews are likely to be secured, including your own ideas based on experience of similar books. This is a horribly competitive area now. Review editors are overwhelmed by review copies, so comparatively few books will be reviewed. It is best to be as realistic about where you are going to send review copies, otherwise you are essentially throwing them away. Still, a really good review is brilliant for any book. A really bad review is the next best thing. That's a very old saying in publishing, and it still has merit: the worst fate for any book is to be completely overlooked.

Events are likely to figure as part of the basic treatment. An event can range from a modest promotion at an academic conference, to a more expensive launch party or a high-profile signing session. The amount you spend on an event will relate to the sales potential of a book.

Digital marketing is now part of most publishers' campaigns; there is more on this below. You are inevitably going to promote a new book through online social websites.

These are the basics – the essentials of a marketing campaign. Not so long ago we would have left it at that, but the big arrival on the marketing scene is digital technology. Digital technology has transformed life in production departments, but its potential for marketing is just as great.

Digital marketing

Digital marketing is not a matter of harnessing a new platform just because it is there. It is about using technology to fit in with what people like to do. No product ever gets off the ground commercially just because it's a new invention. It will only succeed if it fits in with what people are interested in culturally. That's 'culture' with a very small 'c'. This kind of culture is all about what people like, what they do, what they identify with, and what their friends identify with too. A new invention, if it is going to be successful, fits in with the direction people want to go anyway.

Digital marketing not only has the power of websites, social networks and e-mails behind it, it has – and this is a huge advantage over traditional marketing – flexibility and currency. Traditional marketing to *individuals* (in particular for most consumer books) would be hideous in cost and beyond the consideration of any sensible person. It would entail the cost of printing your pieces, putting them in envelopes, and postage. Add to that the improbability of finding out the name and address of every potential buyer of your books, and you can see how that way madness lies. Until now, getting through to those book buyers has mostly meant securing good reviews and excellent display coverage in bookshops. This makes one immediately vulnerable to two key parties: the booksellers and the reviewers. We need them, but we also need to make ourselves less dependent on others.

Note, immediately, that specialist publishers have never been exposed to that kind of vulnerability simply because they can market directly to individuals. Specialist publishers are able to be ultra-focused publishers. They are publishing books with a particular kind of niche in mind – even if it is a large niche. Quite often they have names and addresses of their customers; examples would be school teachers or academics. It does not take a great deal of research to find out the names and addresses of all schools in a country and to be able to mail promotion pieces to the head of English, for instance, or to the school librarian. Similarly, you can mail to any university or college that has a department in, say, mathematics, and address your mailings to the head of department, knowing it will reach the right person. After a while, you begin to capture the names of these individuals and you can put them on your database for future mailings. Despite this closeness to the market that specialist publishing has, the advantages that digital marketing offers are of equal interest to them.

Digital marketing is incredibly effective in spreading the word about a book, and is so widespread now that it must be included in the 'basics' of marketing. A good marketing campaign is of course an integrated one using traditional and digital methods. Online media are currently second only to television in terms of the number of hours people spend on them. You will need to make good use of this:

- Create a Facebook site for your authors if they do not already have one, and use it to feed messages through to the fans.

- Create links between Facebook and your own website so that you, as the publisher, can get maximum benefit from readers visiting it.

- Provide links to people's own sites by creating widgets for their use.

- Set up chats between readers and authors via your website. Give readers plenty of notice, and it is always good to get some questions in advance so that your author can do them justice. This activity now can meet many of the objectives of the author tour or bookshop signings, but with less trouble or expense.

- You can host videos about the book or the author on your website.

These are a few examples. The potential is enormous, and the biggest challenge will be to discipline yourself to use only those routes that will bring benefit.

Social media

Publishers have long been aware of the power of word-of-mouth recommendations. Best-sellers, such as *Captain Corelli's Mandolin* and *The Kite Runner* are examples of books that owed their success to word-of-mouth. Social media are the digital, everyday embodiment of word-of-mouth. Once the message is out and 'running' the potential audience that it can reach is massive. The downside is that these messages can also be negative.

These networks should not be regarded as 'marketing made easy'. Just because you use them for promotion, there is no guarantee that you have done all you need to do. The cost of using these networks is comparatively low, but there must be some sort of strategy behind their use. (Later in this chapter, we cover strategic approaches to marketing.) Although social media networks appear wonderfully flexible, you must bring some discipline and direction to the way you use them. This means:

- knowing the characteristics and attributes of your 'average' customer;

- thinking the way your customers would, instead of imposing your thinking on them. If you do not, you will get their decisions and opinions wildly wrong;

- acknowledging that some people who are intensely involved with social media are not necessarily book readers.

You need also to be aware that some social networks that are popular and powerful now can disappear quite rapidly when a new one appears that grabs all the attention. When the actor Stephen Fry went public about his use of Twitter, he was hugely influential in publicizing and popularizing that network. But his actions were never planned to promote Twitter. So, be vigilant about the speed of change in the popularity of useage of networks, and be aware that this change will sometimes take place in a quite unexpected fashion.

Direct marketing

If you are in the kind of publishing where it is possible to build a close relationship with your customers, then you probably use direct marketing. This involves selling to the customer without an intermediary (a retailer) being involved. Such marketing depends on the availability of lists of names and addresses of book buyers, which means that apart from book clubs that are selling to their members, by and large direct marketing is not the province of consumer publishers; it is a vehicle for specialist books with niche markets. The buyers for these books tend to be keen to hear about anything new that has been published in their field, so they register their names with 'list brokers'. Publishers will pay a fee for using the brokers' lists. In addition to the brokers, publishers can compile their own names and addresses of those who have bought from them. This data is very valuable indeed. Sales can be made without giving discounts, and the sales records provide valuable information for commissioning editors and for planning marketing campaigns.

Digital direct mail is now beginning to substitute for traditional mailings. You have to exercise some care when mailing to e-mail addresses. You need to be sure that the recipient has agreed to receive information of this sort. The law does not allow you simply to e-mail information without this agreement. But whether you are using traditional direct mailing, or digital mailings, your selling copy has to be very focused indeed. The recipient is not able to flick through a book so everything depends on the strength of your copy. There is more on writing copy later in this chapter.

Marketing strategy

The word 'strategy' is often misused and misunderstood. Most people think it means 'plan', others think it means 'tactics'. The original meaning reveals its military origin by referring to the management of an army; that is, the management of its troops in such a way as to force upon the enemy the place and time – the conditions for fighting – that are *preferred by oneself*. In other words, to try to set up the battle so that it is conducted on one's own terms. Today, the 'enemy' is our competitors, and we still retain part of that original meaning by wanting to control, through our publishing and our marketing, the extent to which our competitors can damage us. In essence, for a modern publishing house, this means that the best marketing strategy will be the one that allows us to choose and analyse how we market a book or product instead of being driven into a badly thought through and unfocused plan, running scared from our competitors. Strategy reflects what we want (for example, market dominance, growing a market, changing our market, even downsizing our market) in the next few years. This in turn reflects our own resources and the interests and income of our customers. We have to acknowledge that the strategy will need to be flexible, and will reflect changes in our resources and in our markets. Few things stand still.

True strategy should therefore allow us to choose *how, why* and *when* we deliver our marketing, to ensure the best possible results. This is where tactics come in. We also need to think about the cost of our marketing. It is likely that our strategy will require us to think along the following lines:

- Will our approach be mass market or niche?
- Are we breaking new ground or building on what we already have?
- Are we going to be offensive or defensive in our approach?
- Do we need high quality (with high costs) or will it be rudimentary and low cost, or somewhere in between?

Underlying these questions are further ones about how we can best compete in our chosen market and how can we differentiate ourselves from our competitors. We can only do that if we know the answers to some more questions:

- What do our customers want?

- Do we know what they value?
- Can we deliver what they want and value more successfully than our competitors can?

We should be able to match the considerations in the first set of questions above with those in the second set. For example, if we know what our customers want, that will determine whether our marketing will be full-blown-mass in approach, or whether it will be niche. Do they like to be one of the crowd, or are they very singular? Do they expect quality in most things, including marketing? Then, if we know what they value, we can judge whether they will be turned on by a full thrust, in-your-face campaign, or if they are like cats, waiting to be intrigued.

Finally, if our market identifies some notion of exclusivity, should we deliver our campaign at the very top end of quality, or does our market value something that is modest yet effective? An advert recently shown on British television contains the slogan, 'You don't have to be rich to be posh', illustrating what sociologists have been saying for years, which is that status is not always tied to the possession of large amounts of money.

Marketers sometimes classify potential readers in terms of their personae, not just in terms of where they live, how much money they have or what social class they belong to. They can characterize them as 'joiners, collectors, spectators, creators, passive'. All of these words tell you a little about these people and how they behave. A smart marketer will use these insights to help create a marketing plan to capture the interest of each type.

Two further things need to be said before we move on. The first is that you stand no chance whatsoever in the competitive marketplace if you do not know enough about your customers to be able to answer these questions. In a way, you are building a set of attributes for a typical reader for a book you are publishing. The second thing is that whatever your marketing plan, you must have the resources that you will need to carry it out.

Market segmentation

Now that we are in the realm of being able to spot and identify a customer for the kind of book you publish, we can begin to unpack the other attributes associated with them. They are likely to be:

- age and gender;
- socio-economic status (ie social class, education, and income);

- geo-demographic (ie where they live – town or country, north or south, etc – things that can determine behaviour and attitudes);
- expenditure on things other than fundamentals – food is fundamental expenditure, most other things one can choose to buy or not;
- type of personality or values;
- chosen lifestyle.

Clearly, any marketer would be crazy to believe that a typical customer falls neatly into a descriptive box one has constructed for him or her. There will always be customers who fall partly outside this, but they are usually on the extremities. Imagine your typical customer as being, in every sense, an average! This is an average you had better come to understand.

Marketing mix

Much of what we've written already falls under the heading of what marketers like to call the 'marketing mix', which is a kind of shorthand for all the elements that would encompass the market for a book and how to reach it. This is often referred to as the 'four Ps':

- The *Product* is the book and where it stands in relation to many other similar books. How does it fit in with current demand? Is it doing something new or original? What do we know about these kinds of books and their customers?
- The *Price* of a book is of great interest to marketing. Is it typical? If it's higher, what effect will that have on demand? Some books and subjects are price sensitive. Occasionally a book will have such power in the marketplace that one can raise its price above what the market expects, but the customers will still buy it. Most publishers like to keep in line with their competitors when they are pricing for fear that the market will bite back.
- *Place* is about the channels to the market that will lead to sales. Where does our typical customer for a typical kind of book expect to be able to find and buy it? If you are a publisher who uses direct mail as your main selling vehicle, and you produce a book that needs to go out through the bookshops, this is going to need an abrupt change of selling direction, which you might find difficult to grapple with if you don't keep a team of book reps. If your proposed typical reader is the sort of person who might idly

pick up a book while shopping in the supermarket, then you must have the expertise to sell to those major retailers.

- *Promotion* concerns all those activities that you are going to plan and organize to draw the customers' attention to the book. We've mentioned them earlier – catalogues, advertising, publicity, website promotion and reviews, for example. All these have to be chosen for their efficacy. You cannot do everything and some of it will be a waste of time. You choose and you know why you are choosing, because you know the product and you know the kind of people who like to buy it, at a particular price and at a particular kind of outlet.

These marketing mixes are the building blocks of marketing campaigns. You must not proceed with a campaign until you have them in place.

Marketing budgets

Most publishing houses spend an average percentage of expected book revenue on marketing, promotion and sales. So, if an editor is forecasting £200,000 for a book's sales, the marketing department will fully expect to have £14,000 to £20,000 to spend on achieving those sales. This is because publishers tend to attribute 6–10 per cent of turnover to marketing spend. The percentage will vary depending on the sector of publishing you are in: academic publishers will work with a lower percentage than consumer publishers; as we explained earlier, the former have the relative luxury of being able to be focused, and can make their marketing spend quite efficient. Do not forget that those projected sales are net sales, the sum realized after you have given retailers their discounts.

But why have a percentage at all? Why not just draw up a list of things you would like to do to market a book successfully, and put a cost on that? There are a couple of reasons for this. The first is that publishers, with experience, have discovered that the answer lies in the maths. There just happens to be an average percentage of turnover that seems to work in all sectors, although that average will vary, of course. The second reason is to get us to be disciplined and realistic about how much money we *should* be spending.

One of the axioms of modern life goes like this: the more you spend on marketing a product, the more successful it is likely to be. But think of *Harry Potter,* and that axiom gets blown out of the water immediately. Still, *Harry Potter* could be cited as an exception to that rule; by and large, one must spend a lot of money. We can also turn the axiom on its head and say that if the public does not want the product, the more you spend on marketing it, the bigger your loss. In fact, because publishing is not a genuine mass-market industry, those who work in it know perfectly well that public taste and demand for books is not infinite. We cannot bludgeon people into buying books by flinging thousands of pounds of marketing spend at titles. So, we operate with marketing-spend ratios that experience shows us to be sufficient to get lift-off in sales. We leave out of this, of course, the exceptional marketing spend that will be put behind a substantial purchase; ie a celebrity biography. But even there, a big marketing spend has not always helped a doomed book, and there have been a number of those in recent years. The public was simply not interested.

If you are working with a sum of money that represents a modest percentage of the expected turnover of a new book, let's face it, you are going to have to be clever. And what is wrong with that? Your plan should be cost-effective and demonstrate lots of ingenuity. Nevertheless, you are going to have to make some decisions about how you are going to divide up your budget. You need to attribute expenditure to catalogues, perhaps to point-of-sale materials, perhaps to some direct mailings, even perhaps to some advertising. You won't spend money on all of these, but it will be your decision about how to cut the cake!

You will be asking yourself what sort of marketing strategy and plan you need for the book, how both will address and attack the market for that book, and how expensive that is going to be. Let's look at some activities and where they stand on the resource continuum.

Low cost

Review copies are literally the cost of production of each one, plus post and packing. In addition, you spend time sending them out and choosing where they should be sent.

PR is also cheap, provided a PR executive is already on the staff and is costed as part of the general overhead – otherwise, you will have to spend a lot of money hiring a PR expert. In theory, whilst in-house PR does not cost very much, these professionals have to be very good at persuasion, otherwise this is money wasted.

Catalogues, AIs and flyers will already be part of your marketing overhead – the basic treatment – so there is very little extra cost involved here. E-marketing through your own website should also be part of the basic treatment, and of course, its reach, by linking it to other websites, means it has no geographic boundaries.

Mid-range cost

Doing some direct marketing to bookshops, and not just relying on the reps, is an extra, so we need to put this in at medium cost. But this kind of activity will not remain in the 'mid-range' category if you choose to do some expensive things. Supplying a proof copy of a new book is definitely in the 'mid-range' category, but remember to cost in how you will get those proof copies into the hands of the bookshop managers.

You can support the shops' own catalogues by paying for entries of your books. This need not be expensive, but it will get very expensive for certain seasonal catalogues, especially the Christmas ones. You need to find out costs beforehand.

If you are a specialist publisher, attending conferences can be a mid-range cost unless the staff running the stand have to stay in hotels overnight and there are travel and meal costs involved. These stands need to be looked at in relation to other benefits. It's not just a matter of selling books to delegates: because delegates tend to like to visit these stands, they are often a good source of market research, and from them might spring some future authors. Thankfully, these conferences are often held in universities or colleges, and the display cost is therefore reasonable.

Some advertising does not have to be expensive. If taken out in a specialist journal, for example, the cost may not amount to much more than about £150.

Author signing sessions are in theory very cheap to set up. All you need is a bookshop that wants to host a signing, a large table for a book display, and a chair for the author to sit on. The 'incidentals' or extras are going to be the cost of a few staff dragged from their office desks to support this event; probably a very fine dinner for the author; and if he or she has had to travel far, the cost of a hotel room and travel. In London, or another major city, this could amount to a significant amount of money. You hope to balance this cost with the wonderful sales that will be made at the signing. The bookshop manager will be taking the same view. The cost to the bookshop is minimal, but the disruption will be high. If the signing works, all that will be forgotten. Sadly, very few of these sessions really work. If the author is gigantic, go for it. If not, spare yourself and the bookshop the agony of seeing a decent author sitting all alone.

High cost

Direct mail is always expensive. You are most likely to be mailing leaflets or catalogues. You have to make the catalogues anyway, and even a new leaflet is not going to be expensive. It is the weight, and how that affects postage, that makes this kind of marketing so expensive. However, you have to offset the benefits against the cost. The books sold through this medium are going to be discount-free! What's more, you can really, *really* know who your customers are, because they will order the book through you. Long-term direct marketing of this sort is a wonderful way of building a database of known customers. The web has, in theory, made these hard-copy platforms redundant, but there is plenty of evidence that customers still like the 'flickability' of a catalogue.

Paid-for display areas in prime spots in the shops are always expensive but are becoming the 'norm' for mass-market publishers. Those books do not land by the entrance to the shop just out of the blue, and neither is their positioning just good judgement on the part of the shop staff. The publisher will have competed for and paid for this.

We mentioned academic conferences under 'mid-range cost'. Conferences or exhibitions for professional bodies are likely to be far more expensive. Here the delegates fully expect the publishers' stands to be very smart indeed. Sometimes these conferences are held in hotels or conference suites, which can also add hugely to the cost. The advantages, as with academic conferences, are that they provide a chance to acquire new authors and do some market research 'on the hoof'. You might also sell more books than you thought. There is something akin to the 'souvenir' principle operating amongst these delegates: 'Now I've been able to get out of the office/consulting room for a few days, I'd like to buy something which will remind me of my trip!'

Advertising also comes under 'mid-range cost'. Clearly, if you get a good price for an ad in a journal, it will cost far less than an ad in a mainstream, high-quality publication such as an up-market weekend newspaper. That can cost £10,000 or more. Your book had better be worth it. Rarely do we see or hear book adverts on television or radio, because adverts need to be repeated in order to be effective. No publisher can afford repeat adverts. Where the publisher is likely to pay a high cost is for ads that people can see over and over again, such as on underground trains or stations, or as large billboards at bus stops or on railway stations. Any publisher deciding to use these media is going to have to do some serious work in calculating the cost and how many people will get to see these ads. Do not worry, you will not have to work this out alone. Specialist ad agencies will help you, but you will be left having to make the judgement about what is going to be the best value for money. For instance, never advertise inside buses as passengers are more likely to be looking out of the windows. A large advert on the outside of a bus that is continually moving through a city is going to be worth the high cost.

Point-of-sale material – posters, showcards, bookmarks, spinners – are all going to be expensive. It would be most unusual for a publisher to supply these extras just for one shop: POS material can only be justified for a national campaign. Sadly, although it is costing your company a fortune, this does not mean that the bookshops appreciate what you are doing. Most shops do not have enough room even for the books being sold. They are not likely to get excited about your 'clutter', and most certainly will not unless you brand everything with *their* name on it. So, you need to weigh up the cost of marketing both your book and the bookshop!

Launch parties are beloved of most authors apart from the chronically shy. Amongst the expensive end of marketing activities, they are possibly the least effective. Even if the author is popular enough to have friends and colleagues who will attend, everyone is so busy chatting to each other that few will do more than glance at the book when they arrive, and maybe even pick it up, but hardly any will then buy a copy. They probably think that the author will send them a complimentary copy. Everyone has had a lovely time, you have spent a lot of money on drinks, canapés and the venue, and you will have very little income to count up. However, all this will be forgotten if showing off your author is very important indeed, or the book he or she has written is actually significant.

For books with great commercial potential, publishers will put together a special DVD for sending to bookshop managers. This will involve engaging a production company, whose services will be more expensive than the physical cost of making a DVD or distributing it to the shops. What is in these DVDs? Anything ranging from a feature on the author, to an exciting 'snapshot' of the book's content, to something that amounts to no more than a 'mood' piece whose aim is to raise expectations on the part of those selling the book. This approach can only be used for books where exceptionally large sales are expected.

Even with DVDs, people can be bored with seeing the same kind of thing. The first DVDs that went to bookshops would have made huge impact, but after a while, that impact is blunted. Remember to bring a bit of variety into what you do if you want to keep people's attention.

The marketing plan

We now need to translate our thoughts on strategy and costs into an action plan. Remember that successful marketing means:

- being customer-oriented and understanding what they want and value;
- recognizing that relationships matter;
- bringing logic and method into what you do;
- trying new ideas and being flexible.

Our marketing plan is going to be a written document that will set down marketing activities and how they will be implemented and controlled. The plan will be a reflection of our marketing strategy, and it will not exceed stated costs.

Apart from covering the basics, which we did earlier in this chapter, the marketing plan is going to raise and answer a number of quite specific questions:

- Can we describe the market for this book in terms of segmentation? (*Who is the typical customer, and what do we know about him or her?*)
- What benefits does this book provide for the market? (*Not the benefits I, the publisher, perceive but what the customer perceives.*)
- Who is going to buy this book? (*For example, will it be students, or will it be the lecturers to whom we will promote it? Will it be grannies giving birthday gifts, or will it be their grandchildren?*)
- Where will they buy it? (*In a shop, online, via direct mail?*)
- How will the price stack up in relation to our competitors or as a typical customer spend? (*Just how price-sensitive is this book and does it offer value for money?*)
- What exactly is the competition for this book? (*If we do not know the answer to this question, we should stop now and start again!*)

Our marketing plan is going to be translated into action, which we know as 'promotion'. It is about:

- how we choose to get to our market;
- presenting the right messages to get buyers to purchase the book;
- ensuring it will not cost more to do that than we have budgeted.

Routes to market

They will include some but not all of the following:

Direct mail	Adverts
Publicity	Review copies
Point of sale	Exhibitions and conferences
E-marketing	Endorsements
AIs	Catalogues
Leaflets	Author tours and signings
Launch parties	

You will choose the route, depending on how much you know about your typical book buyer, or your typical 'gatekeeper' (those lecturers and grannies mentioned above).

Communication

This is not just about what you have to say about your books, but how you say it. If you know your typical reader, through doing your marketing segmentation, you should know not only what this person likes/needs to know about a book, but the kind of approach or language that presses buttons for them. We must try to encapsulate in our messages:

- what the book is and what it provides;
- who it is for;
- what is new or topical about it;
- how it fits a need;
- what advantages or benefits come from buying it;
- its value for money.

Clearly, there are some books published that can skip that entire process. Just say the names 'John Grisham', 'James Patterson', 'Stephanie Meyer' or 'Harry Potter', and they set off a series of internal messages for the listener. We are in brand country here. We hardly need to say anything beyond, 'It's here!'

Writing copy for market routes is a skill and we shall turn to it later in the chapter.

Your budget

We have already covered how marketing budgets are calculated (and there is more on a budget for a consumer book at the end of this chapter). By now, you know that the bigger the potential for sales that a book has, the more money you have to spend on it. This looks like a self-fulfilling prophecy but that is not always the case, because a large marketing spend will not rescue a book that no one is interested in. Content is king! You also know that you have to decide how that money will be spent and we gave you a range of spending levels. Whichever way you spend the budget, you are always looking for value for money. Publishing cannot afford indulgences. A higher than average spend might be justified if it leads to sales that bring you a competitive advantage – whether it is in the marketplace or with respect to authors. In this circumstance, everybody needs to understand what they are doing and why they are spending more money. It needs to be understood that this is a one-off budget but that there are distinct aims and objectives behind it.

What comes 'free'

Let us return to what can be achieved without invading the marketing budget significantly. Because it is 'free', it might require a bit more ingenuity.

Reviews are influential. Word-of-mouth is even more influential, but it is very likely that an interesting review might have kicked it off in the first place. Imagine you are the reviews editor of a prominent newspaper. You will be receiving *on average* about 120 books *a day*. How do you choose? It's easy to choose if the authors are mega-famous, but what if they are not. How do you get them noticed?

Feature articles are free but are only written about authors and books that in every sense are exceptional. Your liking the author is not enough to make him or her exceptional to a hard-nosed journalist.

Author interviews will only take place if you have a special book or author to promote. This is a rich seam to mine, however, because author interviewing is something of an industry within radio and television programming. Here you have to be sure that the author is very good at 'coming across'. You do not want your author to freeze on air, or keep repeating, 'As I say in my book ...', because it just sounds too much like a 'hard sell'.

To find yourself in the position of publishing a book on a subject that is just hitting the headlines is good fortune indeed. A few shrewd publishers who had just published books on Islam and politics found themselves with significant sales on their hands following 9/11, although they probably wished that their good fortune had arrived through other means. Similarly, a film treatment of one of your titles is a guarantee of enhanced sales, for which you have had to make very little effort apart from re-jacketing the book to make the film tie-in evident.

What's the magic that could turn the above into a reality? You will certainly want to bring attention to your book by issuing a press release:

- Tailor your press release to fit the newspaper or magazine or radio/television programme to which you are sending it. You should have familiarized yourself with these media and the interests of their readers, listeners or viewers.

- Keep the information concise. Busy people will be reading your press release. Help them by not overloading them.

- Follow it up by an e-mail and then a phone call. If the journalist/ reviewer or producer is interested, they will quickly respond to your e-mail. You have to be prepared to make several calls to get a response. This is known as 'cold calling' and it is not easy to do. In fact, if you are hopelessly shy or 'sensitive', you will hate doing it. It is possible to develop a thick skin and not to take rejection personally. If you know you are unlikely to be able to do this, then do not work for the PR department.

That is the process, but what will make the difference are:

- Good contacts that will help the business of making approaches so much easier. It really does help if people know you.

- An open and friendly personality and a voice that conveys determination and confidence. Would you be influenced by your voice and manner if you had to listen to it on the phone?

- A realistic understanding of what the media is going to be interested in. The successful marketer always asks, 'I'm interested in this, but why should other people be?'

- Setting targets for the number of media and individuals you will contact and focusing on them instead of spreading yourself thin.

Also, do not be afraid of setting embargoes. If you have come to an agreement over coverage with a media contact, your contact will be loath to work with you again if another contact dives in first and steals the show with an early piece.

- The slow but rewarding process of cultivating relationships. Being known to people in the media, getting a response to your phone calls and e-mails, and being taken seriously when you are trying to sell a book or an author is just going to get easier as time goes on.

Writing copy

The original source of copy for any book is almost always the author. In the author's questionnaire, he or she is asked to describe the book, usually in about 200 words. The next person who will work on this copy is usually the editor, who will be asked to turn the author's copy into the jacket copy. In some consumer publishing companies it might be a marketer who does this. Whatever the source, from that will emerge a kind of copy 'meal' off which a number of people and departments will feed. There's the jacket copy, the catalogue copy, the AI copy, the leaflet copy, the advertising copy, the export copy, the rights copy, and so on. When you write copy:

- Try to imagine the readers as real people so you can get closer to them.
- Never patronize them. Write as though you are writing to equals.
- Avoid jargon, because people are tired of it. Keep your English simple and direct.
- Try to write as though you were speaking to the readers. It is the most effective way of drawing the reader in.
- Long sentences are often elegant, but for this sort of writing, keep it short.
- Avoid any usage or particular phrases that are popular in the media at the time of writing. They will quickly pass out of fashion.
- Have a logic or structure to your copy so that the reader can stay with it from beginning to end.
- Remember you are writing copy that is likely to be read very quickly, so you need to make impact.
- If you want to bring energy and directness to what you write, avoid writing in the passive tense.

Writing copy is a bit like writing an angry letter or e-mail: put it aside for a few hours and then re-read it before judging it as appropriate and passing it on. If you feel any uncertainty about the copy, refer it back to editorial. Generally speaking, if you want to reassure yourself about what you have written, ask someone else to read it too.

Once this bedrock copy has been written, it will be adapted for its many uses. With copy for the back cover of a book you have three readers in mind: the rep (who will sell stock to the shop), the bookshop buyer and the eventual customer. The bookshop buyer and the rep care about the speed and clarity in which the book's content and relevance are laid out in the copy, so that the possible customer is motivated to open it. If the copy gets the customer to look inside, we are halfway to a sale!

Copy for direct mailing requires even stronger adaptations, because the possible customer cannot flick open the book. So, your copy should get straight to the point and hit home. Reveal without hesitation the benefits this book supplies. If you can persuade the reader that this book is going to benefit him or her, you are *more* than halfway to making a sale.

Copy for digital marketing is a skill that many are still learning, as website technology and design keep evolving. Without question, being succinct and precise is everything here. The relationship between the eye/reader and this copy is different from that with hard copy. Viewing the screen is transitory in nature so our copy has to hit home quickly and its relevance has to be instantly recognized. We have one end in mind: for the reader to take action. That means writing the bare minimum, tempting as it is to keep elaborating.

The earlier advice about looking at your copy with an objective eye holds for all these adaptations. For every piece you write, return to it later and ask yourself, 'If I wasn't me, working in a publishing house and paid to be interested in what we publish, would what I've just read really arouse my interest? Would I really be prepared to hand over my money to buy this book?' If the answer is 'no', then you had better tear up what you have written and start again. Writing copy is something you can learn to do well. Practice, the ability to be self-critical, and to write copy for the customer and not for yourself will all help you on your way.

Sales

We will be covering aspects of sales in Chapter 5 on the supply chain and distribution, but as the relationship between sales and marketing is so close and strong, we simply cannot omit it here. In particular, we will look at how sales campaigns play their part in the marketing plan.

It will be the sales team that sells stock into the bookshops. Part of the marketing department's activities are designed to help make that happen; the other part is to get customers to buy the books, whichever route is chosen. Marketing can support the sales team with bookshop campaigns, of the sort mentioned earlier – such as POS materials, jackets, AIs, catalogues, proof copies; and if it has budgeted for it, marketing can pay for lead titles to be displayed prominently in certain shops, such as a chain, for example. The book rep really does need that support. Increasingly the rep is being required not just to sell the books but to represent the publishing house in marketing and editorial, giving valuable insights, we all hope, to the bookshop staff about how the books will sell on to the eventual customer.

To get the sales reps fired up, the marketing department must prepare for and help deliver a really good sales conference. The marketing department is not alone in this because the performance of the editors will make a difference – positively and sometimes negatively.

The sales conference

Most publishers will hold theirs twice a year. Not all books that are going to be published that year will feature at the conference: the marketing department will make the choice, based on the sales potential agreed between editorial and marketing. If you are the editor of a featured book, you are expected to present it. Editors new to the job find this very frightening. The reps have heard it all; they have certainly heard all the clichés editors like to attach to books – 'original', 'cutting edge' and 'compelling' being good examples. In many houses, marketing and promotion staff also get to present books, and certainly the detail of promotion campaigns.

What do reps, sitting at a sales conference, want to hear?

- Nothing that is already in the AI, or the catalogue. They've already read them.

- Honesty in your assessment. It is perfectly acceptable to say, for example, 'This book is actually quite dull, but it's everything students need to pass their exams.'

- Exactly what the competition is – title, author, publisher, price – and exactly how your book is going to score over the competition.

- No one who reads their 'script' from a piece of paper. You have to know exactly what you want to say, and to say it apparently effortlessly.

- Someone entertaining. This is not a time to tell jokes – unless you have a really good one that directly connects with your title – but your aim has to be to catch the listeners' attention and keep it.

- Enthusiasm too. Enthusiasm is catching. Now there's a cliché, but it's true. Furthermore, if you cannot show enthusiasm for your books, why should you expect the reps to do so?

- Any interesting snippets, including gossip, that you think the reps will remember. You need to create a kind of 'hook' for each title.

- Just the minimum of what the book is about. They know a lot from the AI and the catalogue, so do not bore them with an endless description.

The presentation (both by editorial and marketing), should not be more than a few minutes in length, unless you have something really exceptional to talk about, and be supplemented by the marketing materials that the reps need. These will be jackets and sample materials, POS materials if you are using them, and a clear summary of what 'extras' the marketing department is running. This could include campaigns to the bookshops, PR, and advertising spend if it is above average. In sum, the reps need to know not only everything that will help them present the same books confidently to the bookshops, but demonstrate to the retailers just how much the publisher is getting behind a book.

Involving the author in marketing

It is not that unusual for both marketing and editorial to want to keep the author as far away as possible from any marketing campaigns. Some authors can write but cannot sell themselves. Some think they know how to sell themselves but, untrained as sales people or marketers, their lack of experience and ability shows. Then there are some authors who believe that marketing has got nothing whatsoever to do with them, and in a way they are correct. It is their job to write the books and ours to sell them. That said, we must not forget that it is the author who knows more about the book and its market than anyone else. We need to make good use of this resource therefore, without allowing him or her to drive the marketing campaigns.

Making good use starts with the editor impressing on authors that filling in the Authors' Questionnaire carefully and fully is going to be the best chance they will have to influence how their books are marketed. Some authors, having toiled through the writing of a book, do not feel very excited about filling in a form about marketing that book. It is vital that the editor gets the author on side. The AQ is going to help us decide:

- where to send copies for review;
- where we might consider spending some money on advertising;
- what our typical reader is (our first attempt at market segmentation), thanks to the author's evaluation of the readership;
- if there are parts of the country, or the world, where this book is likely to be of particular interest;
- what competitive books we need to take seriously in our campaign.

The author's evaluation of the typical reader is probably the single most important information he or she can give us. From that 'thumbnail sketch' we can begin to make some good guesses about how much income that person has, what interests him or her, how well educated they are, what age range they fall into, whether this is a person who likes to be at the forefront of developments or waits to discover whether things are tried and tested. Your marketing routes and your messages must connect with what we know about the typical reader.

Willing authors can also be persuaded to do the following:

- Use both their press and review contacts – this is no time for them to feel shy – to get those features and reviews in print.
- Include a feature on their new book in every e-mail they send out, and most definitely on any digital social network they belong to.
- Take flyers to an event or conference where they are doing a presentation.
- Provide a list of influential people who ought to receive a complimentary copy and whose recommendation has some force. This should never include people to whom it would be 'nice' to send a copy! The recipients ought to be people whom the author genuinely knows, and each copy, preferably, should go out with a personal note.
- Be the highlight of a sales conference if he or she is a really exceptionally entertaining or interesting author. Choose your

author carefully. Not many of them know how to pitch their 'entertainment'. Some think because the audience is a book one, they somehow should become intellectual. Others think that what reps want to hear is a string of dirty jokes. You need to give your author some polite coaching beforehand.

Amazon gives space for anyone to comment on books and your author might be persuaded to join in by way of adding extra information. There is no harm in this, as this information might be useful, but no one should be persuaded to pretend to be a happy customer.

More 'free' marketing

There are a number of organizations to which you will send information, and what they do with it could lead to interest in a title and to sales. It is pretty much mandatory that you send information to some of these places, but others might repay your efforts if you include them.

Both Amazon and Nielsen Book Data come under the heading of mandatory. You need Amazon to sell your books but Nielsen also needs data on your titles so that it can record sales. Both these companies will receive AIs, either as hard copy or, more likely, as PDFs. There are other bibliographic agencies and data suppliers to whom you must send information, such as national libraries. Once these organizations have 'captured' your data, they might use it in ways that could benefit your books.

If you are publishing a book that is of interest to a society, or some other organization of people with a common interest, then do promote your book to them. They are very likely to mention it in their newsletter, website or journal.

These days the biggest source of free marketing of all is of course the digital highway and its websites, blogs and proliferating social networks. Every modern marketer has to devote time to coming up with some very clever ways of getting books noticed via these sites that are not only free, but are a powerful way of getting viral endorsement. Search engine marketing is free, but as mentioned earlier, you need key words that will get you high up on their listings.

It is always worthwhile investigating government-funded organizations. Governments are not allowed to recommend books to customers, but organizations such as the British Council do promote British books abroad.

Two prototypes for marketing plans

Let us now put what we have learnt about marketing into practice and come up with a plan for two books: one is for the consumer market, the other for the specialist market of academic books. Our consumer book is a vegetable gardening book and our academic book is a first-year undergraduate text for social science students.

We are not going to present precise plans here (such as naming TV programmes, magazines or newspapers), because precise plans don't travel and we have to think of our readers who live in other parts of the world. What we are going to do here is take you through the process of analysing the market for these two books and coming up with a marketing plan.

Our gardening book

Gardening books are part of a lively and competitive area, with a few familiar brands such as well-known gardening experts and organizations, for example, the Royal Horticultural Society, and the 'Expert' series. Extremely high production values are, interestingly, not always essential, as the success of the 'Expert' series reveals. There is always a danger that glossy gardening books remain essentially coffee table books. Successful gardening books, rather like cookery books, are popular because they are highly practical. They make you feel you want to do it.

The first piece of analysis that is going to be central to our strategy is to try to define the typical reader. Our gardening book is about vegetable gardening. In market segmentation terms, this is not particularly helpful because people across all parts of society like to grow vegetables. Furthermore, there are no necessary connections with income or geography. The bonus here, of course, is that the market is potentially very wide, but we have little to help us in segmentation apart from one very valuable attribute. People who like to grow vegetables value very highly things that are genuine – in this case, vegetables that have not been flown halfway around the world. They like being in touch and doing things for themselves. Although it takes hard work and effort to grow your own vegetables instead of just buying them from the supermarket, they think this is worthwhile.

We can therefore probably assume that these people also value 'nature' and what is 'natural' and they might also be concerned about issues such as global warming and good health. So in fact we know quite a bit about our readership as a constituency. To make sure the book is a success, we also have to convince these potential customers that it contains everything they need to become satisfied vegetable gardeners. Ultimately, it is the content that will sell the book and not just the association with other issues. Nevertheless, knowing something about what people value is going to help us tremendously with the tone of the marketing messages.

After concentrating on our potential customer, we must now analyse our book against the competition. Every advantage that our book offers must be compared, whether it is through illustration, or text, or the book's structure. The author and the editor should have provided marketing with this analysis. There is scarcely an author who does not start a book of this sort without some notion in his or her mind about writing something that is a real improvement on what is already in print, or is original. It's your job to find out what is different and use it in your marketing messages.

We now need to start translating this into action. We will begin with the basics:

- inclusion in the catalogue;
- AI for the reps and the bookshops;
- entry on your publishing house's website;
- despatch of jackets/covers to the shops;
- conveying of information to organizations such as Bookscan or Amazon, which we mentioned under 'more "free" marketing'.

Where we go from there really depends on our strategy. If this book is taking your company into new territory (perhaps you are launching into gardening for the first time) then everything you do from now on must reflect that. Your messages will be bigger, broader, more encompassing – they will go further than just one book. Your messages will claim that the content of your entry into the gardening world comes with an original approach. Alternatively, is our strategy to push this particular book and this author because we already have a good presence in gardening books?

What you do, and why, really depends on your strategy. One thing you can be sure of is that if it is the former, you will have a bigger marketing budget because you are launching into a new area. That larger budget is going to allow you greater freedom in all areas of expenditure. You simply *have* to make impact.

For the purposes of this exercise, we shall assume that you already have a presence in publishing gardening titles. Your strategy is to maximize the sales for this book, while at the same time consolidating your reputation in the field, the latter being the main aim of your strategy. You have two possible strengths: one could be that the author is a high-profile figure in the gardening world, the other is that the book's content offers real benefits over competing books. In a perfect world, the two combine. Your messages will be designed and written with these strengths in mind.

Our main routes to market might be:

- Advertising in the biggest circulation gardening magazine.

- Review copies to the same magazine (which is bound to be happy with the fact you are advertising there), but also to its main, if smaller, competitors.

- Ads to go in the lifestyle sections of weekend supplements, adjacent to gardening articles. You need to make your very best informed guess at which newspapers more strongly represent your 'typical' reader. In the case of this book, you might contemplate a wider social spread.

- Complimentary copies to all the headquarters of the major garden centre chains. They will be delighted to have some content for their own magazines and newsletters. Don't forget that the media need constant feeding.

- Further complimentary copies will go, along with a note from the author, to all the main gardening organizations. If they like the book, and feature it in their own publications, their backing is going to be important for approval ratings.

- You are going to need your PR executive to get busy with lifestyle magazines. Of particular relevance will be the glossy magazines produced by the supermarket chains. Even if we are growing our own vegetables, we are no threat to their sales. In any case, the strength of these magazines is their ability to reflect the interests of their readers. The very best we can hope for is a feature article and a review, but at the very least we simply *must* get a review.

- Your key account reps need to be told about your PR campaign so that they can feed this into the bookshops.

- Wholesalers that sell books to garden centres also need to be covered by your sales campaign.

- Your reps need to cover retail areas that are not conventional bookshops. This would include the garden centre chains, but even the British Museum stocks a few gardening books, which it considers reflect the interests and lifestyle of its visitors. There is potential here for selling this book in any visitor centre that has a gift shop.

Note that we are not suggesting review copies to newspapers. You have to search hard for reviews of gardening books. It is always advisable to spend your time and the budget focusing on areas where you are more likely to get a result. So, for features on the author (if that person is genuinely well known), your best bet is the garden and lifestyle magazines. Neither are we suggesting signings in bookshops. A garden centre chain, however, might be interested in doing an event that would include a signing session, but this stands its best chance of being successful if the author is local to the garden centre. Other options (if the timing is right) are events at major national gardening shows and the main regional gardening events. Such events tend to feature expert panels and your author could be a prized expert on them. You should hesitate about devoting a very large spend to advertising. Gardening is a good, healthy market, but remember that it is a specialism within consumer publishing. The demand for gardening books is not elastic.

So far we have focused on hard copy and real people. What can we do with e-marketing? In conventional retailing, something called push/pull operates. This means that the publishers push their titles to the bookshops or online retail sites, which once they 'get behind' a title are, in turn, expected to push the sales of the books through to the final consumer. With pull, the publisher excites sufficient interest in titles (through reviews, features and advertising) that the eventual consumer is motivated to 'demand' that the shops supply the books. So, the two sides – the originator (the publisher) and the consumer (the book reader) – put pressure on the retailer or 'intermediary'.

With digital marketing, the push factor is still as important, but whereas the conventional retail bookshop scene is still moderately varied, digital retailing is dominated by one huge supplier, Amazon. This huge concentration of power in one supplier and publishers' relationships with it are 'vitally important', or 'one-sided', depending on where you are standing. For Amazon it is the former, and for the publishers often the latter, as they feel relatively powerless in the face of a retail organization that is completely dominating the e-retailing landscape, and therefore able to demand and receive very large discounts.

At this point, we will concentrate on the opportunities for pull activity as it is in this area that the full flexibility of e-marketing is so useful. Within our publishing house's website, we should be signalling to visitors that this is an important new book from us. This means:

- featuring it in the monthly e-newsletter that comes out on our site, including an interview with the author;
- the placing of a 'top feature' banner on the company's home page during the month of publication;
- the same banner to appear on the gardening list home page;
- providing widgets that allow visitors to your site to look inside the book;
- some attractive offers on the gardening backlist at a special promotional discount to celebrate the publication of the new book.

We need an entry into genuine viral marketing and here we shall use the author. We can almost guarantee that this author has his or her own website – not to have a website is unusual these days for anyone who has achieved even a small degree of celebrity. Our author must fully promote this book on his or her site, or at the very least have a link to our website.

We should also ask our author for permission to use relevant e-mail addresses he or she has, so that we can mail our piece. Life gets slightly more complicated now because we cannot just e-mail indiscriminately, so we need to persuade our author to clear permission for those mailings to go out. For the sake of increased sales, the author is likely to agree.

What will make this more acceptable is to run a competition where the prize will be not just the new book but a set of backlist books on gardening. You will discuss the nature of the competition with your author and come up with something that is thoroughly interactive, where the competitors are motivated to consult the author's website several times over. We also want to link addresses (e-addresses) he or she has for gardening clubs and other well-known gardening writers.

Again, our author has to give you permission to use these addresses. It is unlikely he or she will refuse, or that the recipients will prefer not to hear about the book, but the law requires that permission is cleared. Every message that goes out should encourage the recipient to pass it on to every other gardening enthusiastic he or she knows. The copy in your message is going to be entirely focused. The book is a practical one. Make sure that your copy makes that entirely clear and presents the book's advantages over other ones.

Our academic book

As with our consumer book, we will cover the basics of catalogue, AI for the shops and our reps, entry on our website, a proof jacket for selected shops, some advertising, and the transmission of information to the 'silent salespeople'. This is the 'push' element of our plan. Unlike the gardening book, we will spend less money but we can be focused about what we do and, by and large, that is why we need to spend less money. Large advertisements on the television, cinema, main transport systems, newspapers and magazines – the platforms that are *really* expensive to use – are a complete waste of money when it comes to selling academic books. Either you want/need to buy an academic book, or you don't. Persuasion is very unlikely to make the academic change his or her mind.

Here, also, is an example of marketing to a member of a group that is not likely to be the ultimate buyer. For academic books (indeed for many kinds of specialist books), we need to market heavily to people recommending the books, in this case, the lecturers. The lecturers are the prime gatekeepers in this, as indeed would be school teachers for education publishing. So, we need to consider several things here:

- How do we find the gatekeepers?
- What messages about content will they find persuasive?
- How can we convert their recommendations into sales?

Finding the gatekeepers is not that difficult. The names of lecturers who teach in specific subjects are listed on university and college websites, along with their e-mail addresses. Much of the kind of information you require is listed in the public domain. You can create your own databases of lecturers, and keep it updated. If your academic list is established, you will already have such a database, but it will lose its value if you do not keep it up to date.

The messages will take the form of presenting names or issues that interest these people. Academic readers are as influenced as any other market by 'big names', and simply announcing a new book from a famous academic might be sufficient. That said, however, there are few academic 'superstars' around who can command this kind of appeal. You must use your judgement on this. Mostly your messages about academic books are a combination of the practical and the quality. Certainly for textbooks, the authors will be using their intimate knowledge of how a subject area is taught and examined to inform their writing. Today, most specialist writers no longer have to guess at what exactly is taught in educational institutions – they display the content of their courses on websites. So, an academic author is able to mirror the teaching and learning that goes on within the covers of his or her book. That said, this openness means that writers are all hovering around roughly the same content, and as a result getting the book recognized and chosen is now quite a challenge for both author and publisher.

Here are some other things we should know about this market:

- Academics are under far greater pressure than they used to be. Student numbers at university have increased hugely. Academics not only teach greater numbers but their administrative duties have also grown. Most of them feel they are under great pressure.

- Many of them re-use their lecturers, updating them minimally from the lectures given in the year before. Whatever one's view on this, it's possible that lecturers do this because of pressure of work, or are conservative in their habits. These characteristics make them an ideal audience as they might appreciate help from you via your books.

- Similarly, they tend to present the same reading lists to students year after year, although they do update them.

- Lecturers tend to teach the same subject, so they get to know it very well and your marketing must be conducted at an appropriate level, being selective about what you promote to them.

Our strategy, as with the gardening book, is going to depend on whether we are entering academic publishing for the first time, or whether we are adding a new book to our existing list. Here, we are adding a new social science textbook to our existing list, so we are not breaking new ground. There are two timeframes for marketing to academics: the late spring, before students prepare for exams and will be encouraged by their lecturers to get reading; and early summer, well in advance of when courses begin in the early autumn and students receive outlines for their courses accompanied by reading lists.

There are differences in the way that some universities operate. Most follow the tradition three-term academic year, but some are switching to semester years. Also, not all universities use examinations as their main way of judging students' work. For all of these reasons, marketing in time to anticipate the beginning of the new academic year is probably, overall, the crucial moment.

Because the lecturers are 'known' – this is a market where you can find precise names and addresses – your task is easier because you can get directly to them. This is very different from consumer marketing where, to a great degree, you are going into the unknown.

Let us now think about our 'pull' tactics. Our principal way of promoting to them is, without doubt, what is known as the 'inspection' copy. A copy of your new book will be sent to the known lecturer. The deal is this: if the lecturer reports back that the book will be adopted, and provides the names of local bookshops likely to stock it, he or she can keep it at no charge. If this person cannot recommend adoption, he or she must either return it or pay for it. It is likely that most will adopt the book if it is a good one. However, while genuine interest will lead to adoptions, simply sending the book – to be really effective – is not enough.

These are some of things you need to communicate to the academics:

- Most definitely you need to explain – by examples – how the book scores over competitive texts (this should be covered in the author's questionnaire).
- With a new edition, examples of how it has improved on the previous edition (again this should be in the AQ).
- Content that is going to aid teaching and learning (exercises, case studies).
- Reminders of the success of the author's previous books.
- Strong endorsements of a new author's suitability for writing the book (career, status, prizes, etc).
- Layouts of the text that will aid teaching and learning.
- If your pricing is competitive, say so.
- Name the link to an author website if you have one for the book.

What the academic wants is for you to help him or her make decisions. Anything that makes this easier for these hard-pressed individuals is going to help you make sales, because if they decide in favour of the book, they will push the recommendation towards the student. Students will study book lists and make independent decisions about what to read, but the key to this is that a recommendation from a lecturer is going to be highly influential.

You will have to make a choice about whether to put all this vital information on a leaflet to accompany the book, or virally, by e-mailing the lecturer. There are risks associated with both. Will the lecturer throw away the leaflet, as just another piece of unwanted mail. That might seem perverse, but he or she is more likely to leaf through the book than read your piece. You will need all your design skill here to make that leaflet stand out so that he or she bothers to read it. On the other hand, if you e-mail it, it will be one of hundreds of e-mails that academics receive in a week, just from their own institutions.

You could consider doing both. Send the leaflet with the book but follow it up a few weeks later with an e-mail. There is less risk here that the important messages contained in your leaflet will be lost. Make sure that the book's title is the title of your message if you don't want it to be instantly deleted. You will need to ask the lecturer not only if he or she is recommending the book, but also if he or she is asking the library to order it. Keep your message simple – an enquiry – so that you are not guilty of selling without the recipient's permission.

If feedback is good you can follow up by providing a link to your author's website if there is one. These are now popular add-ons containing information on and chat from the author for anyone interested in the subject of the book. The author's website could also contain a feedback channel that encourages discussion about the book or the author. Customers generally these days are familiar with the 'review' channel on retail sites. More ambitiously, you can have a video of the author on his or her website, or arrange for podcasts or webcasts. These are not uncommon, even for specialist authors. The bigger the name, the more likely the book buyer will look for these significant add-ons.

Finally, some publishers might want to persuade lecturers to take bulk orders for student purchase, at a discount. You should approach this idea with some care, because most lecturers feel that they have enough to do without acting as a retailer. There is always a danger too that the local bookshop will hear about this and be very angry about losing sales. If you decide to publicize a discount for students for sales direct from you, you can tell the lecturers about this, but again, beware of alienating local bookstores.

Conferences

The conference circuit is a staple activity area for academic publishers. In some countries, such as the United States, they are big business because of the size of the conferences. But even in the UK, attendance is seen as essential for most academic publishers. Your display is always very carefully chosen to reflect the interests of the conference and its attendees. If the author of your new book is attending, he or she can usually be relied upon to put a leaflet on the chairs of the lecture or seminar rooms.

You can also consider holding a wine party at your stand, for invited guests only. Unless you specify who should be attending, you will be swamped by roaming academics looking for a free drink!

Finally, you could sell stock at a discounted price, on the day or by using a leaflet, which can be taken away, that features the discount. Attendees have come to expect this, and you will not be losing any more income than you would when you sell books to the shops at a discounted price. Attendees also like to think that when you are dismantling your stand, you will not want the bother of having to transport all the books back to your office or warehouse and that you will want to give them away. Remember the dangers in promoting the idea that books are free!

CASE STUDY   Working through a budget for a consumer book

Our book is expected to sell about 100,000 copies. The price is £15.00 and we expect our overall sales income to be about £600,000 assuming that our average discount is going to be around 60 per cent. The book comes under the genre heading of 'thriller'.

Applying our usual ratio of a marketing spend somewhere in the range of 6 to 7 per cent, depending on the importance of the book, we decide to spend just over 6.5 per cent of our sales income on marketing. We therefore have about £40,000 to spend; of this, we earmark £20,000 to be spent on:

- promotions to retailers;

- prime position in a supermarket chain;

- front-of-shop position in a retail chain.

Each of these items will take up roughly a third of the overall spend of £20,000. However, we want to do more as we have considerable confidence in this book and author, so we want to find an arena for advertising. After looking at the various options available to us – ads in underground stations, on the sides of buses, bus shelters, taxis, cinemas and conventional printed media – we decide to concentrate on a national rail poster. We have decided against one day of advertising on an ISP site because that will swallow up all of our total marketing spend. Television advertising will not work either as we cannot afford repeats. The same can be said about cinema adverts, which will also be very expensive to produce. We have consulted an ad agency and for £15,000 we can get ad posters on railway stations of our choice for two weeks. It has calculated the amount of footfall past these ads, plus exposure to people sitting in stationary trains at railway stations, and we believe that the ad will get total exposure in the region of at least 3 million 'viewers'. This is a kind of 'captive audience', many of whom will be doing the same journey (to work) day after day. The repeat impact, therefore, is considerable and, together with the cost, this represents best value for money. We could get as much exposure (in terms of numbers) by putting ads in the London Underground, but the weakness here is that coverage is just confined to London.

We need to set aside about £2,000 for designing the poster and printing it. We will produce extra proofs for reviews and that will cost us about £1,000. We will allocate a cost of about £1,000 for online promotion through our and associated websites. The design of this and producing copy will require intensive work from our marketing staff but this falls under the overhead of our department.

We allocate a further £1,000 for publicity purposes. This could include a party or any other expenses associated with publicity. Much of this activity will be done by our publicity department (which is part of our overhead), but we think it is sensible to set aside this sum to ensure that the money is there should it be needed. It might be used for transporting the author around for interviews, providing meals with influential people, and the possibility of having to pay for hotel bills around the time of the launch.

This is how we have spent our £40,000. With this amount of money at our disposal, and an important book at the centre of the campaign, we have nevertheless been quite rational about how we have spent it. We have thought through carefully how we make maximum impact and have divided our spend with roughly half going on retail promotion and half on customer promotion – the very embodiment of 'push/pull'.

The money has been spent on tangible things. We have not yet mentioned e-promotion. A successful marketing plan will combine both. At very little cost (£1,000), apart from inputting and creative time, we will also do the following:

- Place regular messages on one of the social media sites – one with book-related pages. There we can also link to any videos and podcasts, interviews and relevant articles featuring our author.

- Our author's blog will link to the company's own website, which will be enhanced by an interview with the author.

- We will feature feedback from readers, booksellers and staff about the book, all designed to create discussion and a sense of momentum.

- This linking will be supported by the 'add this' button, or a similar function, that creates quick links to other social media sites, virally spreading promotion around the web.

This will maximize search engine optimization, and bring readers to our own homepage.

Conclusion

Marketing and editorial are very closely allied, so, for example, when we talk about our marketing strategy for a book, or a list of books, it would be nonsense to imply that this is only relevant to what the marketing department does. Editors, when they are signing up new books with authors, should be carrying that same strategy in their heads. The market they envisage for the books they contract should be the same one that the marketing department envisages. There must be shared notions of market position, segmentation, value, level and quality, otherwise editorial and marketing will be pulling in opposite directions. When this happens, we are probably looking at a publishing house where there is insufficient clarity of goals, and no one benefits from this. So, if you hear anyone talking about marketing as though it is something that only concerns the marketing department, beware.

To recap, marketing is a mixture of everyday routine and the exceptional. Every book gets the basic treatment, but after that, every book gets a little something expressly designed for just it. In our two examples, we have mostly dwelt on what you could do for an individual book through other media and through digital technology, mostly using social platforms. None of these social platforms are named here. The field is so fast moving that some of them will have fallen out of favour by the time this book is out. But this is such a powerful tool: there is nothing that enhances a book as successfully as word-of-mouth recommendation, and that recommendation can now move with lightning speed. This is the 'pull' we mentioned earlier.

But just as much as you care about getting people chatting about your books, you must ensure that the retail trade is ready and waiting to fulfil sales. Without the 'push', you are going to have a lot of disappointed book buyers on your hands. This is the part of the supply chain that people forget about. The books must be available for purchase. Getting those books into the shops is mostly a function of the sales department but it will be your job to give them the messages that they can repeat to the retail sector and will excite them. There is more on the supply chain in Chapter 5.

As you begin to plan, you must have a strategic approach. This might sound rather grandiose (does one book merit this?) but it is vital that you know *what* you are doing and *why* you are doing it. At the start, you need to ask yourself whether you are promoting something that is breaking new ground, or whether you are building on what you have. The answer to that question will determine the size of your budget, your messages to your potential book buyers, and how and where you expect to reach them. There is a logic and a discipline to this. Everything you plan has to be justified in terms of understanding that focus for action.

Overall, we can say of marketing that:

- It involves collaborative and collegial working within a group.
- Prioritization is necessary. Not only is every book different, these books will assume different levels of importance. The different levels may relate to commercial potential or seasonal activity, but you must be aware of this because you cannot give the same amount of time and effort to every book. You have to judge which needs more from you, when, and why.
- It requires planning: of effort, time and timing. Our industry works by lead-in times, often marketing to the retailer six months

ahead of publication or more for a very important book. There cannot be any such thing as last-minute marketing!

- Getting the detail correct is fundamental. Retailers need to know the correct ISBN, the number of pages and illustrations and the price.

- Conviction is a powerful tool in the hands of a marketer. The publishing trade will take seriously and give respect to a marketer who is operating with integrity and not simply trying to fool the market about the value of the books.

Further reading

Baverstock, A (2008) *How to Market Books,* 4th edn, Kogan Page, London

Fill, C (2005) *Marketing Communications: Contexts, strategies and applications*, Financial Times/Prentice Hall, London

Squires, C (2007) *Marketing Literature: The making of contemporary writing in Britain,* Palgrave Macmillan, Basingstoke

Sales, distribution and the supply chain

05

Introduction

In many publishing houses, the sales department will be part of the marketing department. Distribution also often reports to marketing. So why did we not cover them in the previous chapter on marketing? We decided to separate out sales and distribution because their functions are different, even though closely allied to marketing. It is marketing's job to get messages out to the market, to excite interest in a book. Sales and distribution then translate those messages into sales – sales that are fully realized by getting the books into the hands of the buyers. This sequence is often referred to as the 'supply chain'. So:

- How do books get to book buyers?
- How are bookshops, or other outlets, persuaded to stock books?
- How do the books get from the printer to the warehouse and to the buyer?

It's not done by magic, and it's certainly not any bookshop's obligation to stock new books or backlist. We have met many authors who thought it was! While sales reps and what they do are hardly the neglected arm of the publishing industry, not many people give very much thought to warehouses. Yet this aspect of the supply chain is at the core of the successful distribution of book stocks.

The mark of efficient and successful manufacturers is their ability to get their goods to the market. If you cannot get your goods into the hands of the end purchaser, you will go out of business. If you cannot sell your goods, even though you know there will be demand for them, then you cannot get any revenue for them. One of the problems of the old-style economies of the former Eastern European bloc was that distribution was almost non-existent. This is why there were often terrible shortages of food and goods because no one took responsibility for distributing them, or even knew how to do it.

Remember that publishing is a manufacturing business. It makes things (books) and pays hefty bills for their manufacture (usually 30 days after they have been made), so to remain in financial good order publishers need to be able to sell their books as quickly as possible and put the cash into the bank, to pay other bills and overheads. In this chapter, we are going to look at the role of sales in getting books into the retail market, and how distribution gets the books into the shops.

Define sales!

What exactly do we mean by 'sales' here? It is very important that you make a distinction between sales that are made into the retail sector, whether they are bookshops or websites, and sales made to book buyers. It is the latter that ultimately matter.

When it comes to sales, we have two stages. The first concerns sales made into retail outlets, which are almost always made by the book reps. They are usually called 'subs', or subscriptions. Here the retailer is making a guess about how many copies it will sell and ordering the number of copies accordingly. Furthermore, it is ordering for a time span of no more than a couple of months. That is, it is guessing how many copies it will sell in that period. If at the end of that time, or before, it sells all the copies, it is likely to re-order if it has confidence in the title. The retailer will pay the publisher for the stock it has ordered.

Having got the books onto the shelves (or a retail website), the second stage is realizing sales to customers. Those are real sales. Having made a sale, a retailer does not give money back to a dissatisfied customer unless the book's binding is coming apart or there is some other major structural problem with it. The onus for making these sales falls on the retailers, but the publisher's marketing campaign should have played a large part in driving the customers to make a purchase. This is the push/pull sequence we referred to in the marketing chapter.

In this sequence, the publisher gets income from the first stage, and the book retailer gets it from the second stage. This sounds very straightforward, but it is not. There is one significant difference concerning trading between publishers and book retailers and that between producers and retailers in most other market sectors. The difference is this: book retailers may return their stock no later than six months (typically) after they have purchased it if it has failed to sell, and if the stock is still in good condition. Under these circumstances, the publisher then gives the retailer its money back. Therefore, the wise publisher does not regard the sales made in stage one as cast iron. In fact, there are particular dangers for publishers in consumer publishing when a massive marketing and PR campaign can lead to enthusiastic stocking in the retail outlets but the book buyers – ie the public – have failed to be influenced by them. Huge proportions of that stock can go winging back to the publisher's warehouse followed not long after by an invoice for the return of the retailer's money.

This seeming madness is called 'returns'. We will return to it later in the chapter, but for the moment, you need to understand the real difference between 'subs' and 'sales'. Those who have failed to understand the difference, or even worse, forgotten about it, end up in tears when their sales income exits their bank accounts and makes its way back to those of the retailers.

The function of sales departments

So, marketing's function is to tell the market about new books and to raise expectations about them. We hope they will get everyone excited and interested in our new publications. But someone has to make the deal, and this is the job of the sales department. However, long before a deal has been made, the salespeople play a crucial role in determining how many copies of a new book will be printed. When an editor presents a book to a publication committee for contract, the salespeople will have something to say about the viability of the editor's proposed sales figures. Some time further down the road, when that same book is about to printed, the sales department will play an influential role when decisions are made about the size of the print run. Remember, an editor may be hiding behind egotistical concerns – 'back me, back my print run' – but for a member of the sales department there is only one thing that concerns him or her: 'How many copies of this book can we *really* sell?' In some publishing houses, consumer ones in particular, the sales department will have a big say over whether a book should be contracted or not. It will also have views, which others will pay close attention to, about pricing, jackets and even book titles.

Selling to the retail sector

Not so very long ago, our salesperson (called a rep), would visit all the bookshops of any significance within the geographic territory that he or she covered. Appointments for meeting bookshop staff would have been made ahead of the visit. The rep would turn up and take staff through the forthcoming list. There would be time to say something about every title and the authors, and perhaps enlarge on special marketing campaigns planned for specific titles. Reps might also inspect the stock on the shelves and suggest some re-ordering of titles that had now sold out. That kind of selling system gradually eroded as publishers decided that some titles were not worth describing in any great detail, but that reps should concentrate only on potential best-sellers – and the retailers agreed with them. This did not mean that the book was unworthy of being presented but more that the book retailer might not be the prime market for the book; perhaps a library should be. The appearance of software that would keep an accurate tally of the stocks held by bookshops also has meant that reps did not concern themselves so much with stock-keeping.

The relationship between the rep and the retail sector appeared to simplify even more when our reps started to be called key account managers. Here, our rep will talk to a representative of a chain of shops, who is taking responsibility for buying for all the shops, or maybe all the chain's shops in a particular geographical area. However, although the rep is now travelling less and speaking to fewer people, his or her role has become more broad-ranging. The job of the rep here is to actively involve the retailers in the publication of a new book. Selling-in will include choosing to push books that are more likely to be attractive to the customers of that particular chain. The rep will have stories to tell about how the house has conceived of the book in commercial terms. The conversation can turn to joint promotion campaigns – special displays, or an entry in the bookshop chain's seasonal catalogue, perhaps even an author signing session. Both sides will have to bear the cost of that. So, in essence, what does all this mean? It means that reps no longer turn up and say, 'This is what I've got to offer you – take it or leave it.' Now, the rep is trying to interest the retailers by playing to their needs. Does this lead to overall increased sales? The answer to that is 'possibly', but shortly we shall look at what else the retailer wants. This selling-in cycle takes place usually about three months ahead of publication. Amazon is, of course, a key account and business will proceed with them in the same way as it does for other major retailers.

What every rep needs is a good, strong lead title that really engages the interest of the retailer. If you have such a beast on your list, you can raise interest in your other new books because confidence rubs off on everything else. Whilst the role of the rep has broadened and narrowed at the same time – fewer people to see, but more to talk about – there are still fringes of the retail trade where the rep will visit individual bookshops, known as independents. How reps conduct themselves in those shops will not be so different from what they did in earlier times. At both chain bookshops and independents, the rep's objective is to persuade the shop to stock new books. The points of persuasion that a rep will use will centre on most of the following:

- Author's reputation, but only if the author is successful.
- Current popularity of a particular genre of book.
- Information on PR and marketing campaigns that the publisher is going to carry out to support a particular new book.
- Local interest – whether related to the content or the author.
- For an exceptionally commercial title, the rep might also hand the retailer the kind of DVD for a new title that we referred to in the previous chapter on marketing.

Building confidence and trust

A vital part of this persuasive sequence is how the retailer perceives the rep. Trust is the most powerful weapon that the rep can possess. Imagine how it feels for the retailer who has to listen to endless selling pitches from dozens of reps, each calling on behalf of different publishing houses. Decisions have to be made about what to stock (what is going to sell?). Bookshops have limited amounts of space so many new books will have to be rejected. Think of the pressure on that retailer. What the retailer wants to hear is a 'pitch' from someone whom he or she can rely on. The retailer is going to pay a lot of attention to a rep whose persuasion and judgement in the past have proved to be accurate. The job of being a rep means that he or she will return to the same bookshops over and over again, and any rep who has over-sold a new book that failed to achieve good sales is going to be embarrassed to return and have to start the same process again with different titles. Furthermore, this time, the retailer is going to be sceptical.

Trust, therefore, is key to the relationship between the rep and the retailer. By extension, trust in the whole publishing house and its judgement becomes an issue for a retailer. Retailers will most certainly back new books and their authors to the hilt if they have faith in the publishers. This is particularly important if the publishers are launching a first-time author. Getting a first-time author recognized is like climbing a mountain. What is so special about this one amongst the hundreds of others? The backing of a particular trusted and respected publisher will most certainly have an influence, as will an imaginative and energetic marketing and promotion campaign. When this campaign is translated into weekly phone calls updating the retailer about what is happening by way of reviews and media coverage, the retailer's confidence grows. It is often said of publishing that it is a 'people business'. Selling to the retail sector is a very good example of how relationships with people influence how we do business.

Much of this work will have a seasonal aspect to it. The summer is a marvellous time for selling books. People going on holiday love to pack a book or two. The summer is also the time for the unveiling of the shortlist for the Booker Prize. Although this list is always argued over, one can say that these will be, overall, exceptional books, and interest rises both amongst the retailers and the book buyers. The other peak selling time, of course, is Christmas. We like to give a good book as a present. The run-up to this peak is a crucial one for publishers and their reps; indeed the construction of publishers' lists of new books is often focused around it. Every major publisher will also want to have a Really Big Title timed to come out at Christmas and many large royalty cheques will be advanced to authors whose books will be their main feature. Competition between the publishers will be hot.

Sales to non-consumer markets

The two principal markets here are higher education and education. There are other specialist markets, of course, but these are the biggest.

Higher education can encompass scientific, technical, medical, academic and vocational markets. The education market is mostly centred on schools.

Higher education bookshops are by comparison far less plentiful than consumer bookshops and the activity of reps is almost entirely focused on degree courses where the course textbook is the favoured vehicle for teaching students. For the rep, therefore, all sales pitches highlight the suitability of a text for teaching purposes. The higher education bookshop is located either on a campus or in a town centre convenient for students.

There are some reps whose work centres on establishing and maintaining relationships with teaching staff. Here the rep is not only trying to persuade teaching staff to adopt textbooks, but may even be carrying out some market research into what materials a course might need. A supplementary function might also be alerting the teaching staff to other, usually electronic, resources that support a textbook. An additional activity for a rep in this sector might be calling on libraries or library suppliers. Here, as with all specialist selling of this sort, the emphasis is going to be on the essential virtues of the book, which inevitably will be translated into its functionality. It is very difficult to persuade anyone to purchase specialist books out of anything other than necessity. The work of the higher education rep supplements all the promotion and direct marketing work done by the in-house team, which we covered in the marketing chapter. This is where the bulk of the selling is done – through inspection copies. It is only textbook publishing, with potential sales to very large classes, that can support the cost of these reps who make direct contact with the higher education professionals.

The *school book* rep by contrast is going to spend most of his or her time visiting schools. During term time the rep will visit several schools a day in his or her territory. Here again, relationships are crucial. The rep needs to persuade the classroom teacher that he or she understands the teaching and learning requirements and what material is suitable, in relation to which the new textbooks will be presented. The effective rep is also listening carefully to what the teachers might be saying about their competitors' texts, and this will be fed back to the commissioning editors at the publishing house. Like the higher education rep, the school book rep is very likely to be offering a support service for digital learning products that the publisher has sold to the school.

Both these specialist reps will have their work dominated by the academic year. Higher education reps will concentrate their efforts from the early summer onwards, building up to the start of term in September. There will be another push after the New Year to coincide with courses run on a semester basis. For school book reps, the spring is likely to be the busiest time, because annual school budgets begin then. In quieter times these reps are likely to attend or set up local conferences with the aim of showcasing books, or to try to deepen the relationships they may be forming with members of examination boards or of local education authorities. These reps, therefore, like their colleagues in consumer publishing, are acting far more as representatives of their publishers than just as salespeople.

So you think want to be a book rep?

Being a rep can be a first-class grounding for work within a publishing house, both in marketing and in editorial. A rep is seeing the business at 'the sharp end', something that other professionals in publishing can be shielded from, especially editors. A young editor should be encouraged to go and spend a few days with a rep, to see just how tough it is out there in the market. This experience is likely to prevent anyone from forming over-optimistic views about a book's potential. Yet this does not mean that working as a rep kills off enthusiasm or commitment. A really good rep possesses both, but they have been tempered by reality.

To thrive as a rep, and certainly to enjoy being a rep, you will need the following:

- Plenty of energy because the work involves 'performance' – that is, pitching for sales, which is hard work. It also involves a lot of travelling, which is always tiring.

- Self-motivation, because although some books can help you feel enthusiastic, others will not. Yet you have to feel motivated about all of them because that is your job.

- Good organizational skills are needed because the rep has to organize his or her time to fit in with the requirements of the retailers. This means making plans well ahead of the dates on which you wish to visit them, getting there on time and with all your selling materials and information to hand. You need to be able to show, for example, book jackets, and talk about marketing and promotion campaigns without hesitation or bumbling.

- Communication skills are essential. You will never become a rep if you are unable to express yourself clearly and succinctly. The average retailer wants to hear good, plain English, and he or she does not have time to listen to you droning on and on. So, you need to be able to pack a communication punch.

- Knowledge about the typical reader for any book he or she is presenting to a retailer is always convincing. The retailer is going to feel far more confident about this than a vague pitch about who is going to buy the book. This means, as a rep, you have to put in some hard work to ensure you have grasped the readership and the level for any book. The more knowledge you can display about the typical reader and the market for a particular genre of book, the more confident the retailer is going to feel about you.

- A good sense of other people's psychology is extremely useful. This allows the rep to exercise judgement about how a retailer might react to a particular kind of pitch. Some might like an 'in-your-face' pitch; others something more seductive.

- You also need to be sure of your own psychology. You need to be strong enough to negotiate should the retailer wish to 'discuss' terms. This might not mean caving in immediately but being prepared to argue on behalf of the publisher. You should also be strong enough to know when to stand down when a retailer is making a really good case for an increased discount.

- Independence of spirit and mind are also required. You will spend a lot of time on the road, and often speaking to people you do not know very well, trying to persuade them to stock your books. Only someone who is capable of being on their own and finding their own motivation can do this. If you are shy and constantly need the company of others to keep you happy, this is not a job for you.

- Lastly, honesty is essential. If retailers suspect you are not being entirely honest with them, you will become a liability to yourself and to your publishing house. It is very easy to exaggerate a book's potential, but if you are over-selling, you will not be given a fair hearing the next time round. It is also very easy these days to check on the sales of real books through online sales data providers such as Nielsen Bookscan.

We hope it is becoming clear just how important are those links to the sales force mentioned in the editorial and marketing chapters. However well motivated, intelligent and hardworking the reps are, they are handicapped if they do not receive good, clear and supportive knowledge about the books and the markets from both editors and marketers. Even a brilliant rep cannot make up effective sales pitches from thin air. We hope too that you can draw the right conclusion that an effective rep is someone who enjoys his or her job. Negativity always comes through however much one tries to disguise it. All-important commitment and motivation must be genuine.

Not everyone is suited to being a rep. If you are, and if somewhere further down the line you feel you could make a successful transfer to editorial or to marketing, repping will have given you a really strong grounding.

We now turn to the things that book retailers want in addition to best-sellers.

Discounting and returns

The two are linked, and not always to the publisher's benefit. Generous discounts to retailers give them plenty of encouragement to buy stock and to sell it hard. It therefore encourages them to take a risk. It is not a risk in the real sense of gambling, however. If you gamble on horses and you lose, the bookie will not give you your money back; if you 'gamble' on your book stocks and fail, the publisher will give you your money back.

In an ideal world (a world that many publishers would love to inhabit), the reward for giving high discounts to retailers would mean publishers not having their books returned. At the time of writing, this ideal world does not exist. The publisher sells to retailers at the most competitive discount it can afford and then waits, with some anxiety, to see if those highly discounted books will be returned three to six months later, depending on its returns policy.

Why is publishing a rather unusual industry in allowing returns? The origins are honourable: returns allowed retailers to 'have a go' with some books that were not going to be immediate winners. These are books that may, like good wine, take some time to give of their best. By honouring returns, publishers and retailers were both attempting to keep the publishing base as broad as possible. This is an eminently good intention. The history of publishing is full of examples of hugely successful books that did not appear either at first or second glance to be winners, but publishers and retailers were prepared to back them.

Such well-meaning optimism seems quaint these days and is mostly absent, but its supreme representative – returns – is still with us.

Intermittently, both sides of the trading equation initiate discussions on setting up a hard-and-fast relationship regarding returns, but the issue remains unresolved. The idea of encouraging retailers to 'have a go' with some books remains a commendable one. With it these days, however, comes a price – even higher discounts. There might be other complications too. There are books that simply do not merit carrying an exceptionally high discount – specialist books for example. Any publisher has to question whether even higher discounts on books that are not speculative are justifiable. It is not an accident that the returns rates for specialist books are far lower than they are for consumer books. Look at it this way: if you are a publisher of books that are least likely to be returned, do you really want to give a retailer a higher discount in order to eliminate returns? This might look like giving away even more money to the retailer just to keep the status quo as far as you are concerned.

High discounting does not have such a deep past. Until the early 1990s, most European countries exercised some method of price control over books. When a book was published, it had a 'published price' and no retailer was allowed to sell the book at a lower price. The thinking behind this 'retail price maintenance' was similar to that behind returns; in this case it was intended to counteract any possible 'pile 'em high, sell 'em low' tendencies. The supermarket approach to selling was seen as completely inimical to bookselling because the range of stock in publishing is far, far wider than anything you will see in a supermarket. A supermarket makes money because it stocks a limited number of items in all the ranges it covers, but in bulk. This allows the supermarket to price everything much lower than the corner shop can.

If publishers and book retailers adopted such an approach, the number of books published would have to plummet and the kinds of books published could only be popular books – the sort of books that appear in the best-seller charts. Life in publishing is more complicated than that. Publishers produce books for a variety of audiences, of different sizes and at different levels. There is a market for many sorts of books and it is the function of publishing to provide them.

The name given to this retail price maintenance in the UK was the Net Book Agreement. Although it was investigated several times because of claims that it was a restrictive practice, those claims were not endorsed. The NBA, however, was simply an 'agreement'; it was never a legal requirement for publishers to follow it. Eventually the NBA was broken by several of the large publishing corporations, which in effect meant that it was destroyed. It was impossible for some parts of the publishing industry to follow the NBA and for others to discount their books as much as they liked.

The effect of the abolition of the NBA is debatable. Some believe that in opening up discounting on price, the market for books was extended. The market was certainly extended through the non-traditional retailing sites. Supermarkets started to stock books and the pre-eminent digital bookselling site – Amazon – took advantage of the ability to use price as a selling tool. Market statistics, however, show that the number of books sold has not increased significantly, so one could claim that discounted pricing has failed. It has not made bookselling any more prosperous, and since sales have not increased significantly, the publishers have not got richer either. The only beneficiary has been the book buyer. High discounting allows book retailers to sell us books often at very low prices. It could be said that these very low prices have devalued books in people's eyes. Interestingly, some European countries that abolished their own NBAs around about the same time as the UK did have reintroduced it, because they feel that books and authorship have not benefited.

One further thing to consider about discounting is that publishers are known to price their books higher than they otherwise would in order to compensate for high discounts. Any frequent visitor to bookshops will observe that a remarkable number of new hardbacks are priced at £25 and yet strangely the discounted price is usually somewhere between £12.50 and £15. The effect is to make the book look like a real bargain. Are we looking at a marketing ploy or a genuine enticement? The approach is too consistent to feel that it is the latter.

Further discussion about the benefits of discounting and whether returns should be abolished is not appropriate here. These are matters of opinion as much as practice, but readers of this book must be aware of the financial consequences of both in the supply chain. Discounting and returns are certainly regarded by book retailers as essential for their ability to do good business. Providing a good deal for the customer has become the mantra for booksellers, and represents a massive cultural shift in bookselling from the old days of indifference to book buyers. Here again, you will find differences of opinion on the best way to sell books and give the customers what they want. Not all book retailers believe that discounted pricing is the best tool; some believe that providing good, broad stocks on the shelves – stocking in depth, in both new books and backlist – along with expert sales staff and first-class customer care, is the way to sell books.

Special sales

Not all sales are made through the usual retail sites: the sales department will also be serving the demands of other book buyers. The most common are:

- special offers to newspapers and magazines (buy the newspaper and get a book either free or for a bargain price);
- special editions of books to be given away by a company (travel books that come with your documentation for your holiday);
- bulk buys of textbooks to institutions;
- sales to direct-selling companies that take stock they have bought to offices, factories and occasionally to schools;
- book club sales, often the province of the rights department.

These special sales provide welcome extra income for the publisher, but not all new books are suitable for this treatment. Inevitably, these are books sold at very high discounts to the organizations buying them.

How is the sales department organized?

One of the first things to grasp is that not all publishers have a sales department. A company may be too small to afford such an overhead. In this case, it will contract with a freelance sales company that will do all the work that one would expect from a sales rep but for a percentage of the turnover or income made from the books it sells to retailers. For the publisher, this means that the company does not pay salaries or travelling costs and only pays the freelance company for the sales it actually makes. This can be a really good solution for small publishers, but inevitably there are downsides.

The first is that a freelance company and its staff never quite have the same relationship with the publishing house, its staff, its authors and its books as an in-house sales team. The second is that these freelance companies are inevitably carrying the lists of other publishers. This raises issues about priorities, loyalties and commitment. A rep cannot give his or her best to every book when several lists are being carried. While this issue can just as well apply to in-house reps carrying many books for the company that employs them, there is a degree of supervision and control that sales managers can exercise over their own reps. You have to accept that you cannot control a freelance rep in the same way.

What a small publisher can rely on is that the freelancers must make sales to survive: this is payment-by-results after all. But there is another way forward for the small publisher – one pursued by a number of them – and that is to form a consortium, together employing and paying the overheads of their own combined sales force. The economies that come from this are available to the small publisher and so is the management and control of the reps. The more astute these consortia are, the more discriminating they are about the small publishers they are prepared to let join them. They have to ensure that everyone in the consortium is going to perform, by way of sales, as well as the others in the group. They will not be able to afford to carry passengers.

Both in-house and consortia sales teams will have a sales director, usually with sales managers reporting to him or her, depending on the size of the publishing house. It will be the sales director who will negotiate overall sales terms (discounts) with the main book retailers and the supermarkets. The key account managers referred to earlier, and who are geographically organized, will negotiate on sales of particular titles with their counterparts working in the shops of the bookselling chains. In practice, most chains allow their branches to make their own purchasing decisions even though it is head office that will do the purchasing.

With supermarkets, it is not uncommon for the sales director to do the negotiating, and similarly with Amazon. Inevitably, they want big discounts, requiring a decision at a high level. Some supermarkets are also known to demand their own jacket on a book to which they wish to make a big commitment. This is a tricky area. Who is really the publisher here? How will the author feel?

Selling internationally

For English-language publishers the world is its territory. As a result, most of them will have made arrangements for selling their English-language books in overseas markets. These arrangements are, of course, quite separate to the selling of translation rights. We must also distinguish between an international sales force that reports to the UK office, and the sales force that will work for an international distributor. We shall be looking at international distribution later.

For the export sales staff, there will be a requirement to spend time travelling in the territory they cover and most will cover several countries in a particular region. There are many similarities between selling in the domestic market and selling overseas. The export rep needs to be as thoroughly familiar with the books and the lists as the 'home' rep, and the necessary characteristics and challenges can be remarkably similar, but the need to be utterly realistic about a book's selling potential is probably more acute when selling to overseas markets. There are real differences between these countries and the domestic market, as follows.

Export reps really do have to be self-reliant as they are likely to have to spend a fair amount of time on their own, and in a culture that is different from their home culture. This is not at all like going to another country for a holiday.

These reps have to put in a great deal of hard work researching the bookshops that will be realistic sources of sales. Sometimes the sales are not made where you expect to find them. Of course, there are sales to be made in tourist areas, but specialist sales often flourish in quite small bookshops tucked away in towns and cities serving enthusiasts hungry to get their hands on books on the history of coins, or architecture, books by certain novelists, play scripts – the possibilities are endless but they need to be discovered and then worked on. An export rep can build longstanding and quite close relationships with bookshop owners. The same issues concerning discounting and returns will also feature.

Unlike in the domestic market, the export rep might encounter political or social issues that can influence what he or she might try to sell in an export market. There are some countries where certain topics are absolutely forbidden. The export rep needs to be sensitive to this, which means acquiring a proper knowledge about the territory.

For small companies that cannot afford to run an export sales department, the situation is comparable to how they deal with this issue in the domestic market: they can engage freelance export reps – usually called agents – to cover particular territories for them. There are the same strengths and weaknesses to consider. As in the domestic market, the agent will expect the publisher to mail catalogues and leaflets to the main retail customers, although in this case the mailings may go in a wider circulation. For UK publishers this will include the British Council's overseas offices, which work to support British publishers and authors. Just like the freelancing rep in the UK, the overseas agent will be paid by results, but often a small retainer will be paid to help with overheads. This is perfectly justifiable as an agent is likely to be covering a large territory, with all the travelling and accommodation costs associated with that.

Sales targets

Both home and international reps are likely to be set sales targets. These targets are arrived at quite simply through the accumulation of sales assumptions, which are set every year for both new books and backlist. Sales directors will break them down for particular territories, probably setting territory targets in line with sales achieved in previous years. They are very likely to set a target slightly above what has been achieved before, but with the prospect of a bonus for the rep if these figures are met.

What if the figures do not materialize? This could be an issue of performance: the rep is simply not making enough deals. However, if they do not materialize across the board, then it is not the rep who is at fault but the books. They have not met expectations. At this point, we have to go back to basics and question the quality of our book commissioning.

Having explored how books are sold into the retail sector both at home and abroad, we now turn to how those books get from the printer into the bookshops.

Distribution

Small independent publishers, usually at the start-up stage, often charge ahead trying to entice authors to join them, taking receipt of scripts, looking for printers, designers – you name it – but forget entirely about what they will do when the books have been printed. There was one small publisher who tried keeping the books in the basement of his house until he ran out of room. Then he went and knocked on the doors of the houses in his road begging his neighbours to store his books for a small fee. Surprisingly, he did find willing neighbours but they discovered that books are bulky when they arrive in their hundreds, and they also suddenly remembered that they are a fire risk. So eventually, this small publisher had to find a distributor to store his books.

Distributors always have warehouses. This is where the books are kept until they are moved out to the shops in response to demand. Sadly, some books never find their way out! Warehouses are very big places, storing millions of books. Most people, when they see the inside of a warehouse full of books for the first time, are truly astonished.

The job of a distributor is to:

- fulfil orders accurately;
- send out books to the customers quickly and reliably;
- ensure that books are kept safe – dry, free from dirt and fire hazards;
- ensure that books are transported and received in perfect condition;
- do all this as efficiently and cost-effectively as possible;
- take care of the customer, whether it is the publisher or the book buyer.

Distribution is a specialist activity. Amazon made no profit at all in the early years of its existence because it simply did not know how to run a distribution business. It learnt, slowly, and having developed expertise, its financial performance was transformed.

When a book has been printed, it is transported from the printer to the publisher's warehouse where it is stored until all its copies have been sold. For most of the time, books are stored in the warehouse in packaging, in the area known as 'bulk storage'. Computers essentially run warehouses, through complicated systems that show exactly where each title is stored. When titles are ordered, copies are retrieved from bulk storage and taken to what are called 'forward racks' where they will eventually be packed and sent out to whoever has ordered them, mostly to retailers or sometimes to individuals. This process is known as 'picking and packing'. In a modern warehouse, the operatives, sitting in small, computer-driven trucks, will be guided to the exact spot where a particular title can be found. The systems are extraordinarily efficient.

Further efficiencies are found in the flow of books out to the retailers, amalgamating orders wherever possible to get economies of scale. Publishing has steadily been improving its fulfilment times for orders. In the latter half of the 20th century is was not uncommon for bookshops to have to wait two weeks for books on order to be delivered; nowadays two days would be the norm, and at certain times of year where there is great pressure to get books through to the marketplace with all speed, such as Christmas, one would expect the turnaround of orders to be no more than a day. Books are transported to retailers by secure delivery systems (using vans and lorries) and not by conventional mail. Individual orders, made by a non-retailer, will be sent out through the mail and the purchaser charged for this. As well as fulfilling retail and individual orders, the distributor will also receive returns from the shops and place them back in storage and reimburse the retailers on behalf of the publishers.

A distributor will be prepared to do meet most reasonable requests from their publishers, including putting promotion leaflets within new books, or questionnaires to book buyers, or checking copies of books if anyone has reported a problem with, for example, the bindings. In this case, the publisher needs to know if a rogue copy has come to light or whether the binding problem is more widespread. For all these services, the distributor will charge a fee, which is always a percentage of the sales value of books moved out of the warehouse to the market.

The fees charged vary with the warehouse chosen. It is not always a good policy to go with what appears to be the cheapest: publishers need to choose their warehouses carefully. There might be a basic fee but then warehouses will vary in the extra charges they make, for example, for the kinds of jobs mentioned above. Also, when a publisher negotiates with a distributor, there will be assumptions made about the total quantity of books the distributor will have in storage, on average, in the warehouse. If the publisher's books do not sell as well as expected, the warehouse finds itself storing more books than expected, and for that extra storage, the distributor will make a higher charge to the publisher.

A distributor's geographical location is something the publisher needs to think about too, although there are many examples of good distributors who are *not* located right in the middle of the country. Neither is the biggest distributor necessarily the best. Certainly, a publisher that is essentially a specialist publisher should think long and hard about whether a distributor, the majority of whose clients are consumer publishers, is the right one for it.

No publisher should ever choose a distributor without getting an opinion from its customers on the quality of service offered. Publishers are happy to exchange experiences with other publishers because they know how important it is that their distribution is good, effective and efficient. The overall fee charged by a distributor ranges between 11 and 13 per cent. Eleven per cent sounds better but the publisher needs to question whether the figure is lower because the operation is very efficient, or because it is an enticement. The distributor must charge enough to keep the business in good financial shape. There are few things more disastrous than a distributor who goes bankrupt. In the process of bankruptcy, the stock of a bankrupt company can be sold at any price, and to anyone, to generate some income to pay the creditors. This means that a publisher would lose complete control of the stock:

the choice of where to sell the books and at what price is lost because the bankruptcy administrator has been given responsibility to sell the assets of the distributor to realize some income. You could suddenly come across your books at a car boot sale.

Wholesalers

Wholesalers add another level to the distribution structure. They only operate in consumer publishing, buying stock direct from the publishers at a high discount. They then distribute these books to anyone in the retail market who wants to do business with them. There appears at first glance to be no need for such an operation (are they not duplicating what the publisher's distributor does?) but what wholesalers do is to offer very fast distribution to the retail market. They are effectively pledging to go one better than the publisher's own distributor. To date the evidence is that there is a niche of sorts that the wholesaler is occupying successfully.

Overseas distribution

For the significantly large publishing groups, whose books have a genuine potential for sales in overseas territories, the solution is to find a distributor in that territory, or to set up one of their own. If you are looking for a distributor, you have a choice of going with a publishing house similar to yours and making their sales team, warehouse and distributor part of the package, or you can set up your own operation creating all the basic components from scratch. Clearly this is going to be very expensive indeed, not just in monetary terms but also in knowledge creation terms. For example, a UK publisher that decides to set up its own operation in the United States is going to have to recruit local professionals. Operating in another country and in another culture, the UK publisher is very likely to make some poor judgements about who it hires. Any mistakes will take some time to surface, but they will eventually become clear and it will prove to be very expensive. This is all part of the 'cost of entry' into something new. Going into business with another publisher is probably the safest way forward, provided you think you really do know that company and its management.

If you start your own distribution company overseas, you bear the full cost of setting up and running it, and it is not possible to put a figure on that. Only you know how much you can afford to spend on this – if you can afford it all. This really is the province of the big and financially successfully publishing groups. Where would they be most likely to establish overseas bases? The answer is, in large territories where English is the chosen language. For UK publishers, such overseas offices are frequently based in countries within the Commonwealth.

If you cannot afford this kind of expansion, and you enter into a distribution deal with another publisher, it will charge a percentage fee based on the amount of revenue your books make. Again, the same issues will come into play as those that feature when you are choosing a domestic distributor. Finally, you need to be aware that overseas distributors also expect to exercise returns policies!

The supply chain

By now we hope you have some sense of what the supply chain is. It starts with the publisher, although through the publisher, the chain actually starts with the publisher's printer. The printer makes the books, delivers them to the warehouse (or distributor), who then delivers them to the retail market. For fast-moving consumer books the wholesaler is another possible link.

As well as the physical activity that is going on, there is an accompanying plethora of paperwork, mirroring the movement of books, and a financial trail. The paper trail would typically involve:

- invoices (stating the payment required for goods supplied);
- delivery notes (providing evidence that the goods were delivered);
- credit notes (showing how much money a party is owed, perhaps for overpayment of an invoice or for the value of returns made);
- authorization of returns (where a sales rep signs to say that the publisher is prepared to accept the returns).

The returns process is often handled electronically these days and credit notes are issued immediately once stock has been returned. Of huge importance in the paper trail is the clear and accurate inclusion of the ultimate identifier of any publication, the International Standard Book Number (ISBN) and the International Standard Serial Number (ISSN) for journals. Without these numbers it is impossible ultimately to recognize a particular book. We can guess that there is probably not another novel in existence called *Portnoy's Complaint*, but we can imagine that there might be dozens of titles called *An Introduction of Psychology*. Which one do we mean? It is *essential* that the correct ISBN appears on *all* paperwork.

Recently the Association of American Publishers proposed a 'micro-level identifier'. This MLI would contain not just the ISBN but everything else of acute value such as the publisher's name, who owns the copyright, and the terms and conditions for buying the publication. Whether this is adopted or not, in a publishing world that seems continually to be expanding, absolutely accurate identification is necessary, otherwise the errors in the trading process will be endless. This is why, in the editorial chapter, we stressed the importance of the correct ISBN being put attached to a book project right at the beginning of the paper trail.

The financial disciplines of the supply chain

The word 'disciplines' has been used deliberately. A typical trade transaction in publishing is quite complex compared to other industries. As well as the expected issue of 'demand' and 'supply', we have another significant one, which is timing. We are not referring here to the timing for a product to be introduced to the market, but the timing of revenues (both receipts and payments), which is very much affected by returns.

As we mentioned earlier, if you are in a manufacturing industry, you need to make money as soon as possible after you have manufactured your goods and paid the bills. In publishing, the receipt of income is usually quite a prolonged process:

1 A publisher will pay the printer about 30 days after manufacture of a book.

2 A retailer will be invoiced for the books it orders from the publisher but will not be required to pay for them until 90 days later.

3 The retailer will pass payment to the distributor, who then pays you 30 days later.

This is the first significant gap. The publisher has to wait to be paid 90 days longer than the printer has to wait. This is an uncomfortably long time to be kept waiting, but what makes it worse is returns:

● a retailer can ask to return stock between three and six months after paying for it, and immediately be refunded for it;

- if a publisher accepts returns after three months, the retailer could be paying for stock (within 90 days) and then being refunded for returns a week later;
- if the publisher only accept returns after six months, it has about three months to enjoy the income taken from the retailer before possibly returning it back to them.

It is for this reason that a prominent publisher some years ago referred to the publishing industry as acting as bankers for the book retailing industry. We receive their money and take care of it, but then we give it back to them when they think they need it.

For publishers that rely on international sales the situation is even worse. First of all, high discounts are the norm (to give them even more encouragement!), so one is making less profit on every copy sold. Second, the lead-in times for payments are roughly double what they are in the home market. One can wait 180 days for overseas distributor to pay up. And as was mentioned earlier, the distributors fully expect to operate a returns policy.

How do we describe this or make sense of it? Money is shuttling to and fro. Publishers and retailers are acting within their rights of course, which are based on established custom. We could be kind and say it is odd or eccentric, but it makes controlling and managing income quite difficult. Imagine you are a managing director. The news from the distributor is that you have sold X thousand books this month and you know that within 30 days you will be paid for these sales. Where life becomes difficult is when returns intervene within this period, in which case you will get your expected payment for sales, but minus the value of returns. Your income, therefore, could be very different from what you expect or what you budgeted for.

It is wise, therefore, for you to assume that every month your income will be diminished by returns, and since you cannot guess what the level of returns is going to be, you need to work out what your average returns figure is. Within the publishing industry, returns tend to run at anything between 13 and 20 per cent of income, but this can fluctuate tremendously. Why is this? It could be a result of weak books being published, or a book shop chain deciding that it would shorten the amount of time that books are exposed on the shelves, or even shops finding themselves short of cash and looking to find it wherever they can, including through returns. If you are sensible, you will look to see what your average returns figure is and, when assessing your income for the next month, automatically deduct that figure so that you have a more accurate picture of how much cash you are likely to receive.

Publishing is a game only for those prepared to live with the long haul and who have strong nerve, because the management of cash flow is particularly difficult.

The supply chain as a food chain

At every point along the way, someone is deducting a percentage of your sales income for services rendered:

- The largest 'meal' will be given to the retailer, by way of discounts. Discounts can range from 20 per cent (rare and most likely for high specialized and highly priced books) to 70 per cent or more.
- Your distributor by comparison will seem less needy and you are likely to be providing fees of between 11 and 13 per cent of your sales income.
- Your overseas agents or distributors will be paid an amount similar to your UK distributor.
- Your UK reps will be included on the payroll if you have your own in-house team. If not, you will be paying your freelance team between 10 and 13 per cent of the sales income they make for you.
- Your in-house team will get bonuses in addition to their salaries if they meet or exceed the targets set for them. This, however, is not a problem. They will have earned that extra expenditure.

This picture represents a lot of people eating off the same plate – the book sales. One does not have to be a mathematician to work out that if you add up all those percentages, it does not leave very much from our book income to pay for all the publishing house's bills: salaries, the cost of making the books, running our offices and paying the authors their royalties.

Publishing, therefore, is endemically a low-profit industry involving many parties. However hard people work, it is difficult to drive up profit by increasing efficiencies. The supply chain includes the flair, hard work and drive of the book reps (helped, we hope, by marketing and editorial) and the agonizing uncertainties of payments and returns. It is a strange way to make money.

Digital distribution

Everything could change dramatically if and when e-publishing really takes off. Theoretically, it would be possible to eliminate large parts of the retail sector, and warehousing too. Digital distribution presents a real possibility of publishers having direct contact with their customers.

Already we have seen examples of bookshops printing copies of books to supply customers' needs. Customers go to the shop, say what they want, and if it is digitally available, the shop prints it off for them. There are several issues here that need acknowledging. First, retailers, including their demands for discounts, remain in the supply chain. Second, the quality of these printed books at the moment is variable, and can be of concern to a customer who likes production values to be high. Third, book production is not the core business of retailers. How will they organize their staff, because some of them will need to be on the shop floor, dealing with customer enquiries and sales of books in stock? How would they cope if hundreds of people came in every day wanting books that will be have to be printed by the retailer? Finally, their shops will have to be fundamentally reorganized to make space for this printing and binding activity.

Still, this model could be made to work if the technology is improved and some financial sense could be made of the relationship between the retailer and the publisher. Providing even higher discounts to the retailer would compensate the publisher for having to make the usual arrangements with book manufacturers, or paying for stock to be distributed to the shops. The publisher is still left, of course, with the job of pre-press work. One can envisage a situation where the publisher makes a charge to the bookshop for the use of the material, leaving the bookshop with decisions about what price to put on a book.

More attractive is probably the way most media futurologists conceive book publishing developing. We will have two ways of obtaining our content: we can either go onto the publisher's website and, for a price, download content we want, or we can buy handheld devices preloaded with content. Journal publishers have, of course, for years been selling content to their readers who read it online, with the option of buying hardcopy if this is material they think they will need to refer to often. The nature of journal publishing is that it is based on articles, not whole books. The relationship of the reader with the content is different than that of whole books. Some specialist publishers are already providing whole books online for no cost, with the option of ordering and paying for a print-on-demand copy subsequently. It will be interesting to see how that business model works out, but for the moment there are many questions in the air about how to make money out of it.

The real difference to sales and distribution will come if hand-held devices prove popular with the reading public. First, the cost of them has to come down if they are to be successful. Second, of course, readers must be happy to read their 'books' on them. If you have purchased your device, it will be perfectly possible to order and receive your chosen content. Will you be able to buy individual books or will you have to buy multiple titles, some of which you may not want? Exactly when will you be able to buy these titles? Will publishers stick to the old tradition of issuing a hardback book first, with the digital version coming later, as the paperback does now? What implications will this have for pricing? If you choose not to make hard copies of content, then your costs will come down. Will the prices? For the same reason (the driving down of manufacturing costs) will the authors expect to be paid higher royalties?

It is easy to provide digital versions of current books, but many books were not originally produced in digital format and the cost of scanning them for digital purchase is going to be very high. Will publishers be expected to provide 'extras' for the customers for digital versions – the ability to make notes on the device or even to change content, for example (which raises huge issues about copyright)?

Payment direct from customer to publisher for content will require vastly expanded customer service and payment departments. This may be worthwhile given all the other savings the publisher is making.

What role will bookshops (and Amazon) have? Strictly speaking, there could be no need for either. The main exception would be if publishers used the retailer as stockists of pre-loaded content, or if they used them for providing top-ups. You go to the retailer with a request for specific titles, which they supply, and you pay them – rather like going to a petrol station with your car. But then the question of discounts or fees appears again, both for pre-loaded titles and top-ups, and publishers could find themselves back in the eternal struggle of living with the retailers' drive for profit while trying to maximize profit themselves.

At the moment we do not know, yet it is clear that we are on the edge of something revolutionary, *if the book buying public wants it –* everything will eventually be determined by what the customer wants. While people still want traditional books, there is a place for retailers, and the supply chain will continue as ever with its discounts and its returns. But a future of hand-held devices eliminates the need to manufacture books, to store them in warehouses, to sell them into the shops, to provide discounts to retailers, to sell and distribute them all around the world. For many chief executives of large publishing houses, this is a very attractive future.

Conclusion

The special characteristics of the way publishers sell and distribute their books are currently not only a challenge to the industry but an object of some curiosity to those who work in other manufacturing industries. Many have made observations on the sanity of publishers who continue to sell their guaranteed best-sellers at high discounts instead of capitalizing on their profits. It seems that publishers have adopted the habits of supermarkets, but despite the discounting incentives, the market for books has not greatly expanded.

The returns policy in publishing astonishes many when they first encounter it. Publishers appear to be acting as private bankers to the retail industry, but unlike bankers they are not making themselves fabulously rich. Yet the returns process is so well established as part of the selling process that it appears to be indestructible, despite many efforts made to change it. We might make a guess that the onset of e-publishing could provide a catalyst for that change.

Further reading

Allan, B (2004) *Guide to Export for UK Publishers*, The Publishers Association, London
Anderson, C (2009) *The Longer Long Tail*, Random House, London
Book Marketing Ltd (2005) *Expanding the Book Market*, February, BML, London
Holman, T (2005) The returns journey, *The Bookseller*, February
Linacre, S (2007) Wholesale changes, *The Bookseller*, March

Publishing services and production

06

Introduction

A senior and respected figure from the world of publishing began his career as an editor. His four-year-old daughter was curious to know where her father went every day, and why he was normally only there to see her in the evenings and at weekends. She had just started to read, and loved having books read to her by her parents. 'What do you do all day, Daddy?' she asked. 'I go to work in an office, and I make books – a bit like the ones we read together,' he explained. One of the books they had just been reading was about a blind watchmaker. The little girl knew that a watchmaker made watches, so she told all her friends at her birthday party the following week that her father was a bookmaker. After that, one or two of the editor's and his wife's friends seemed a little cooler towards them than they had been previously. The irony of the bookmaker and the business of risk that seems so apt to the world of publishing does not do much to explain to the outside world what exactly it is that a publisher does to the book. If the author writes it, the printer prints it and the bookshop sells it, what is the publisher's role? Hasn't technology removed the necessity for a publisher anyway?

Some people will understand the idea of making judgements, investing in risk and adding value by improving quality. However, given that so many famous classics have apparently been turned down by publishers at the outset before finding a sponsor or a champion, it is not surprising that the time between an author finishing writing a book and its appearance on the shelves in the local branch of Waterstone's or W H Smith remains such a mystery. For some, the idea of becoming your own publisher seems much more attractive and feasible now that the technical business of 'making a book' has become so much easier.

Different kinds of editor

In Chapter 3 we explored the crucial process whereby the commissioning editor and the author together set in train the creative process that produces the typescript. We described the editor's role as one of gatekeeper, striking a balance between the aspirations of the author and the commercial goals of the company for which the editor works. The editor organizes the resources and draws together the commitment – financial, commercial and practical – that will be needed to bring the book or project to market. The editor is responsible for persuading colleagues that the book he or she is asking the company to invest in meets a market need, and will succeed. Such success, so long as it follows, will allow all to share credit – or, if not, the editor will suffer alone.

In this chapter we explore the way that a typescript, once delivered, is turned into a book or finished product. We look in detail at issues of quality: is the content good enough? Is it well written, and have all the errors of grammar and spelling been removed? If the work is non-fiction, are the facts accurate?

Design quality

What do we mean by design? For books, we need to ask, has the content or information been well laid out so that the arguments are clear, the headings logical and the route through the book – the navigation – simple and easy to follow? If the publication is a printed book, does the buyer or reader feel the physical product has been well made and is reasonable value for money? Are the production specifications acceptable? Is the paper opaque enough, and is the binding robust? In this chapter we try to explain what happens to a raw typescript before it can be brought to market in a way that satisfies the reader (and the author!), and makes an acceptable return for the publisher.

The process of making books was for many years entirely linear. It often started with an author submitting his or her idea (or typescript) to a publisher. Once the project had been accepted, the author set off on the solitary task that is writing – with, if he or she was lucky, occasional contacts and expressions of interest (or concern) from the editor. On completion, the typescript (disks or piles of paper) was submitted for acceptance. Changes were probably made once the work had been edited.

A designer put together grids for a layout and started work on a jacket or cover. Production provided estimates, costings were completed, the edited typescript was typeset, illustrations commissioned, photographs hunted down and permissions cleared. Once the art and text were brought together (sometimes in what was called a 'paste-up'), page proofs would be produced and checked, and the author (sometimes even the editor) restrained from making last-minute changes.

Early copies of the finished book would be sent out to sales reps and submitted for review. Bulk stock would be delivered to the warehouse, bookshops would subscribe to more copies of the book than they could sell, and the book would be published (on a Thursday). Invoices would be adjusted for returns, and a couple of months later the publisher would receive cash for a project that may have been set in train two, even three years earlier. Small wonder, then, that commercial book publishing has proved such a hard field in which to make serious money.

This only slightly exaggerated sketch of the old production process in publishing is drawn to make one or two important points (apart from the difficulties of cash flow in publishing). It is tempting to assume that technology has changed everything. Certainly, the mechanics have been simplified with what in most companies is now a digital workflow. The word processor has taken over from the typewriter; desk top design and illustration together with page make-up have replaced galleys, em-rules and cow gum; and digital files now take up so much less space than films and plates.

The speed and ease of communication via the internet have revolutionized and should have accelerated the production process. But the stages that an author's creation needs to go through before it can be turned into a saleable product remain essentially the same. The same kind of flawed thought process that predicts the end of the book now we have information and entertainment 'at the click of a button' tends to assume that producing a book must now somehow have become a simple, easy and quick process. This, as Barbara Horn has put it, 'is to mistake the tool for the skill'.

Another feature of the old linear approach to publishing was its departmentalized hierarchy. We implied in our opening chapter that publishing was once riddled with class prejudice and snobbery, making editors the ruling elite and other departments the lower orders of mere service and fulfilment. A result of this stereotype (not entirely eradicated from some publishing companies) was that people worked in independent and separate groups, isolated in 'silos'. It is significant that publishing services and production are still referred to by some senior managers as back office functions – the parallel with 'below stairs' is hard to resist.

It also meant that the stages of production were strung out in a long line, with projects at different stages of development or completion being handed over by one department to another. Indeed, some companies still have 'handover forms', which makes the process sound like a relay race, with runners literally handing on the baton to the next member of the team. It also led to a certain degree of rigid demarcation, with editors never being allowed to decide on design issues, and certainly forbidden from speaking directly to typesetters or printers – just as production staff could never be allowed to communicate directly with authors.

Once again, technology may have lowered if not removed some of the walls that separated departments, but it has not changed what are essentially three elements (not necessarily sequential) in the 'production process':

1 fixing the words in a publication – accuracy, style and complexity, grammar and spelling;

2 deciding on the appearance of the product – design, layout, illustrative content; and

3 turning the raw material into a finished product by manufacturing it – estimating costs, typesetting, printing and binding, and delivering the result to an agreed schedule.

So, yes – it may still be convenient to think of these three stages as editorial, design and production, but the metaphor works less well if the end product is not printed at all, but part of a new website or a digital database that can be accessed by customers. Yet the medium in which the finished material is produced is actually less important than the process by which it reaches that finished state. So, for the time being, we will stay with those three sections in this chapter.

Editorial

Introduction

In Nathan LeStrange's western, *Showdown at Gold Creek*, the author makes special use of the word 'edited' in that thrilling story. Don, one of a gang who betrays the others after a bank robbery goes wrong, is on the run. Jip, the self-elected gang leader, is determined to find and kill him. 'I don't mind how it's done, I just want him *edited*.'

For both publishers and those outside the industry, the word 'editor' and the process of editing remain confused, even if the activity is less bloodthirsty than in LeStrange's book. The public at large mainly think of 'editing' in the newspaper context: deciding what story to lead with, cutting pieces and making punchy headlines so that they fit the available space, perhaps even setting a tone or giving the paper a political or establishment leaning. In the 1930s, Geoffrey Dawson is said to have often written editorials for *The Times* from home, while contributing to the feeling that the paper was a mouthpiece of the establishment. The Canadian Lord Beaverbrook in *The Daily Express* was a loud voice for Empire up to and during World War II, and his membership of Churchill's War Cabinet was not seen as a conflict of interest.

Defining different editorial roles

In Chapter 3 we dealt with the editor as someone who commissions or acquires authors and projects for the company. This process cannot realistically be separated from the next stage in the editorial process – working on content submitted by authors so that it is factually accurate, readable and grammatically correct. Yet the sheer proliferation of job titles for this function makes its purpose unclear. Consider these; no doubt you can think of others:

Publisher	Senior editor	Managing editor
Junior editor	Copy-editor	Desk editor
Content editor	Picture editor	Project editor
Production editor	Assistant editor	Associate editor
Editorial assistant	Publishing services manager	Editorial services controller

Organizational issues

Two important points need to be made immediately. In some companies, each editorial team is led by a publisher (or editorial director) and may include one or more commissioning editors, as well as more junior people who work on the typescripts once they have been delivered by the author. These assistant or junior editors will be responsible for the content of new projects, and will be in regular contact with the author. In time, they may take on increasing levels of responsibility before themselves becoming commissioning editors. In the meantime they work closely with both the author and the commissioning editor, acting as a bridge between the two as the new book passes through production.

One of the reasons for this lies in the role of the commissioning editor being essentially a marketing one. It makes sense, then, for that person to spend a lot of time outside the office – in the marketplace, meeting new authors and planning new projects. Few good ideas can be generated by spending all day huddled over a screen, despite the strength of the web as a rich source of market information. In the commissioning editor's absence, then, the process of working on projects in development requires the editor to be present, working at a desk in an office (hence the job title 'desk editor' in some companies), and liaising with other colleagues in the production chain.

Some companies have gone further and created an editorial or publishing services department, detached from the commissioning role. New projects are handed over to services controllers once the commissioning editor is satisfied that what the author has delivered broadly corresponds to what was agreed in the contract.

The argument here is that working on a new project does not just involve editing it. What is often called 'pre-press' covers design and artwork, picture research, photo permissions, typesetting even – many of which functions can be freelanced out of house, or accommodated in a desktop publishing programme. Besides, in large companies there may be dozens, even hundreds of new books going through production each year, so it can make sense to have a pool of skilled controllers who can be deployed to handle a range of different projects according to demand.

Opinion remains divided on the effectiveness of these two structural choices – is it better to have editors working on a list in close contact with their commissioning colleagues, or a services department handling all aspects of pre-press so that commissioning editors can be literally freed from their desk to go out into the marketplace, where they belong?

Authors may feel a greater sense of belonging if the editor working on their project is part of the commissioning team. Publishers adopting the second method have been able to make efficiency savings and sometimes improve margins.

Content editing

Let us for the moment go back to the close relationship that can develop between authors and their editor when it comes to fashioning the typescript. There are perhaps two aspects to this personal and difficult task. Some authors need more than just friendly encouragement while they are writing. They may benefit from someone who has the courage to judge whether or not ideas are working, or if characters are believable, dialogue is realistic, or treatments of difficult scenes are effective. Someone like Max Perkins, the editor of Scott Fitzgerald, amongst others, had the unusual ability of helping an author by encouraging and criticizing, making judgements that the author accepted and trusted. It was a way of keeping the author company, so to speak, during the long (and often lonely) creative process.

The second (more obvious) stage is to criticize a completed typescript and suggest ways it could be improved. We take for granted that an editor, on behalf of the publisher, has a role (even a right) to make such suggestions. After all, it will be a condition of most contracts that the publisher will only publish the author's work if it is 'acceptable' (see Chapter 7 for a description of how such acceptability can be defined and achieved).

The extent to which the author fixes it him- or herself or the editor improves and corrects the original will be determined in part by the amount of work that is needed to make the typescript acceptable, or just more suited to the needs of the market. The editor's first task will be to identify what is missing, what has not been done well, and what is excessive – bearing in mind that the commonest problem faced by publishers is a typescript that is over length, sometimes by as much as 20 per cent, or a fifth.

In the past, when authors saw publishers as merely their agents in ensuring what they had written reached their readers, it was often unusual (even unthinkable) for an editor to reshape what an author had written, except perhaps tactfully to correct spelling and punctuation. When Harold Nicolson was writing *Some Lives* in the 1930s he made an entry in his diary that indicated his displeasure at having something he had written altered – he clearly did not expect an editor to tinker with his writing, and having been a journalist he was used to getting copy 'right'.

How much editing?

Nowadays, editors working on educational or academic books will often be dealing with novice authors, or with those who have no professional experience of writing a full-length work. Both author and editor will expect there to be substantial editing, perhaps even a major re-write or re-casting of chapters and sections. There may even be occasions when people in certain official roles need, for political reasons, to be shown as authors of a work but who have little time or no ability to finish the job. In these cases, editors may almost take on the role of ghost writer.

In many companies, this editing of the content or 'copy' is outsourced to freelancers, and is usually accompanied by instructions on the extent to which the work needs to be edited. A light edit would involve little more than checking facts and spellings, adjusting sentence or paragraph length, and possibly helping standardize the organization and headings within the work. Authors with a reputation for submitting well-prepared finished typescripts will often only need this light edit; or they may be hostile or sensitive to more major changes.

Medium or heavy editing is used if the editor who commissioned the work feels the typescript needs significant improvement. Such a judgement may have been made by an external adviser who has read the text. The changes may be essential to make the book acceptable to the market, and in some cases the typescript will be returned to the author for him or her to undertake this further work. Sometimes, however, a detached professional outsider – an editor, no less – will do a better job of undertaking these necessary improvements.

If the editor is up to the job (and the author accepts his or her intervention), this 'intrusive editing', as it is sometimes called, still needs to be done with great care and sensitivity, and the reasons for doing it explained carefully to the author. The work also needs to be done without losing the author's 'voice'. Most authors have a distinctive style, and even radical changes need to be made without this voice being lost. It has been said that the good copy-editor has been everywhere and is revealed nowhere.

Proofreading

People from outside of publishing sometimes confuse the role of the copy-editor with that of the proofreader, although the same person, whether employed in a company or working freelance, may do both tasks. It is true that the skill involved in both roles needs a meticulous eye for detail, but someone correcting proofs is making a strict comparison between an approved original and a typesetter's rendering of that original, while the copy-editor may be allowed more room for intervention and initiative. Besides, making editorial (or author) changes at proof stage (late in the production process) is generally regarded as a serious crime, as it will certainly add to cost and may delay the schedule.

Whoever does the job and however extensive the editorial work is, the common aim remains the same: making the author's work as good as possible so that it meets the needs of the reader and the market, and reflects well on the reputation of the author and the publisher, both of whose names will be on the cover. If you talk to authors about their experience of good copy-editors, they will always be grateful for the same thing – sensitive but firm intervention that reflects the editor's detailed knowledge of the book as well as sympathy with what it is trying to do, retains respect for the author's creativity, and unobtrusively and anonymously adds value to it.

A partner in this process of making something of quality even better were the printer's readers, a companion to the typesetter (or even the compositor) whose purpose in reading galley or page proofs was to minimize mistakes (and thus reduce the typesetter's costs). They also had a habit of sometimes spotting a mistake in the content. One printer's reader left a marginal note in pencil on page 433 of a set of page proofs which said, 'I think you will find the relationship of Philip to de Vere is *nephew,* not cousin. See page 109: "... having no father, Philip was inclined to think of de Vere as his favourite uncle ...".' Modern typesetters and printers are less likely to have the resources (or the time) to employ someone with that attention to detail.

Does accuracy matter?

Does editing to this level of detail really matter? Are the army of pedants who write to the newspapers about trivial mistakes of spelling or usage part of a dying breed whose concern is exaggerated? There can be no question that good editing of a book – or any publication – does add to its value, and to the reputation of its author and publisher. Conversely, a book with errors of fact and mistakes in spelling or punctuation will probably alienate its readers.

Consider this metaphor: imagine you are about to take off in a plane on a 12-hour flight. As the aircraft is taxiing down the runway, you turn on your reading light – only to find that it is not working. Never mind, you think – I'll watch the movie and go to sleep. But then you begin to wonder: if the reading light is not working, how can I be sure the engines have been properly serviced and maintained? Will the wings and tail survive mid-air turbulence? In other words, your confidence in the whole journey is undermined by what seemed like a trivial shortcoming – and most evidence suggests that a badly edited book is unlikely to secure the approval of critics or the confidence of its readers.

In the end, it may come down to cost. Perfect quality with no mistakes may be an unattainable (or even an undesirable) goal. We argue that an edited typescript should have the status of a first set of proofs – in other words, second thoughts by the author, changes for change's sake later on must be avoided, and this is part of the way editors and authors need to work together: authors respecting editors' needs and constraints as much as editors responding to author demands.

Managing or doing

What does a managing editor do? People who come to this role have sometimes previously worked as a 'desk' or 'content' editor. The danger for them is knowing when to stop doing and when to stick to managing. The temptation to re-check a freelance copy-editor's work can be strong, but must be resisted. We have only to think of the frustration we can feel when seeing someone else failing to do a job well or on time that we know we can do with our eyes shut – we have an overwhelming urge to take over the task ourselves.

An important thing we need to consider is the way typescripts are edited – who manages the process, and who does the work. These will normally be two (or more) different people. In big companies the process of editing, designing and producing their publications is often referred to as 'publishing services'. Here the controllers and managers may be more traffic controllers than editors or designers, farming out the work to freelances and focusing their attention on schedules and budgets. Yet this whole publishing process cannot really be managed by someone who does not know how all the stages work, and how a change in one area may impact on another.

An editor who is managing the production process or overseeing the pre-press stage of a new project finds themself in the middle or at the hub of the process. This editorial hub is at the centre of a whole range of interrelated activities – parts of the publisher with whom the editor needs to be in constant communication. We have already seen how someone in this position can be the bridge between the author and the commissioning editor. Also essential to the process will be links to the design team for layouts and covers, and for artwork and photos if the book has illustrations, and most critically to the production department. Other 'spokes' from this hub may also connect to sales and marketing colleagues who need Advance Information sheets (see Chapter 4, page 99), completed author questionnaires, and copy for the jacket or cover that may form the first part of the publicity.

It may help if a managing editor knows or understands how the various processes work, but it is important too that he or she can remain detached from the actual process of copy-editing or deciding on layouts and typefaces. It is only too easy for managers, having delegated or outsourced a piece of work, to feel they should check it, and even go over it again. Their real value, however, lies in the overview they can have of the whole process. This is sometimes referred to as 'taking the helicopter ride' – travelling over an area of land, in this case the whole publishing programme of a division or even a company, and being able to spot where problems or hold-ups could develop or have already occurred. This in turn allows an objective assessment and a measured decision on what should be done to deal with the problem.

Design

If the editorial process is concerned with making the best of the textual content of a book or any publication, then design focuses on the visual effect and impact of it. Like good editing, good design is an understated, even silent element of the finished product – and, similarly, you can always tell when its beneficial effect is absent. Design is never a dominant or strident ingredient, and must always complement the finished book's impression, not make an impact in its own right.

Layouts and covers

The role of the designer, whether a member of the in-house pre-press or publishing services team, or an independent freelance working to a company brief, is concerned primarily with the layout of the content and the cover (or jacket) of the publication. Even a 384-page paperback thriller will need decisions taken about the choice and size of typeface, and how headings like parts in the book, or chapters, are going to be set, where page numbers are going to be placed and so on. Other books without illustrations may have a range of sections and subsections with tables, all of which will need different types of heading. These need to be standardized and placed in order (the 'hierarchy' of headings, as it is known). All these layout decisions are part of the navigational tools the reader will need to make his or her way through the book. If they are done badly or missed out, it will be like walking in a strange city without signposts or street names.

The cover is one of the key marketing components of a book. First impressions do count, and market research will confirm how swayed we are by the cover of a book as we pick it up. What do we do? We look at the title, and the author (rarely the publisher!) We turn to the back cover and read the blurb. What's the book about? Who is it intended for? What do the reviews say? We may flick through it, even (if we are of a certain generation) raise it to our face and sniff the smell of paper and fresh ink.

There are three vested interests that must be satisfied when finalizing a cover or jacket: the author, the sales and marketing department, and the designer. Authors have been known to insist that an unsuitable photograph they took should be used, designers sometimes hold out for the aesthetic over the functional, and we have heard marketing directors make generalizations such as 'green doesn't sell'. If the cover *is* that key selling tool, the sales and marketing director should probably have the last word, but be prepared to negotiate.

Illustrations and photographs

For books with illustrations, the designer's role is to commission the illustrator to create drawings or artwork, and to choose or oversee the choice of photographs, either from an in-house bank with minimal or no copyright restrictions or selected by means of a non-exclusive licence (and a fee) from a picture library. Illustrations need to be sized and scaled to fit the layout of the book. This was sometimes done by means of a paste-up where text proofs were literally stuck down on double-page sheets to show the exact space left for the pictures.

Most book illustrators are freelances who used to submit flat artwork on boards, sometimes with overlays to separate second colours, but the whole process has now been largely digitized using onscreen desktop systems and proprietary software programs such as QuarkXPress, PhotoShop and InDesign. The same is true for photographs from picture libraries or photo agencies. Black and white photos were 'halftones', while full colour slides were known as 'trannies' (short for 'transparencies'). Both would be similarly sized or scaled for colour separation (known as 'repro') before being returned to the agency.

Now 'low res' (low resolution) images are sent through for picture editors or researchers to choose from. Only once terms and a fee have been agreed will the 'high res' version be supplied to the publisher, a version sharp enough to reproduce from. The process of screening, scanning or colour separating, and separate four-colour film-making has been exchanged for sizing and positioning electronic images and creating digital files that can be uploaded directly on to the printer's server for printing and manufacture.

The drawing together of these components – text, artwork and photos – into what was known as 'page make-up' is still principally in the hands of the designer, but his or her work will be part of a digital workflow; see Figures 6.2a and 6.2b on pages 184–85. The input may start with the edited typescript from the editor in a program like Word and the output for printing and binding or uploading onto an aggregator's server, or on to the company website, may be a PDF or XML file. The procedure is broadly the same, but there are important differences at the production stage that make the process more circular than linear.

Production

This department's descriptive label, though still widely used in publishing companies, is probably the least accurate of the three (editorial, design and production) as the 'production' department's role has broadened. It has taken on some of the distribution functions of a warehouse, especially when the finished product is a file that must be compatible with an e-book outlet, an aggregator's server, a print-on-demand station – or a manufactured book destined for the warehouse, a wholesaler or a bookshop.

The head of production may now be called a Business Operations Director because a lot of the functions that were separated into 'pre-press' and 'manufacturing' have merged. Just as the typesetter needs to work from files that the editor has specified to the author, the art and photos will be in compatible formats for reproduction and printing, and the end result will be a store of digital assets that need identifying and defining. The digital asset management system must meet the twin demands of in-house availability for re-use and outhouse acquisition for licensing or other authorized consumer use.

Essential roles of the production staff

Production controllers do still work to these main three skills:

1 Commercial (providing initial and final estimates, controlling manufacturing budgets and end quality).
2 Technical (knowing which supplier will best meet the specification requirements of different projects).
3 Scheduling (establishing 'by when' or milestone schedules, then critical paths).

In many companies, estimates will be done at two separate stages. The first conceptual stage will provide some benchmark costs in enough detail for the editor to make a proposal to the editorial board which, if approved, allows an author to be commissioned and a contract issued. Once the typescript is received and accepted a comparative and more detailed estimate will be created. This will in turn be checked before 'press' – ie before the books are manufactured or the XML file uploaded.

Some companies use these three stages – conceptual, pre-press and manufacturing – not only as points to review costs, but also as stages in development where a project that should be abandoned can be cancelled, with minimum loss. Such a system, known as RF1, RF2 and RF3 (where 'RF' stands for 'revised forecast') is a simple way of literally cutting your losses. These reviews can also be a judgement on the effectiveness of an editor or member of the publishing services team controlling a budget, as the differences between the various stages are a comment on the extent to which minds have been changed, or costs omitted or underestimated.

Plant and manufacturing costs

A typical costing for a print product will normally comprise two sections – pre-press and manufacturing, sometimes known as PPB (standing for paper, print and bind). The main reason for this distinction is to highlight two kinds of cost: those that are generally incurred only once when a new book is produced, and those that recur every time the book is printed. For many kinds of publishing, the best profits are still derived from backlist reprints. These can often show a better margin once the initial or 'start-up' costs have been covered.

First costs, non-recurring costs, plant costs – different names for essentially the same thing – include the cost of copy-editing and design, basic typesetting, layouts, cover images, and the fees paid to illustrators for providing artwork. Permissions for third-party text extracts, or picture permission fees for photographs from libraries or agencies will also be part of these first costs, but they are often not 'one-off' fees. Re-use of these images may well incur further charges. Plant costs may also include one-off author fees where the copyright is assigned to the publisher – sometimes known as 'work-for-hire'. However, royalties paid on sales of the book (including advances) form part of the recurring costs.

The manufacturing costs or PPB cover the printing and binding of the book and the materials used to create it – paper, board for the cover, ink, thread, glue, or wire for binding, and usually shipping costs from the printer's factory to the publisher's warehouse. For many books, especially those printed in full colour (that is, usually, four colours), there are big savings to be made on the cost per copy simply by printing more copies, as the expensive element (known as 'make-ready') is spread over a longer print run and the unit cost will fall.

This economy of scale – the more you print, the lower the unit cost – has caused problems for publishers over the years. They have sometimes been reluctant to reprint a book until there was sufficient demand to produce a reasonable unit cost. Some author contracts even included what was known as the 'small reprint clause' – a provision to pay a lower royalty when and if the publisher is forced to reprint an uneconomical number of copies. The technology behind 'print-on-demand' has now largely removed this problem, at least on books without colour illustrations. Now very low quantities – even as few as half a dozen – can be printed at a unit cost only 10–15 per cent more than if a longer, more 'economical' print run had been approved.

Calculating gross margin

The ratio used by most publishers to judge if a project can be approved is the gross margin calculation. A gross margin (sometimes, inaccurately, referred to as 'gross profit') is the sum left after direct costs are deducted from net sales revenue after discount. Those costs include expenditure on plant and PPB as well as royalties. If sales are 100, direct costs are 35 and royalties 10, then a margin of 55 (55 per cent of 100) is left. If company overheads are running at 40 per cent of sales, then – theoretically – there is a 15 per cent net profit left. Table 6.1 on page 179 and Tables 6.2 and 6.3 at the end of this chapter show how these figures work.

To the unwary editor, the economies of scale derived from increasing print runs present a temptation that can be hard to resist: let's print more copies to make the margin look better. If we had only one commercial message in this book to give to those involved in fixing print runs, it is not to increase the print run simply to lower the unit cost and make the margin apparently better. Print runs must be set to meet market needs, and for stocks of books to be cleared in a reasonable time.

Many publishers print stocks of books for a year, or at least aim to. More often than not, those stocks last for 18 months or longer. If too many are printed, the notional saving in a lower unit cost is dissipated by the expense of storing unsold books, and eventually by having to write off their stock value, as this simple example shows.

Our sales and marketing colleagues give an initial forecast on a new book of 1,250 copies in the first year with further sales over the next two years of 750. The logical number to print is thus 2,000 copies. However, the unit cost for printing 2,000 copies (including plant costs and author's fee) is £1.50, while if the print run were extended to 3,000, the unit cost drops to £1. (Sharp eyes will have noticed that the cash outlay – £3,000 – is the same in both examples.) The selling price is fixed at £5.95, and the average discount known to be a modest 30 per cent.

The decision is taken to print 3,000 copies. When the book is published, it sells 1,500 copies in the first year, but sales then fall sharply. Year 2 sees sales of only 350, and this drops even more to 100 in Year 3. With luck, we may sell another 50 copies. We have managed to sell 2,000 copies over four years, and still have 1,000 copies in the warehouse. Compare the different gross margin calculations in Table 6.1.

TABLE 6.1

Example 1 (theory)	
Print 3,000 copies @ £1	(3,000)
Sell 3,000 copies @ 70% of £5.95	12,495
Gross margin	*9,495 (76%)*
Example 2 (theory and reality)	
Print 2,000 copies @ £1.50	(3,000)
Sell 2,000 copies @ 70% of £5.95	8,330
Gross margin	*5,330 (64%)*
Example 1 (reality)	
Print 3,000 copies @ £1	
Sell 2,000 copies @ 70% of £5.95	
Write down 1,000 copies @ original cost of £1 Incur warehouse costs of 15% of £4.17 *(unit sales value)* on 1,500 copies *(quantity left after first year's sales)* 8,330 – 3,000 [2,000 cost of sale, 1,000 write down] – 938 = 4,392	*(Gross margin: 53%)*

We need to add to this the fact that the cash represented by the stock of bound copies has been tied up in unsold stock sitting in the warehouse for four years. It is rather as if we had locked up 50 £20 notes in a box and hidden the key. At the end of the four years, we find the key, unlock the box, take out the £20 notes and burn them – not a sensible use of cash; and it is cash and cash flow that are many publishers' main priority.

Finding suppliers

Production managers and controllers used to have the role of placing work with the most suitable (or sometimes the cheapest) supplier, whether a typesetter, a printer or a binder. In past times, this is why in the run-up to Christmas, a production department was the place to go for a drink, as past, present or aspiring suppliers would leave lavish gifts of champagne and spirits in the hope that they would get more work next year. Now companies tend to work not only to standard formats (page size, paper quality) but also with a select group of known and trusted suppliers who will be sent the bulk of a company's work, depending on the type of project (continuous black and white text, or integrated four-colour) and continuing evidence of performance to time and budget.

The hunt for low-cost quality production supply never ceases. In the 1960s Paul Hamlyn discovered good colour printers in Eastern Europe. In the 1980s, almost all colour printing was done in the Far East. Now the spread is broader, and Europe and the Middle East play their part, as there is no longer the time available for shipping huge quantities of books halfway round the world – nor from an ethical point of view is it wise to create such a large carbon footprint.

Production staff are responsible for balancing three things – quality, cost and speed. Pressures on costs can force companies to make savings in the short term that can harm longer-term reputations, or even brand image. A poetry publisher with high-price but high-quality books alienated its market by moving to a cheaper paper that yellowed after only a few years. Low-cost binding may cause your books to fall apart in use, and give you a reputation for poor quality. Printing colour books in China in the 1980s saved 30 per cent on printing costs, but by the time freight costs and the six-week shipping delay had been factored in, the savings were sometimes not so impressive.

Scheduling

A few years ago, in a publisher's production department in Harare, Zimbabwe, a sign greeted visitors to the manager's office. It read: 'Your lack of planning does not automatically translate into my sense of panic.' This was a blunt message to editors in the company not to expect production departments to recover time lost by an author's late delivery or an editor's underestimation of the time taken on the pre-press stages of a project. Nowadays, it is usual for a consensus on timing and schedules to be reached, and for editors to sign up to the culture of punctuality by assuming as keen a sense of keeping to timetable as anyone else in the company.

At the conceptual stage, production controllers will often create a milestone schedule. This outlines the main stages of a project, and is created backwards. That is to say, if it has been agreed to publish a book in March 2013, by when do we need to pass the proofs for press? By when must the page make-up be completed? By when does the author need to submit his or her typescript? – and so on. These 'by when' dates will be the basis of a more detailed schedule created once the typescript is received, and its acceptability for processing established and agreed. Detailed schedules form a set of critical paths: a linear depiction of the various stages of projects to show if there is overlap either with key dates (annual holidays or Christmas closure), or clashes because the same group of people could be working on different stages of different projects at the same time. Figure 6.1 shows a critical path schedule for producing a book.

The art of scheduling has been studied for many years. Planning, preparation, communication and team work – the standard stuff of project management – have proved to be the most effective way of inculcating a general attitude that expects things to keep to time. This approach is rather like the familiar road journey that takes half an hour if you allow three-quarters, but can last for 45 minutes if you allow only 30. And editors may need to consider whether they should lie to their authors. Do you let an author notorious for late delivery know that you *must* have his typescript by 31 July when you know, in your heart, that if you got it on 30 September you could still meet your production deadlines?

Our experience is that contingencies, whether for extra time or extra expense, are best avoided. Adding in a bit of leeway in the schedule or the budget leads to a false sense of confidence (even complacency) that in turn can create a lackadaisical approach to controlling. While accepting that delays can occur and costs do sometimes go over budget, a culture and attitude that these things are in normal circumstances unacceptable has proved the better way of maximizing profitability in a publishing business.

Ordering faulty widgets

On budget contingencies, the following story illustrates two approaches to the business of allowing error, or expecting to avoid it. The stereotypes involve, on the one hand, an indulgent, contingency-based approach, and on the other, a strict expectation that things will be done precisely according to the budget, schedule and terms of the contract.

A manufacturing company needed to order some components ('widgets') from a supplier in a foreign country. After the terms and costs had been settled, the buying manufacturer sent the foreign supplier

FIGURE 6.1 A critical path schedule for producing a book

Title and spec	January				February					March				April				May					June				July
	3	10	17	24	31	7	14	21	28	6	13	20	27	3	10	17	24	1	8	15	22	29	5	12	19	26	3

Here's to Your Health!
256 x 170 mm
304 pp
125,000 words
75 colour a/w
300 colour half-tones

text — assess — edit

proof 1; collate — correct — proof 2

check set — in & passed

permissions — list — clear

index — create — edit set — proof

a/w — prepare briefs & check with author — prepare visuals — check visuals — prepare final a/w — check

photography — prepare briefs — shoot — check

picture research — prepare briefs — research — 1st selection — fill gaps — final selection

sales conference

London Book Fair

Bologna Book Fair

public holiday

public holiday

BookExpo America

public holiday

project manager

an agreement in which it stated that it would accept a margin of tolerance on the quality of the finished components of 5 per cent – in other words, it was prepared for only 95 per cent of the widgets to be supplied in perfect condition, as ordered.

The order was duly signed, and three months later the foreign supplier delivered the components. In the packing case were two boxes, one big, the other very small. In the big box the complete order had been supplied in full and all the components were exactly as specified. In the small box were a quantity of faulty additional widgets equating to 5 per cent of the order. Attached to the small box was a note which read: 'Here are the faulty components you ordered. We are not sure why you want them, but are pleased to supply them as requested. Assuring you of our best attention at all times …'.

Circular not linear

At the beginning of this chapter, we likened the publishing and production process to a long, linear activity, with people standing in a line, handing each other bits of the project as it evolved. Publishers are having to change the way they supply their products to their market. Originally, they just produced books that arrived in the warehouse from the printers, and were then supplied to wholesalers, bookshops and customers as and when the items were ordered. Until recently, additional material – audio tapes to go with language textbooks, follow-up exercises on a CD-ROM – were dealt with separately, but in the same way: as items produced in quantity and supplied when ordered.

A whole different approach is now needed because the end product is no longer necessarily the printed book (or other artefact). It is a digital file expressed in a standard format that will be put to a wide range of uses, both internal (that is, used by the company itself) and external – for all kinds of 'customers'. The digital workflow that allows this process is much more circular than linear, as the end point (the digital file) may prove to be the starting point for the next iteration of the project; see Figures 6.2a and 6.2b.

The key to this process is standards. What this means is that each stage of the development of a project has to be produced in a way that is usable by or compatible with the next stage, and that the end result is in a common (standard) format that allows maximum connection to people or systems that want to make use of that finished product. This involves a fundamental change to the way publishers think about finished products.

FIGURE 6.2a Editorial workflow

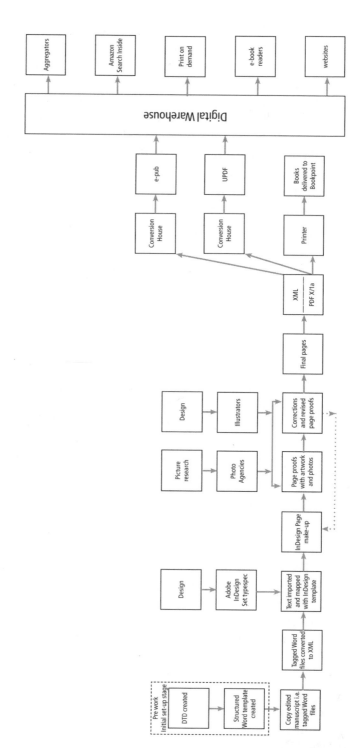

FIGURE 6.2b Editorial workflow

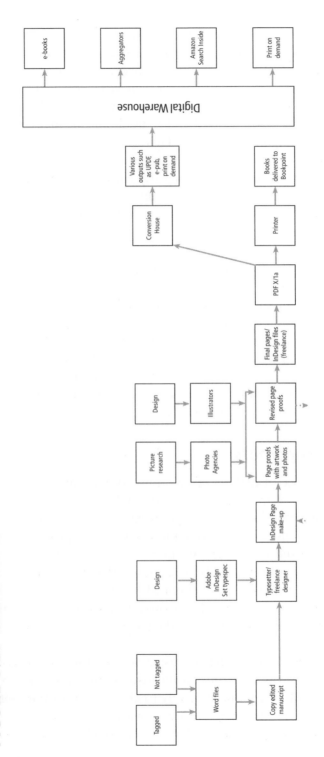

If the starting point was the book, any exploitation of the rights acquired from the author (either by licence or acquisition) would mean starting again: 'We've done the hardback, now we're going to do the paperback.' It is possible that in recent years, vertical grouping (with hardback and paperback imprints in the same group) allowed the film of the typesetting to be re-sized and re-used, but for many years separate paperback companies would need to re-set the text. A different approach was needed for serialization or translation, but then these new formats and new versions were generally produced by someone else. Dramatization and film rights presupposed that the cost of reworking the original would be undertaken elsewhere, and again at somebody else's expense.

Nowadays, the starting and finishing point has to be the digital file. To create this file, all the stages of pre-press and manufacture have to be linked compatibly. The Word file created by the author has to be tagged and marked in such a way that the desktop editor can work on the typescript and the typesetter can then use that file at the next stage with minimum change and re-working. The designer's layouts produced on Quark or the cover designs laid down using PhotoShop must similarly be captured, as will the artwork from an illustrator or the photographs from a picture library. Both need to be incorporated into the finished page as it will appear in the book.

The end of proofs

A consequence of making up the finished page on screen had been the almost total disappearance of proofs, what are sometimes nowadays called 'wet proofs' – text or images printed on paper. There were several stages of proofs. The first were known as 'galley proofs' (long strips of paper from the typesetter, whether working in hot metal, photo- or litho-setting) or 'page proofs'. Page proofs that included integrated four-colour images were usually supplied 'unimposed' – that is, not in the position on the sheet that they would need to be for final printing (so that when folded and trimmed, the pages of the signature ended up in the right order).

A final check was often made using ozalids, also known as 'blues' (the ink for these was sometimes a blue-ish colour), and more recently as 'plotter proofs' – produced merely to check the position that had been 'plotted' for the final pages. Occasionally proofs or running sheets of colour books are provided so that they can be checked for 'register' – the way in which each of the four colours is laid exactly over the others, without the slightest misalignment. Even a tiny slip could lead to a blurred or fuzzy finish. Register marks for each colour can easily be seen at the edge of running sheets. They are similar to the coloured bullets – black, blue, magenta and cyan (blue) – to be found at the edge of newspapers or magazines.

The finished file may be a PDF (portable document file), but this will not be as useful or as compatible as an XML file. XML is a file 'language' that can be uploaded and used by a wide variety of external users. Those customers may need the whole thing (the complete 'book') or only parts of it; they may want to create an e-book, or upload sections on to a website; the publisher may want to offer digital bits of the product, equivalent to chapters from the book. And publishers will need to agree a scale of charges and prices so that these customers can be invoiced and money collected from them.

To achieve this, a file management system needs to be created. It is not as simple as a digital rights management system (or DRM), which over the years has become a way of restricting rather than enabling use by such customers. More valuable is a system of digital asset management that allows external users to access (and if necessary pay for) the material, and means that the assets can be stored and re-used by the publisher in other formats and at a later date.

All this change means publishers have to embrace a strange and unappealing world – the world of standards, metadata, taxonomies and classifications: in short, the defining and tagging of 'bits' of their 'stuff' that allows access, recall and transmission. These identifiers may take the form of existing definitions: international standard book or serial numbers. Alternatively, the products may need digital object identifiers (DOIs) to break down further the granularity of their products.

This is more than just a technical convenience. It denotes a fundamental shift in approach to what the publisher actually has to do nowadays. For years the publisher set all the rules: to supply the whole work, on its terms. In other words, it was the publisher that decided the final content of the book and insisted that – even if the buyer only wanted Chapter 8 – he or she had to buy the whole book (or go to the library). Nowadays readers used to finding information on the internet want three things above all: the bit they want, immediately, and at very low or (ideally) no cost.

Managing digital files of publications means at least five issues have to be addressed and resolved:

1 The format and scope of the material, and details of which parts of the whole are available, and how users (customers) can access them.

2 The right and licence of the publisher to offer this material, and confirmation that it is legally allowed to offer all the components in the desired format.

3 The identity of the user or customer and evidence that he, she or it has authority to gain access to the material and make use of it in specified ways (personal download, electronic distribution).

4 The use to which the customer wants to put the material (private study or non-commercial research, or incorporation into an online learning program).

5 Mechanisms for buying and selling the material in whole or in part, and collecting payment (credit or debit card, online account).

CASE STUDY: Worked examples of gross margins

Comparative gross margins: Example 1

Publishing proposal

A new title is proposed, *A Guide to World Art*

Original specification

256 pages, royal octavo, section-sewn, cased plus four-colour jacket, including a 16-page four-colour section tipped in as two 8pp half sections.

Publishing details

First printing, 3,500 copies @ £14.99 (100 gratis), average discount 40 per cent. One reprint, 1,500 copies @ £14.99 (no gratis), average discount 40 per cent.

TABLE 6.2

	First printing	**Reprint**
COSTS		
Royalties	£3,000	£1,300
Plant cost (exc. plates)	£1,250	£125
16pp plate section	£1,500	£150
PPB 3500 @ £2.43	£8,505	£3,915 (PPB 1,500 @ £2.61)
Total	*£14,255*	*£5,490*
REVENUE	60% of £14.99 x 3,400 = £30,580	60% of £14.99 x 1,500 = £13,491
MARGIN SUMMARY		
Revenue	£30,580	£13,491
Costs	£14,255	£5,490
Write offs (5%)	£1,529	£675
Gross margin	*£14796 (48.4%)*	*£7326 (54.3%)*
Gross margin over two printings	£22,122 from sales of £44,071 *(50.2%)*	

Comparative gross margins: Example 2

Revised specification

224 pages, royal octavo, burst-bound, 215gsm card four-colour cover, UV varnished, including one 32-page four-colour plate section, tipped in as two 16pp half sections.

Publishing details

One printing of 4,000 copies @ £18.99 (250 gratis) at average discount of 45 per cent.

TABLE 6.3

COSTS

Single printing		
Royalties	£3500	
Plant cost (exc. plates)	£1250	
32pp plate section	£3000	
PPB 4000 @ £1.98	£7920	
	Total	*£15670*

REVENUE

Single printing	55% of £18.99 x 3750	£39167
Gross margin		*£23497 (60%)*

Variable factors to consider are: reduce plant cost (cheaper elements); reduce print costs (reduce estimate, lower spec., cheaper binding); trim royalty or author cost; trim discount; increase price. But never increase the print run to make the gross margin look better!

Conclusion

One thing that you should draw from this chapter is the way that 'production' has moved from being a back office service department to a front office partner in product development, along with the commissioning editor and the design team. The end product may be in print form, or even still a book, but this is just one of several choices that the publisher has in offering works to the public. It is significant that when the 2003 Copyright and Related Rights Regulations were enacted in October that year, the definition of 'publishing' included for the first time the phrases 'making available' and 'communicating to the public'.

In earlier days, the following example was sometimes given to emphasize the importance of all stages in book production – editorial, design and production – working closely together. The designer could not produce a cover or jacket design until the width of the spine had been decided. The width of the spine could only be fixed when the number of pages and the weight and gauge of paper had been decided. This, in turn, depended on the editor giving a correct estimate of the number of pages that the typescript would make, by doing an accurate cast-off for a project that might have been contracted but not yet written.

Nowadays such a simple task could be done in seconds on screen, whatever the final length of the typescript. The shift in thinking is of a far more fundamental kind. What is required of course includes the normal ingredients of good project management – planning, clear briefing of participants, and good continuing communication. What is additionally needed is a much broader understanding of the process of developing publications, as well as complete competence and confidence in the technology of digital production workflow and management. Skilled practitioners in their own narrow field or people who were happier working in their independent silos are no longer required.

Further reading

Horn, B (1997) *The Effective Editor's Handbook,* PIRA, Leatherhead
Horn, B (2006) *Editorial Project Management,* Horn Editorial Books, London
Peacock, J (1992) *Book Production*, Blueprint, London

Acknowledgement

Figure 6.1 on page 182 is reproduced from *Editorial Project Management* with kind permission of the author and publisher, Barbara Horn (Horn Editorial Books). The editorial workflow examples in Figures 6.2a and 6.2b on pages 184–85 were developed by Hodder Education.

Why publishers need to know about the law

07

Introduction

Publishers have never had an easy relationship with the law. Perhaps the outdated stereotype lingers on: publishing is a gentleman's profession in which your word is your bond; no need then for complex legal documents. The keystone of most publishers' businesses – the professional agreement between author and publisher – was often based on acquaintance or friendship. The relationship between Frederick Macmillan and Thomas Hardy, for example, was a personal one. Cynics, however, would often describe the publisher as a parasite, feeding on the creativity of authors, liable to take advantage of the innocent writer struggling to make a living, and prone to meanness or deception.

It is as if a faint mist lies over the whole process of publishing: because it is a creative process, it attracts people who may have decided not to work in hardcore industry or commerce, and for whom the rigours of finance and the law are unattractive. Yet scarcely can there have been a time when it was more important for publishers as intermediary between creator (writer) and reader (user) to be crystal clear about the rights they own or acquire, the licences they negotiate, and the sound legal foundations they make for their business.

So what are the key aspects of the law that publishers need to be familiar with? Copyright is the bedrock of the publishing business, and an awareness of its central principle – the creator as first owner of copyright – is essential at all levels. Libel and defamation are well-known topics that many presume are the only things publishers really need concern themselves with, while obscenity and blasphemy have become rarer problems today, at least in some parts of the world. For educational and academic publishers, these prominent issues do not arise very often. For them, liability for what they publish is much more important – mistakes in medical or engineering publications are obvious examples of possible negligent mis-statements.

In the last few years, issues to do with the protection of personal data and cases dealing with human rights such as privacy and access to information have grown in prominence. The internet has made us much more sensitive about who is using our personal and private information, either in their publications or to reach us and persuade us to buy them. Publishers also need to take into account laws governing trade and commerce, competition law, consumer protection, and trade descriptions. It is illegal, for example, for publishers to band together and agree on prices for a group or type of publications.

The internet is a tremendous source of information. There is really nothing you can't find if you're prepared to look, and the temptation to cut and paste other people's stuff, adjust it slightly, and claim it as your own can be overwhelming. But technology has made discovering such plagiarism – simple breaches of copyright – much easier. The hope that you can do something quickly and on the cheap, and get away with it, is becoming more forlorn.

Copyright has been called a 'trading system for works of the mind', and certainly in the UK and most of the northern hemisphere the law focuses on copyright as a method of protecting intellectual property and expecting it to have an economic value, expressed in terms of cost and price. However, in many parts of the world the emphasis is on the creator as a person with a reputation, whose standing in the community may be at stake if his or her copyright is infringed. These moral (as opposed to economic) rights are just as important, and much legislation, including that in the UK, encompasses both in copyright law. We talk about rights *owners* in whom copyright is vested, and for whom breaking the law will be an *infringement* of their copyright. What constitutes copyright infringement (and remedies) is something all publishers need to be alert to.

There is a widespread belief that the entire landscape has been altered by digital technology and the web, and that as a result the ground rules have all been changed. In fact, the principal tenet of the Berne Convention, which is one of two attempts to provide copyright equivalence across national boundaries, remains that of giving the creator the exclusive right of authorizing the reproduction of his or her works. Certainly copyright and other regulations to protect intellectual property have been put under enormous pressure by the sheer ease with which we can now access vast amounts of other people's intellectual property. Yet that speed and simplicity are deceptive: just because you can find information quickly does not automatically mean that you can use it. An author who says to you, 'It's all right, I found it on the web' should ring alarm bells in every editor's mind, as the general assumption that web material is somehow open and free can be misleading or just false: free of access, perhaps; free of the need to seek permission or pay a fee, not necessarily.

The web has also brought into sharp focus the difficulty of controlling copyright and other intellectual property measures by national laws. The principle of territorial integrity – rights granted or reserved according to national boundaries – has effectively been destroyed by the global nature of digital creation and distribution, allowing border-hopping to any destination (or origin) you please. Public opinion (although often ill-informed) has moved to regard copyright as an old-fashioned and perhaps obstructive piece of legislation, and Google's mission to inform the world by unlocking knowledge has not helped maintain respect for copyright.

In addition, the music business has gone through radical change following its ill-starred response to early illegal file-sharing. Although that process in now reasonably well regulated, the idea that downloading music should be easy and cheap, preferably free, has taken hold and influenced people's attitudes towards the written (or printed) word. Some markets in publishing regard copyright as an unfair trading standard kept in place by greedy publishers, ignoring the fact that most rights holders are authors rather than publishers.

These issues are still being debated, and established principles and practice may still be some time off. In the meantime, publishers need to give more thought to applying technical protection measures, as well as wrestling with the growing problem of community publishing, user-generated content, blogs and both the opportunities and threats posed by Web 2.0.

Contracts, especially those between authors and publishers, are at the centre of most publishing businesses. Publishers on the whole outsource almost all of their operations, including writing (and printing), so it is extremely important that the main source of their 'supply' – authors – is properly overseen and regulated. Good fences make good neighbours, as the cliché has it: a good contract, fairly constructed and clearly understood, is an essential part of the publishing process. Contracts express mutual obligations on both parties: the author to deliver and the publisher to publish. And unless the publisher has decided to go for outright copyright acquisition of an author's work, the licensed rights granted by the author to the publisher need to be well understood by both sides.

If the pen really is mightier than the sword, it is important for publishers to be familiar with the basics of copyright and other publishing laws. No one needs to acquire a law degree to understand the principles, most of which are based on simple common sense combined with standard ways of doing business with others, and reaching agreement with them. Nor is it necessary to read and absorb the detail to be found in the standard British work on copyright, *Copinger and Skone James on Copyright* (Walter Arther Copinger's original first edition was published in 1870). But like someone about to go for a walk in a dangerous place – be it a snake- or a spider-infested jungle, or some rough urban back streets, it is better to be prepared; to wear protective clothing, so to speak – and to be alert to the perils and dangers you might meet. Many of the problem areas in publishing law can be anticipated, in the strict sense of the word. Given the cost of legal disputes and the harm they can do to business reputations, the watchword of this chapter might be 'Be prepared!' Prevention is better – and cheaper – than cure. If you want a clear and comprehensive book outlining the risks you face, the admirable *Publishing Law* by Hugh Jones and Christopher Benson (2006) is by far your best companion guide.

Copyright: the bedrock of publishing

In general, the creator of any work – text, pictures, maps, a DVD, or articles and images on a web page – is the first owner of copyright in it. Owners have the exclusive right to copy, publish, broadcast, adapt or perform their works, and authorize others to do so (or not). Copyright exists (it does not have to be registered) in literary, dramatic, musical and artistic works, but not in ideas, titles (of books, for example) or unregistered names. Copyright in works created by employees of companies or organizations 'in the course of employment' does not belong to the individuals concerned: it is owned by their employer. The phrase 'in the course of employment' is generally taken to refer to someone whose contract of employment specifically states that creating works is part of that employee's job, not merely that they create something during working hours.

Since 2003, in the UK and Europe, rights owners have gained a further right of communication to the public. This means items posted digitally or electronically on a website or other portal have the same level of copyright protection as material on a printed page. It is easy to assume that because web material is so easy to find and download for personal use, copyright regulations have somehow been eased. For publishers, however, it is likely they will be 'treating' or 'dealing' with material – disseminating it, certainly, and possibly adapting it. In most cases, they will be selling it too.

Conventions

Although copyright laws are applied at national level, most countries share the principle of creator as owner, and this equivalence is reflected in two main international conventions. The older of the two, and the one most people are familiar with, is the Berne Convention of 1886; the other is the Universal Copyright Convention of 1952. This requires the inclusion of the © symbol (together with the rights owner's name, and the date and place of publication), but works that lack this mark may still be protected by copyright. Countries (or territories) sign up to one or other (and in many cases both) of these conventions – hence, the familiar wording in many publications: 'This work is copyright in all countries that are signatory to the Berne Convention.'

Copyright has two distinct aspects: it is an economic right that protects and values intellectual property ('works of the mind'), and rests upon the principle that creators of works have spent time, effort and original creativity to 'make' them, and that such creations thus have a value (and may have a price). Copyright (in Britain, only since 1989) can also protect the reputation of creators, who have moral rights that forbid others from misusing their work, and harming their reputation or lowering their standing in the eyes of their peers.

Creative and performing rights

As well as protecting creators' rights, copyright applies to performers' rights, principally of course in the area of musical and dramatic works. A performance of a contemporary song may thus have many copyright interests within it: the composer, the lyricist, the singers, the orchestra, the conductor, and the recording company, and it is these multiple copyright interests that need the greatest care when authors or publishers want to make use of 'third-party rights'.

Legal term of copyright

Copyright is not perpetual. Generally, the legal term of copyright in a work lasts for 70 years from the end of the year in which its creator died. Thus, the work of someone who died on 1 February 2010 will remain in copyright until 31 December 2080. The works of Pablo Picasso (died 1973) and George Orwell (died 1950) are thus still in copyright, while those of Rudyard Kipling (died 1936) and John Singer Sargent (died 1925) are not. Bear in mind that it is often the copyright of the *photographer* of an artistic work whose copyright permission must be sought.

Works in the public domain are freely available to copy once the copyright term has expired. Copyright in the typographical arrangement of a work – its layout, design and printed form – lasts for 25 years from first appearance. It is important to realize that copyright exists in typefaces, or fonts. While it would be hard to enforce copyright protection in widely used typefaces such as Times New Roman, some decorative fonts with a distinctive design may be rigorously protected. An example is the 'Johnson' typeface used by Transport for London on the underground system.

The 70-year *post mortem auctoris* rule applies throughout Europe, and now also in the United States. Elsewhere, the term may be 50 years. The copyright term in works not created by a single author (or joint named authors) will usually be measured from the 'date of first appearance', and in many parts of the world, the legal term remains at 50 years. In the UK, copyright also protects government and parliamentary publications through Crown Copyright; this normally lasts for 125 years from first appearance. Most countries protect their official publications, and some may be regarded as confidential or even secret. In contrast, freedom of information legislation in, for example, the United States, has the opposite effect – material is much more accessible and is made freely available to any user.

Third-party rights

In preparing material in any format, printed or digital, authors and publishers need to be aware that including items owned and controlled by third-party rights holders – whether those items are passages of text, a photograph or video clip, two lines of a song, or an item found on a website – may require permission, acknowledgement and the payment of a fee.

Copyright subsists in both the components and the overall organization or presentation of a work, sometimes referred to as its 'arrangement'. A typical college textbook, for example, may contain separate copyright interests owned and controlled by the author (text), a picture library (photographs) and the Ordnance Survey (maps). In addition, the publisher will own copyright in the arrangement of the published work, even if it may have only a limited non-exclusive licence to publish the embedded copyright works owned by third parties. We look in more detail at these rights in the next chapter.

However, the medium in which a work is published is sometimes less important, in that the same copyright rules generally apply whether the format is a book, a CD, a video or DVD, or the page of someone's website. Publishing or republishing parts of a website will almost certainly require permission, and the owner or manager of the website will probably be the best initial guide as to who owns which parts of it.

Moral rights

The economic value of copyright must be considered alongside the way it can also protect a creator's reputation or standing in the eyes of other people. These are known as 'moral rights', and their origins lie in the code of honour and the *droits moraux* of medieval France and Spain. Moral rights in UK law were introduced only in August 1989, when the 1988 Copyright, Designs and Patents Act was made law. It is important to remember that the creators of works made before that date cannot seek redress under moral rights legislation.

There are four moral rights that we need to consider: paternity, integrity, false attribution and privacy.

1. Paternity

The first is the right to be identified as the author or creator of a work: the right of paternity. Authors normally assert this right by having wording printed at the front of the book (usually on the title page verso) that reads, for example: 'The author, Gill Davies, asserts her right to be identified as the author of this work in accordance with Section 77 of the 1988 Copyright, Designs and Patents Act.'

2. Integrity

The right of integrity concerns the creator's right 'to object to derogatory treatment', in other words subjecting a work to change that could damage that creator's reputation. This might mean editing a piece of writing badly so that the balance of an author's argument was distorted, or part of it missed out altogether. Cropping a photograph or reproducing a painting with poor colour values could also be an infringement of this moral right. In the contracts section of this chapter we refer to the right of copyright owners to allow (or not) someone – a publisher, for example – to adapt their work. There is obviously a close link between the right of adaptation and the moral right of integrity, so it is important that change of any kind is done with the author's agreement.

3. False attribution

The moral right of false attribution involves attributing a work to someone who is not its creator. Let us say Professor A writes an article, published in a medical journal, describing the merits of a new drug. This drug appears to be a wonderful cure for a certain disease. Ten years later, Professor B writes another article highlighting the serious side-effects of the drug and refuting the claims for its merits and quality. A year or two after that Professor C writes another article citing the original positive review of the drug, but wrongly saying that Professor B was its author. Professor B might sue Professor C for falsely attributing the positive review to him, and harming his reputation because he appeared to be praising a drug now seen to have serious problems – especially as it was he, Professor B, who had in fact highlighted its negative qualities.

4. Privacy

The moral right of privacy has quite a narrow definition, and should not be confused with legislation concerning people's individual rights to privacy, now increasingly covered (in Europe at least) by human rights law. In this case, the rights apply to a person whose photograph is taken (with permission) by a photographer who states that he or she is taking the picture for personal use. If that photographer subsequently uses the photograph for commercial gain – by licensing it to a magazine or newspaper, for example – then the subject of the photograph might object that his or her moral right of privacy had been infringed.

These four moral rights can either be asserted or waived. In the case of the right of paternity, this has to be asserted in writing – hence the wording inside many books. Waiving moral rights does not mean transferring them to someone else; it means the owner of the right chooses not to exercise it. Authors sometimes assign rights to publishers in exchange for a fee, but moral rights cannot be assigned. They are inalienable, meaning that they are personal to someone in particular. As a result, publishers often seek a waiver of moral rights, especially the right of integrity, as it removes the obligation for them to check back with an author if they want to re-use a work and modify it for another audience.

Exceptions and infringements

There are exceptions to copyright, most of them quite limited. The reporting of news, the use of extracts in the setting of examinations (but not in sales of past papers), and freedom for teachers to copy up to 1 per cent of a work in any quarter of the year are all exceptions. The most common exception, however, is known as the 'fair dealing' provision by which it is permitted to copy an insubstantial part of a work for the purposes of criticism and review, or for private study and (since 2003) non-commercial research.

Fair dealing and substantiality

The origins of this concept of 'fair dealing' lie in the world of scholarship and research, and date back to the time when an academic in a university needed to take a single copy of part of a work so that he or she could continue studying even when the library was closed. The fact that it was librarians who often took these copies (on the earliest kind of photocopier) has led to the phrase 'library privilege' when considering what constitutes fair dealing.

Once you move this into the publishing field, the concept of a single copy disappears, but the principle of copying only a small ('insubstantial') part of a work has remained. Authors often want to include parts of other works, or photographs and illustrations from other books, in their publication. Editors or permissions staff need to make a judgement about whether or not these third-party items are substantial (and need permission) or insubstantial, and can thus be included under the fair dealing provisions. In the next chapter, we explore when and how fair dealing can be applied, and when permission needs to be sought. In either case, acknowledgement is essential.

Infringements

Outside the realm of fair dealing (or permission), we need to consider what is meant by copyright infringement. If you break copyright law, what is it you are doing – and what might be the consequences? An infringement of copyright is an illegal use of someone else's intellectual property. An author who used a substantial part of another writer's work without permission (and without acknowledging its use) would be infringing the copyright in that writer's work. The publisher who published the book containing the extract would also be infringing copyright. Writing and publishing a work known to contain illicit material (in other words, where copyright has not been cleared) is called a 'primary infringement'.

A wholesaler might then buy bulk stock of the work and sell it to booksellers who in turn would sell the book to customers: these parts of the supply chain are committing a 'secondary infringement'. The publisher who publishes and the bookseller who sells a work *known* to contain infringing material are both breaking the law, even if they did not know that it was an infringing work (the key word is 'known', not 'knowing' – in other words, they *could* have known, even if they did not know at the time).

Plagiarism

Plagiarism and passing off are also forms of copyright infringement, and both involve a deliberate deception. In other words, the author who infringes another's copyright is deliberately either disguising its true origins, or passing off another author's writing as if it were his or her own. Note that the plagiarism has to copy the actual arrangement of the words used by the original author. It is not enough to copy merely the ideas contained in a work, as two writers Bagent and Leigh, authors of *The Holy Blood and the Holy Grail,* found when they sued Dan Brown, the author of *The Da Vinci Code.* The judge in that case ruled that Dan Brown had merely copied the *ideas* in the earlier book, not the actual arrangement of words. Moreover, the ideas – that Christ did not die, but married Mary Magdalene and had a child – were hardly unique even to the Bagent and Leigh book: these had been discussed over many years by people in the Roman Catholic Church.

Copyright infringement has to show that the author or creator whose work has been infringed has either lost value or suffered harm to his or her reputation. Using a work without permission usually means that the proper owner has been denied payment of a permission fee. It may even be that he or she might have chosen to withhold permission – which makes the misuse doubly bad. Most instances of copyright infringement do not get as far as the courts, as that would often involve costs to both parties that might well exceed the value of the unpaid permission fee. Sometimes the infringing publisher will offer to pay double what would have been the original fee, as a way of acknowledging an element of penalty in the payment.

A copyright item used without permission and the consequent loss of value to the owner is not the only type of infringement. An author's moral rights may have been infringed, and thus his or her reputation may have been harmed. Often it is the moral right of integrity that is at issue. This is the one that allows a rights owner to object to derogatory treatment of his or her work. A scholar or researcher whose writing had been edited badly, or changed in a way that made him or her seem ignorant or even ridiculous, could easily constitute such an infringement. Cropping or tinting a photograph, or reproducing it too small, might also be considered an infringement of the photographer's moral right.

Remedies for infringement

Occasionally a rights owner may not be satisfied with a publisher or author merely apologizing and making a retrospective payment. He or she may feel the infringement is so serious that he or she must ask a lawyer (who must agree on its seriousness) to place an injunction on the publisher. This means that the publisher of the infringing item must cease publication of the work containing it, remove all copies from the market (or the warehouse) and even deliver the copies to a place of the rights owner's choosing (usually a solicitor's office). An injunction of this kind drawn up by a lawyer has to be delivered to the publisher, and it must act immediately in accordance with its terms. This is generally known as the 'cease and desist, and delivery up' method: in other words, 'stop publishing, remove all copies from sale, and deliver up as many of the offending copies as can be traced'.

Much the same principles of identifying copyright infringement and dealing with it apply on the web, although many people imagine that misuse of copyright works is less of a problem here because rights owners are generally more willing to let their work be used freely in a digital environment, especially if the use is personal or educational. This is a dangerous misconception, and it cannot be stressed strongly enough that the same rules apply to material used on the web as they do in print. In other words, the rights owner still has the exclusive right to authorize (or not) the use of his or her work, be it substantial amounts of text, a piece of artwork, or a photograph.

And do not imagine that in the speedy freewheeling digital world no one will notice the occasional unauthorized use. The reality is that just as the web has proved itself a brilliant discoverer of facts, images and information generally, so too is its capacity to spot infringements – a kind of spy in the sky. Software now exists to detect digital plagiarism, whether the theft is of the text of a published work used by a university student in a hurry to complete a dissertation, or the professional pianist whose husband put out recordings of her performances that had been stolen from the repertoire of other pianists. Moreover, owners of registered names, brands and marques may be extremely vigilant of unauthorized use of their property, and now have a means globally of detecting such misuse very quickly.

The mechanism for dealing with infringements in a digital or web context has been incorporated into legislation drawn up and enacted in the last 10 years. The European Copyright Directive of 2001, now incorporated into most countries' legislations (and into the UK's Copyright and Related Rights Regulations of October 2003) contains the principle of 'notice and takedown'. Like the 'cease and desist' approach, the 'notice' takes the form of a legal injunction, usually issued to the webmaster of a site, who is obliged to remove the offending item. This 'takedown' or removal of the infringing work has to be done immediately. Indeed, in the 2007 case of the Belgian newspaper proprietors versus Google (which the newspaper proprietors won),

Google had to remove the offending headlines and news stories within 24 hours, under a threatened penalty of €20 million a day.

What's in a contract?

At the heart of most publishing businesses lies the formal relationship between the main supplier – the author – and the publisher. The importance of negotiating a fair and reasonable agreement with your authors cannot be overstated, and yet it is often a source of uncertainty and a cause of ill-feeling. The relationship has always had its problems, with each side bemoaning the traditional weaknesses of the other. Publishers, it is said, are sometimes arrogant or patronizing, poor at keeping an author informed and involved, and on occasion downright mean. Authors, meanwhile, have little idea of the professional process of publishing, often deliver typescripts late, and seem to be unaware that most editors have many projects in their care, and cannot be expected to lavish individual attention on every book.

The first thing to emphasize is that a contract, whether it's a simple letter of agreement confirming a fee and a transfer of copyright to the publisher, or a full length licensing and royalty agreement, should be the concluding confirmation of a series of discussions in which terms have been debated and agreed already. The contents of a contract should never come as a surprise, nor should a contract be a long legal document with which to threaten or browbeat an author. Reaching agreement on terms is a way of consummating the relationship, so clearly described in Gill Davies' *Book Commissioning and Acquisition*.

Key legal preconditions

Leaving the relationship aspect to one side for the moment, what are the key legal issues that must be established before any kind of agreement is reached?

Authors first need to confirm that they are free to make the agreement, are a 'qualifying person', and that the work they are providing to the publisher belongs to them and is free of problems or trouble. It is important to check if an author is free to make an independent agreement with a publisher. Some employers might consider that the author's work belongs to them, and could claim copyright in it. Just as important is getting the author to affirm – warrant, indeed – that the work being presented for publication is theirs. There are normally two things that need clarifying: the first is that the author has not plagiarized another person's work – copied it, in fact. Copying ideas, facts or historical events is not plagiarism. Copying an author's *arrangement* of those ideas, facts or events by using recognizably the same words in the same order could be plagiarism.

The second thing that an author must warrant is that material whose copyright belongs to a third party – text extracts, photographs, images or web content – has been identified. The contract needs to specify who is going to be responsible for clearing and paying for any permissions to use that third-party material.

The author also needs to confirm that his or her material does not contain any 'trouble'. The most common type of trouble is using somebody else's copyright material without permission. But libel, slander, blasphemy and obscenity may be issues, as well as liability for mistakes that could lead the reader of the book into risk or danger to health and personal safety.

The grant of rights

At the beginning of most author-publisher agreements the grant of rights has to be stated. As we saw at the beginning of this chapter, the author – creator – of a work is the first owner of copyright in it, so a publisher seeking to make use of that creator's material has to make some kind of agreement that grants it the right to publish the work. This grant of rights is usually accompanied by what is known as the 'consideration' – in other words, payment:

> In consideration of the payment hereafter described in Clause X, the author grants to the publisher the sole and exclusive right to publish the work in all forms including print, digital and electronic, in all territories of the world and in all languages.

These are the words commonly used at the beginning of a contract in which the author licenses the publisher to publish his or her work. Under the terms of this licence agreement, the author retains copyright in the work, and the publisher is granted an exclusive licence. Now the publisher, when the work is published, also has copyright in what is sometimes known as the 'volume edition'. Effectively, then, there are two parallel copyrights (they are not *joint* copyrights, each is separate but linked) – the author has copyright in the content and the publisher in the 'published edition'. This also means that neither party can act outside the terms of the contract without referring back to the other party.

Assigning copyright

A simpler form of grant of rights can take place whereby the author assigns or transfers copyright to the publisher, usually in exchange for a fee. Under this process, copyright is transferred from the author to the publisher, which will now usually control all rights in the work without further reference back to the author. Although it seems odd for an author to want to abandon rights in his or her work and to forego any further say in how it is used, there are several types of publishing where this is the norm. And although a fee is often paid in exchange for the assignment of copyright, the work is often provided without payment – researchers writing articles for journals, people penning short pieces for an organization or charity they support; and it is here, sometimes, that the problems begin.

People assume that because no payment is involved, no copyright procedures need to be followed, and a verbal understanding is all that's required. This can lead to acrimonious disagreements if an article is subsequently found to be very popular, is then bought by another publisher, and money starts to change hands. Who, after all, 'owns' the article? And to whom should any subsequent income be paid? Should it be shared? Without a formal agreement – even a simple one-page signed letter – misunderstandings and ill-feeling can easily arise.

If you decide to write for a publisher of non-fiction titles aimed at pupils wanting to find information in the library for a school project, you will be invited to submit your work to a well-defined and exact formula – word-count, page layout, language level and so on will all be prescribed – and your agreement will require you to assign copyright in what you have written in exchange for a one-off fee. One of the reasons for this is that the publisher may want to negotiate a co-edition and produce multiple editions in other languages.

Assignment of copyright also applies to research scholars writing for journals in that they are normally required to assign copyright to the publisher. In this instance, however, no payment is made to the author. Indeed, in some regimes, particularly in the United States, the author or his or her department or funding body pays for publication. The publisher asks for a copyright transfer agreement so that when the article is republished as part of another publication (like a monograph), placed on a website, or added to a subject-based collection of articles, the publisher does not need to go back to the author (or, in some cases, several authors) for permission each time. Meantime, salaried researchers are more interested in their department's prosperity through publication and citation of its members' articles, or their career advancement, than in receiving payment.

Moral rights in copyright assignments

In all cases of assignment, or transfer, of copyright, an important additional step needs to be taken. This concerns the author's moral rights. In many cases authors will be asked to waive their moral rights, even though publishers will normally credit them by publishing their name (the right of paternity). As far as the moral right of integrity is concerned – the right to object to derogatory treatment – most publishers ask authors to waive this right. This means publishers can use the piece later in other edited forms without constantly having to check that the author agrees with the changes.

Many author bodies recommend their members resist the requirement to waive their moral rights, arguing that authors' reputations may be harmed by indiscriminate changes made to their work. Journal publishers argue that constant referral back to authors would add hugely to their costs, and thus to the price of the journal. Most publishers of reputable journals would be at pains not to edit scholarly work in a way that might harm an author's reputation. After all, it is likely that the brand value of the journal has been developed through years of publishing high-quality articles that have been carefully reviewed and meticulously edited. But it is easy to see why the two sides do not always agree on this point.

To overcome resistance to copyright assignment, some publishers seek to agree a 'right of first publication'. Under this procedure, the publisher has an exclusive right to publish the article for the first time. Thereafter, each party has what amounts to a non-exclusive licence to continue using the work. The publisher is free to republish the work, add it to a data collection, or otherwise exploit the article commercially. Meanwhile, the author remains free to use his or her own article for all non-commercial activity: posting it on a university intranet, adding it to conference papers or using it in teaching or lecturing.

Main elements of a licensing agreement

Granting or reserving rights

As we have seen, the grant of rights in a licensing agreement often begins with the words 'In consideration of the payment hereafter described in Clause X ...' and this 'consideration' makes the contract legally binding under contract law. However, a letter of agreement about an article for which the author receives no payment would still have the force of law, so long as it was signed by the two parties.

There then follows the section in which the author grants the publisher the exclusive licence to publish the book. The word 'exclusive' is important, as the publisher will wish to protect its investment in the author's work by keeping the field to itself: in other words, no other publisher should be granted the right to publish the same or a very similar work in competition with this one.

The right to publish must then be qualified, and the rights granted described in detail. Authors may grant rights to the publisher to publish in all territories of the world and in all languages, and further to license editions of the work 'in whole or in part', in all forms, including print and electronic form, and all other media 'known or hereafter developed'.

Authors working with consumer or trade publishers may be reluctant to grant all these rights in a blanket fashion. They – or more commonly their agent – will reserve many of these rights. As a result, the rights granted to the publisher may be limited to publishing the 'volume' edition (the whole work in book form) in the territories of the United Kingdom and Europe, and in the English language.

These secondary or subsidiary rights can take many forms – different formats of the book, extracts serialized in newspapers and magazines, audio rights for disc or radio broadcasting, and options to develop a film or television version. Recently, the most contentious rights (though so far not often the most lucrative) have been digital or electronic rights, either of the whole work, or of extracts, or – more commonly – adapting the original to make a new interactive product. These rights are analysed in more detail later in the next chapter on rights and permissions.

In the run-up to agreeing the terms for a new project, and before the contract is signed, there is a possibility that an editor, keen to attract a new author to the company, will make promises, give assurances, or even exaggerate what the publisher will do for the author's book. This is very risky, as letters, e-mails, witnessed conversations or even recorded telephone calls could be construed as a contract.

In a 1990 case, an author sued Oxford University Press for breach of contract. The editor concerned had made enthusiastic remarks in a letter about the author's new work and then, in a phone call to the author (which was recorded), agreed that for a book of this kind and given the author's track record with the company, a sizeable advance would probably be appropriate. But OUP then decided not to go ahead with publication of the book. It was later agreed in court that both these items – the letter and the recorded phone call – constituted a contract, although no formal contract had been drawn up or signed. It is important that all correspondence with authors contains the words, ideally as a heading, 'subject to contract'. Most contracts also have an 'entire agreement' clause in which all previous correspondence is superseded by the formal contract, somewhat along the lines of the words 'this is the last will and testament of ...'. The terms of this final contract override anything that may have been unwittingly agreed in an earlier 'unintended contract'.

Competence and delivery

The interval between signing the contract and receiving the typescript is the most critical and difficult in a project's evolution, and it is essential that the agreement is transparent and that both parties understand each other's priorities. Knowing that the author is competent is an essential element of the process, especially if he or she has not written before. Technical knowledge is one thing, but can the person write well? Does he or she understand how important simple language may be for pupils, particularly those reading in a language that is not their mother tongue? A good teacher is, in part, a performer. There is no guarantee that he or she will be able to capture that performance well in written form.

These features of competence can be hard to capture in a contract. One of the best ways of doing so is to draw up a comprehensive brief, and attach it as an appendix to the contract. Such a brief might include a maximum (and minimum) number of words, and specify the internal organization of the work (chapters, sections and headings). Presentation is important, too. Publishers usually ask for the work to be submitted as both a typescript and a digital file, with the written content double-spaced and on one side of the paper only.

The brief should also specify the market for the book. Who is going to want to read it? Who will buy the publication? A phrase that can be useful here is the 'reason and need for publication'. In educational and academic publishing, the brief may get very specific on details such as the precepts of a national curriculum, or examination and qualification requirements. The language level is critical, too. A chemistry textbook for 16-year-olds in school may be written by a professor at a university, but if that professor pitches the writing level at an undergraduate audience, the book will fail.

Many publishers will tell you that their greatest problem with authors is the late delivery of typescripts. Ideally, the delivery date in the contract will have been discussed and agreed by both parties, but what if the author delivers late? And what are the reasons for this consistent problem? Inexperienced authors often underestimate the sheer amount of uninterrupted time they will need to complete a full-length work. Most authors, particularly in the educational, academic and professional fields of publishing, are in a real sense 'amateurs'. That is not to say they are incompetent. It is just that, for the majority of authors writing books in this field, the revenue that they will ultimately receive will form a small part of their overall income. As writing is not the main part of their job, their priority is more likely to be focused on teaching, lecturing, or conducting research. So, time for writing is inevitably forced into so-called 'leisure hours' at weekends and in the holidays.

What can a publisher do if a typescript is delivered late? Most contracts contain a clause that makes this lateness a 'material breach' of the contract – in other words, serious enough to cancel it. If all publishers who ever received a work late from an author cancelled the contract and refused to publish, there would be a dearth of new books (no bad thing, perhaps). But in reality, publishers will often wait, and agree extensions – though checking up on progress during the writing period can be a good way of anticipating delay, and perhaps even offering help.

Judging what is 'acceptable'

Getting the typescript in is one thing. Assessing its suitability for publication, judging its acceptability – that is quite another, and can prove contentious. Stanley Unwin once described the good editor as 'one who is good at judging other people's judgements', and the key to acceptability can be what other people think of the work. In consumer publishing, a contract will often not even be issued unless the submission is good, and outside readers may make this initial assessment. But with commissioned works in the educational and academic areas, it is more a matter of judgement when the typescript has been completed, and editors normally seek the opinions of two or three referees – usually professionals expert in the same field as the author.

So what can an editor do, legally and contractually, if the work is just not good enough to publish? Most contracts stipulate as a condition of publication that the work has to be made acceptable before the publisher will proceed. The author has to be given the chance to make the necessary improvements, in the first instance. If the work is then *still* not up to the required standard, contracts will usually state that the publishers shall be free to approach a competent third party, and to get this outsider to fix things. The author is normally shown this third-party work to approve it, but if he or she does not accept what has been done, the publisher must be able to have the final say. The work carried out by the third party is usually paid for out of the original author's royalties or other income.

Disagreements about quality are time-consuming and can lead to acrimony between author and publisher. Ensuring the author is competent in the first place (even inviting him or her to submit some trial material to judge that competence), and spending time devising and agreeing a detailed brief are good ways of reducing the likelihood of an author delivering a poor piece of work. The opinions of outside professionals are crucial, but the publisher's ability to have the final say is critical too. The publisher is putting up the money and taking the investment risk: in the end, it must be confident that it is committing its funds to a potentially successful project.

Warranties and indemnities

Publishers need the author's undertaking that what he or she submits for publication is 'safe' and, as far as possible, 'trouble-free'. The main thing that an author has to attest or warrant (effectively, promise) is that he or she is the author of the work. Plagiarism of other people's work is a common problem these days, as the internet provides such a rich source of other people's writing, and some authors 'copy' material from this source almost without realizing they are doing it.

Authors have to be a 'qualifying person' – over 16, for a start; neither an undischarged bankrupt, nor certified criminally insane. Current or former prisoners, however, do qualify. Putting these unlikely disqualifications to one side, publishers also need to check that authors are free to submit their work in their own right, and that they do not have a contract of employment with an institution like a school or university that might claim ownership (or copyright) in what the they have written. In UK legislation, copyright in a work created during the course of employment belongs to the employer, and case histories suggest that 'in the course of employment' means that writing forms part of the person's job as defined in the contract of employment, not just something written in working hours.

Avoiding 'trouble'

Another key part of the warranty that an author has to make concerns third-party material that may infringe other people's copyright, or be a breach of some other law. Few works will contain things that are obscene, defined in English law as 'a tendency to deprave or corrupt', rather than material that is merely offensive or disgusting. However, in many parts of the world cultural, religious and moral standards apply that make what might seem harmless and acceptable in one country unacceptable or highly offensive in another.

These moral issues do not merely relate to subjects such as nudity or the sexual act: in some parts of the world, illustrations showing the use of alcohol or tobacco may not be acceptable. In Britain recently an educational publisher decided to modify a historical photograph. The celebrated engineer, Isambard Kingdom Brunel, is shown standing in front of one of his steamship's anchor chains with a cigar in his mouth – except that in the textbook, the cigar has been airbrushed out of the picture.

In another instance, a children's story (*The Machine Gunners* by Robert Westall; published by Macmillan Education) set in Newcastle at the beginning of World War II included the word 'nigger'. The word is used affectionately by local children who for the first time in their lives meet a black boy who has been evacuated from the blitz in wartime London. Although the word was historically correct and not used in a derogatory way, its modern connotations made the word unacceptable for some people, particularly because the book was used in schools. The dilemma of historical accuracy and what has become almost an obsession with political correctness remains a difficult one, but for which the law itself is no help.

The same problem presents itself concerning blasphemy. Under English law, blasphemy in published material applied only to the Christian religion. In a famous case in 1977, Mary Whitehouse, a stalwart campaigner against broadcasts and publications she found offensive or unacceptable, sued the publishers of *Gay News* for publishing a poem about the homosexual feelings of longing the centurion at the foot of the cross had for Christ crucified. Her action was successful. This law was repealed in 2008.

More recently, there have been occasions when the principles of Islam have been threatened by unsuitable publications. For believers in that religion, it is a very serious offence to reproduce any depiction of the prophet Mohamed. Oxford University Press published a book in the United States that included a reproduction of a 14th-century painting of the prophet, while a Danish magazine produced a cartoon that showed a caricature of the prophet. In both cases, feelings of offence ran so high that the publications led to physical violence against the publishers, and even rioting. Publishers that operate internationally need to consider issues that go far beyond a mere interpretation of the law – religious, cultural and moral issues must all be taken into account.

Publishers as well as authors have a responsibility to ensure that what is published is accurate and correct. In most contracts, authors must warrant that what they write will not harm readers who follow information or instructions in the publication. Obvious examples include recipe books that specify using a fish or vegetable, part of which is edible while another part is poisonous. In medical or pharmaceutical textbooks, dosages of drugs or other medicines may be critical in an emergency or in the treatment of seriously ill patients. This liability for inaccuracy is sometimes called a 'negligent misstatement'.

In the 1970s an educational publisher was successfully sued by a local education authority for publishing a chemistry textbook that included an incorrect quantity of a highly volatile liquid to be used in an experiment undertaken by a teacher in a school laboratory. The liquid concerned was concentrated nitric acid (HNO_3), and the quantity was misprinted by a factor of 10: the decimal point had been put in the wrong place. The correct amount should have been stated as 0.5 ml, but the book gave the figure as 5 ml. The possibility of there being a serious accident is obvious, but who was to blame? In legal terms, the author (whose copyright the book was) and the publisher were jointly responsible, even though the mistake was made by the typesetter and subsequently by a freelance copy-editor not checking the proofs carefully enough. In this case, the publishers did not sue either the typesetter or the editor (but they probably did not use their services again!) All copies in stock had to have an erratum notice inserted, including those books already sold that had to be recalled from schools. In addition, the publisher had to publicize the mistake to all customers who might have bought copies – a tiny mistake, perhaps, but an expensive error, and harmful to reputation as well as sales.

Libel and defamation

Equally important is what is published about people, and the effect this may have on their reputations. If you publish a magazine article that states someone is a liar and a thief, when they are neither, then you have committed a libel against that person, and they may sue you for defamation. Of course, if you can prove that what you have published is true – the person in question is both those things – then there is nothing they can do. The strongest defence against libel is truth. Libel can be directed only at a living individual (not groups or classes), and it must be possible to identify who is the subject of the libel, even if he or she is not named. Although the problem is most commonly found in publications dealing with contemporary issues (newspapers and magazines, principally) a book about a notorious public figure will need to be carefully scrutinized by lawyers before publication to make sure the author has got all the facts right.

Privacy issues

In recent years, celebrities have managed to resist reports or block publications about themselves, even when the stated facts are true. They will argue that publication of these usually unwelcome revelations is an invasion of their right to privacy. In Europe, privacy is regarded as a human right, similar almost to education or access to medical care, while in the United States there are much stricter rules on what constitutes an invasion of privacy. If a famous singer is photographed leaving a clinic renowned for treating alcohol and drug dependency, is that picture an invasion of the singer's right to privacy, or is it – to use the phrase usually applied to unearthing political scandal – 'fair comment on a matter of public interest'? Once again, this reinforces the importance of publishers being active assessors of risk, rather than relying on a narrow interpretation of sometimes imprecise legal statute.

When authors give these warranties – promises, in effect – they also agree to indemnify the publisher against any cost that may arise from their breach. Although the practical implications of this are rarely tested, it may not be realistic to expect an individual author to be able to pay these costs, which might include legal fees and amount to a large sum of money. In recent years some organizations have insisted that writers (such as teachers in schools) take out indemnity insurance against this possibility, but that too could be impractical, especially if a teacher is being paid a modest sum for a small contribution to a publication, some or even all of which could be swallowed up by the insurance premium.

So much of what contracts contain is a statement of what is reasonable, and both authors and publishers need to be practical and realistic about the issues. Descending into a detailed analysis of legal minutiae or insisting on the strict interpretation of a particular clause can rapidly become counter-productive. On the other hand, this is not an invitation or an excuse to be casual about formal agreements: most problems to do with author-publisher relations stem from a lack of clear documentation about what has been agreed. It is, as with so much in professional publishing, a matter of judgement.

Subsidiary rights

A licensing agreement needs to specify which other rights have been granted to the publisher by the author. For contracts dealing with educational and academic publications, few authors will want to do anything other than grant these rights in the hope that the publisher will be in the best position to identify any possible opportunities for translation or adaptation in other markets. However, few schoolbooks these days travel well outside the immediate territory in which their curriculum-focused content applies.

As we have seen, authors working in the trade and consumer or children's field, where many opportunities for exploitation could exist, will often reserve some of these rights. They (or their agents) believe that by going direct to customers seeking rights deals, they will maximize their benefit and income. It can be a negotiating issue, however: the publisher may not feel it can get a proper return on its investment unless it is given a range of rights and licensing opportunities through which it can recover that investment.

Whatever is agreed, the contract needs to state clearly which subsidiary rights have been granted to the publisher and which reserved by the author. It also needs to specify the shares of income each party will receive from any subsequent sales of these rights. The author will rarely get less than half of this revenue. A fuller description of these subsidiary rights and how they can be negotiated, sold and managed appears in the next chapter.

Competing work and first option

Most contracts try to prevent an author from writing a work that could compete with the one described in the contract. This is why the grant of rights at the beginning of a contract refers to an *exclusive* licence – no publisher would want its investment in a new work to be put at risk by the same or a very similar work competing with it. Yet many authors write many works in their field of knowledge or scholarship, and it can sometimes be hard to define what exactly is meant by a 'competing work'.

The following contract wording is generally agreed to be the most effective: 'a work likely to compete with or to affect prejudicially the sales of the Work'. In other words, for a successful claim to be made, the original publisher might have to show that it had actually lost sales of a publication as a direct result of the competing work. The truth is that a successful author who writes prolifically may actually be helping promote his or her earlier books by writing a so-called competing work.

Many contracts contain an option clause by which the author is required to offer his or her next work to the publisher. This is sometimes called a 'first refusal' clause. Opinions differ about the value of this clause. Obliging an author to submit his or her next work before the publisher has even received (let alone published) the first work is full of risk, especially if the next work is not any good. Besides, it is not a commitment to *publish* the work, merely to consider it. Some editors would rather build up their relationship with an author by doing a good professional job on the book. Only then might an author want to continue to work with and then offer his or her next work to the same publisher.

This option clause is not the same thing as a two- (or three-) book contract. Here the publisher is making a commitment to an author for more than one book in the hope and expectation that the sequence will be very successful, either because the author is well known or has a track-record with another publisher. Making such a commitment (usually accompanied by a sizeable advance) can be extremely risky.

Copyright infringement

Contracts normally spell out what should happen in the event of an infringement of copyright of the author's work – perhaps the publishing of a pirate edition of the book. In a licensing agreement, copyright in the content of the book remains the property of the author. So the publisher must have the author's permission to take steps to pursue infringements of copyright on the book, especially as it will usually be the publisher who first becomes aware of any problems.

The clause allows the publisher to take action in the author's name, but at its cost. It is, in effect, a joint attempt to track down and stop the problem, but to do it with the full agreement of the rights holder – the author. If as a result of a successful prosecution the publisher receives payment in compensation, this money is shared with the author once all costs have been paid.

Revision and termination

Some works, especially academic or educational textbooks, need updating and revising so that new editions can be published. Publishers will want the author to agree to work on producing these new editions when the time comes, and this does not usually cause any problems. After all, it is just as much in the author's interest as the publisher's to keep the book up to date and in print so that sales can continue to generate royalties.

With the passage of time, however, authors may no longer be in a position to work on the book. They may simply have retired, or even died. To protect the publisher's continuing interest and investment in the book, a clause is included in the contract which states that if the author is 'unwilling or unable' to work on updating his or her work for a new edition, 'the Publisher shall be free to employ some other competent person to do the necessary work, and that any costs incurred in producing this new material may be deducted from the author's future royalties'.

Neither party to a contract will wish to end it unless there is a 'material breach' – in other words, a breach of the terms in the contract so serious that one or other side may end their commitment. Certainly the failure by the author to deliver the typescript or the publisher to publish it might be a reason for this. More often, however, the contract ends when the book goes out of print and is no longer available.

The procedure in most contracts is that the author requests the publisher to reprint his or her book. The publisher may refuse because, in its view, there is no market for any further sales. If it does refuse to reprint, the mechanism for ending the contract is set in train. One result of this termination is that the rights originally granted to the publisher revert to the author, who is then free to do what he or she wants with it – including offering it to another publisher.

The rights reversion clause, as it is known, has caused some problems in recent years because of publishers' ability to issue very short print runs, or even to print on demand, yet still to make an acceptable margin. Occasionally publishers have not played fair with authors, instead acting rather like the 'dog in the manger' – refusing to let a book go out of print by keeping very small stocks of it so that rights cannot revert to the author.

This act of bad faith is quite rare now, and agreement has been reached that moves the emphasis away from just keeping a book in print towards making it clear to everyone (including an outside arbitrator) that the book either is or is not 'commercially available': this would mean that it continued to be marketed by appearing in catalogues or on websites, and was being actively marketed.

Preparing accounts

Fees

For some works, especially those where the author assigns copyright to the publisher, a single one-off flat fee is paid. This fee may be paid as a lump sum, either on delivery of the work in acceptable form, or on publication. To help the author's solvency and the publisher's cash flow, this fee is often split three ways – a sum on signature of the agreement, a further sum on satisfactory completion of the work, and a final sum when all the loose ends (captions, glossary, index, checking proofs, etc) have been tied up and completed, or the work has been published.

Very occasionally, repeat fees are paid, but the norm is for the author to receive only one payment. Then, even if the book is a great success, or it is translated into several other languages, the author won't get anything more by way of payment. The advantage for the author of course is that he or she gets paid whether or not the book goes on to become a success. The advantage for the publisher is not having to pay repeat fees if the book reprints, often leading to an improvement in margin and profit.

Royalty rates

Royalty payments often go hand in hand with licensing agreements, and both symbolize a desire on both sides – the publisher's and the author's – to form a long-term working relationship, and for the author to commit to making the book a success. This will mean that if and when sales increase, the author can share in that success, especially if the book becomes part of the publisher's backlist and goes on selling year after year. When J D Salinger died in February 2010, it was revealed that he had published no books since 1965, yet his best-selling classic, *The Catcher in the Rye*, originally published in 1951, continued to sell many thousands of copies a year.

Royalties are calculated as a percentage of sales, with 10 per cent a typical mid-range rate. But there is a choice as to how the calculation is made. For authors of trade and consumer books sold in the home market through bookshops, it is normal to pay a royalty based on the retail selling price of the book. However, for export sales and any outlet where big discounts have to be granted to suppliers, either a lower royalty rate or a different basis for calculation is used.

This different basis is usually calculated on the net sums received by the publisher after discount, widely referred to as 'net receipts'. This can be a more realistic way of sharing the proceeds from a book's sales. In educational and academic publishing, the discount may be quite low – between 20 and 30 per cent off the selling price. But to get books into chain bookstores and supermarkets, discounts of as much as 60 per cent or even 70 per cent are sometimes given. Even at 50 per cent discount, the publisher making payments based on selling price ends up paying a much larger actual royalty.

From a publisher's point of view, paying authors on 'net receipts' means its payments are kept more closely in line with the funds available from actual sales. However, authors might argue that their income should not be dependent on how big a discount the publisher has to make – they should be getting, as far as possible, the same amount on every copy of their book that is sold. Examples of royalties paid by each method are shown at the end of this section.

Scaled royalty rates

Sometimes scaled royalty payments are made: a low rate – say, 5 per cent – is paid when the book is first published, and increased as and when sales grow and pass certain thresholds. These break points, as they are known, may be in step with reprints. So the low 5 per cent rate is paid for the first printing of, say, 2,000 copies; this increases to 7.5 per cent for the next 2,000 copies, and finally rises to 10 per cent once sales of 4,000 have been achieved. This rising royalty rate is sometimes applied when initial costs (of colour illustrations, for example) are high. Once these first costs have been absorbed, the publisher can afford to raise the rate of royalty.

Shares of other income

Authors earn additional income from their share of the sale of subsidiary rights, and some titles lend themselves better than others to this exploitation and additional revenue. School textbooks have very limited potential outside the country and the curriculum for which they are written. Children's story books based on fantasy characters (and thus with no specific national or cultural 'identity') can have international appeal, as can books on topics like ancient history and (to some extent) on food and wine, cookery, wildlife and tourism. Celebrity biographies lend themselves to lucrative serialization deals with newspapers. Mass-market paperback fiction may attract high fees in options from film and television companies.

Shares between author and publisher will rarely be less than 50 per cent payable to the author, and the more sensational the content, the more eminent the author, and the greater the possibilities for rights sales, the higher will be the share due to the author. A world-renowned fiction writer will expect his or her agent to insist on 90 per cent of the rights income from a rights sale to a US publisher, and for serialization and translation deals, a 75 to 85 per cent share is the norm.

Paying advances on royalty

Advances are payments made on account and in advance of royalties earned from sales of the book. They are not separate or additional fees. There are contrasting issues to be considered here. The author (particularly a professional writer living by earnings from his or her writing) needs money on which to live while writing the book. On the other hand, the publisher may have to put up a large lump sum as an advance two or even three years before the book in question has been written and can be published. For established authors or great celebrities, the amounts can be very big, and all but the largest publishers will find such a drain on their cash difficult to sustain. As with flat fees, it can help to pay an advance in stages.

Timing

Publishers normally produce accounts of sales made and royalties earned twice a year, and pay any sums due to the author within three months of that date. For publishers whose accounts run for the 12 months of the calendar year (January to December), royalty accounts would be sent out in early January and early July, with payments made by 31 March and 30 September. Payments received from subsidiary rights sales would be made at the end of the next accounting period.

One or two publishers prepare accounts and pay royalties only once a year. This helps the publisher's cash flow as money received in January may not be sent on to the author until the end of March of the following year – nearly 15 months later. Many authors and most author groups feel this is unfair, and provision is made in some contracts for lump sums over a certain amount to be paid out more promptly.

Other kinds of contract

In some genres of publishing, such as trade or consumer books and in academic markets, especially in the United States, there has been pressure in recent years to provide agreements that are 'fairer' to authors. This begs the question of what is meant by 'fair', and implies that existing contracts may be unfair, which, if authors are prepared to sign them, cannot be generally true. It boils down to whether or not the author should get a larger share of the value chain.

MTA

In the UK some 20 years ago, the Minimum Terms Agreement (MTA) was drawn up and adopted by some publishers. The language of the contract was written in simpler wording and was accompanied by explanatory comments intended to help authors understand the issues being agreed. Royalty rates were sometimes higher, with 10 per cent seen as an absolute minimum. The legal term of copyright (50, later 70, years following the author's death) was exchanged in favour of a term of 10, 15 or 20 years from first publication.

Accounting was invariably done twice-yearly, and payment made more promptly – bearing in mind that the original three-month delay between sending out accounts and paying the amounts due had a reason. Bookkeeping and clerical calculations might take a long time for a company with perhaps hundreds of authors on its lists, a reason now sounding more like an excuse to hold on to the money, given that spreadsheet software can produce accounts and make payments in weeks if not days. For some years, the Society of Authors in London had a roll of honour in its offices listing publishers that had adopted the MTA and nearby a rogues' gallery of those publishers still paying out royalties only once a year.

Creative Commons licences

Creative Commons is a not-for-profit organization with origins in California that 'increases sharing and improves collaboration' by allowing writers to offer their material for dissemination when any financial consideration or motive for profit is absent. 'Share, re-mix and re-use' is one of its slogans, and the site (www.creativecommons.org) offers a range of model licences that allow creators to choose how much of their material they are prepared to place in the public domain, and how many rights they wish to reserve. A key condition is attribution – in other words, the creator must be named. Creators can insist that material is not adapted or changed, but only re-used 'as is'. Each licence is accompanied by a range of symbols that are easy to understand. The most common of them, not surprisingly given the name, is a dollar sign in a circle with a line through it – indicating that money cannot be charged for any use of the material.

Open Access issues

Although not a licensing system in itself, the Open Access movement needs to be considered by publishers, especially those involved in disseminating scholarly information through online journals. Once again, it is the academic community (particularly in the United States) that has been pressing for change. Many protagonists see the process whereby scholarly writing is reviewed by other scholars before being accepted for publication (the 'peer review process') as slow and restrictive.

An established journal, like *Nature,* rejects the majority of the submissions it receives. There may be a delay before a journal can find room for an article, even when it has been accepted, so the time between submission and publication can seem unacceptably long. Some academics also argue that publishers control the channels for dissemination of research too tightly, and that journal subscriptions are too expensive. Given that scholars writing for the journals do not receive payment, these grumbling complaints might seem legitimate.

Part of the problem is that publishers have always done a poor job of explaining what it is they actually do to justify the fact that they keep any margin or profit from the scholarly publishing process. A clue lies in the fact that *Nature* (and other top scientific and medical journals) rejects so many submissions. The truth is that scholars and the universities and organizations that employ them are judged not only by the number of articles that appear in a prestigious subject journal, but the extent to which they are cited by scholars in other journals.

Reputation of both individuals on a career path and of institutions whose funding depends, in the UK, on the RAE – the research assessment exercise – provides the compelling need to be published. The fact that Macmillan has spent over 150 years making the brand that is *Nature* so strong and well respected is in the end down to the publisher's initial investment in the risk of publishing a new journal, and its subsequent marketing efforts to generate (and hold on to) subscriptions. Journals' success is measured by what is known as the 'impact factor' – how many people have read and noted the article (by referring to it, or citing it).

None of this justification cuts much ice with the Open Access movement, still less those from what is sometimes known as the 'copyleft' – extremists in the scholarly community who see copyright as an outmoded publisher-driven obstacle to the free flow of information and, ideally, the flow of free information. They also complain that not only do researchers not get paid for their writing, they also have to assign copyright to the publishers by signing a copyright transfer agreement. However, attempts to speed up and liberalize the publishing of journal articles have generally not been successful, particularly when undertaken by people or groups who know nothing about the real costs of establishing and publishing a journal. Even the Public Library of Science – a US initiative to make scientific information from many different journals more freely available – depended on major government funding when it was set up.

'Author-pays' models

From a rights and licensing perspective, there have been some changes. Some publishers and journals now operate an 'author-pays' model, whereby contributors (or their employer) pay for the article to be produced so that on publication or shortly afterwards the journal is available via open access – without charge. Other publishers offer their writers an agreement whereby the contributor retains copyright in what he or she has written, while the publisher secures a right of first publication. Once published, the article can be used by each party to the agreement under what amounts to a non-exclusive licence. This allows the publisher to continue to exploit the work commercially (by re-publishing it, or including it in a database) while the contributor also continues to make use of the research article – in lectures, at conferences, or by posting it on a secure network, such as a university intranet.

Recently, British and European government-inspired investigations were set up to look at whether a larger share of publishers' proceeds from publicly funded research should not be ploughed back into the research process itself, rather than being pocketed by publishers. No conclusive or mandatory change arose from these investigations.

Data protection, human rights and patent law

Beyond copyright, there are important areas of the law that publishers need to consider. Some of these issues have been brought into prominence by the internet, which makes it much easier for us all to look at and check up on what we and others write and publish. This transparency has also made individuals more guarded about their privacy – not only data about themselves (and what they look like), but keeping control of any rights they may have in what they have created.

Protecting personal data

Data protection is subject in the UK to two Acts passed in 1996 and 2003 by which people have a right to control what others do with their personal data, and to insist that it is used only with their 'informed consent'. What are personal data? Your name, address and date of birth are all personal to you, especially when these data are linked. Generally we do not mind giving these details to someone if we want to be sent information or goods. Obviously issues to do with your religious or political belief, medical conditions, financial situation or physical appearance can be highly sensitive and private matters, and ensuring they are kept secure is a key part of data protection.

For publishers, the common situation where data protection needs to be understood is in the gathering of personal data for marketing and promotion purposes. Keeping details of customers and clients does not usually cause any problems, but they must give you the information about themselves freely and know to what purpose you are putting it. Also, they may be interested to know how carefully those data will be looked after, and whether they will be stored for a long time or passed on to others.

Normally, we as customers must opt in and give personal data only by affirming that we agree to the terms, and that we want to be sent information or goods. The process of opting out – telling someone only when you don't want to partake or receive information – is illegal now.

Nor can publishers (or anyone else) use data collected for one purpose for another. Storing names and addresses of scientific researchers to whom publishers then send details about science publications in their field would be an acceptable activity. Mailing them with leaflets about renting cottages in the country for them to do their research in peace and quiet would not.

Personal data about children are especially sensitive, for obvious reasons, and might include their physical appearance. Publishers planning to use photographs of individual children in their publications – pupils working on a maths problem in a classroom, for example – will need to seek permission not only from the school and the teachers involved, but also a parent (or guardian) who must give informed consent if a child of theirs under 16 is going to be shown.

European human rights legislation

Linked to the issue of data protection, particularly concerning what we look like, is the new European legislation on human rights. These rights include those you would expect, such as freedom of speech and access to education. But increasingly they are also being applied to our right to a private space or not having private facts about us made public. In the United States, there are strict privacy laws that on the whole do not apply in the UK. Instead, people who wish to preserve their privacy have sometimes resorted to human rights law to try to conceal facts about themselves from being revealed more widely.

Patents

Strict controls also exist on the use of pictures (photographs or illustrations) of registered brands. Under patent law many manufacturers or owners of valuable brands can register both the product (or service) and the many features that go towards making that brand instantly recognizable. These features may be unique, and can include the name or the colours of the product, a marque or logo (the distinctive Penguin on both the book and the chocolate biscuit), even the typeface or an accompanying jingle or strap line such as, 'The world on time', 'Every little helps', or 'I'm lovin' it'. Certain designs, such as the shape of the Coke bottle, are also protected under patent law.

Worked examples of rates of payment

Fee-based payment

Some kinds of publishing (children's non-fiction, for example) pay contributing writers a fixed one-off fee. For books with several different contributors, each writing separate chapters or sections, the payment of a fee based on the length of the piece or the time taken is a practical and acceptable way of working. How should the amount be calculated, and where should such payments appear in a publisher's accounts?

Rates of payment

Many professional writers work to a standard range of payments based on the numbers of words, usually calculated per thousand. The sum per 1,000 words might be between £150 and £250 (though much lower – and higher! – figures are common). The publisher may have to pay more if the writer is an expert in his or her field, or is required to do the work quickly because there is pressure on a deadline. Some kinds of publishing projects almost always carry a fixed fee. Authors of non-fiction titles for school pupils or children are typically paid a fee for the whole job, and this includes help with finding illustrations or photographs, writing captions, producing a glossary and index, as well as researching and writing the book.

A 32-page 6,000-word book might earn a fee of £1,500 (or £250 per 1,000 words). Normally, fees are paid once only. They can be broken down into staged payments, for example, 25 per cent on signature of the agreement, 50 per cent when the publisher receives an acceptable typescript, and the balance when the additional work (including checking proofs and layout) has been completed. At £100 a day, this is not a large sum of money for 15 days' work, but it is paid regardless of how the book sells when it is published.

But it *is* a one-off fee, and the writer will not normally be paid anything further, even if the title is translated into many different languages. In Table 7.1 a margin has been worked out to show how these fees are included in calculations – and the benefit to the publisher of having to pay the fee only once. The gross margin when (if!) the book reprints can be substantially higher, as one-off costs, including the writer's fee, do not normally recur.

TABLE 7.1

		3,000 copies @ £15 recommended retail price First printing	1,500 copies @ £15 recommended retail price Reprint
Origination costs	Writer's fee	2,500	-
	Art and photographs	2,500	1,500
	Design & typesetting	1,000	-
	Origination	1,250	250
	Total	7,250	1,750
Paper, print and bind costs	Print and bind	3,600	1,980
	Paper	400	200
	Freight	600	300
		4,600	2,480
	Total cost	**11,850**	**4,230**
	Unit cost	*£3.95*	*£2.82*
Sales revenue	1,000 home sales @ 35% discount	9,750	500 @ 35% d/c 4,875
	1,900 export sales @ 60% discount	11,400	1,000 @ 60% d/c 6,000
	(100 gratis)	-	-
	Total revenue	**21,150**	**10,875**
	Costs	11,850	4,230
Margin	Gross Margin	9,300	6,645
		(44%)	*(61.1%)*

Royalty payment

Royalties take the form of a percentage based either on the selling price of the book, or – more commonly with academic and educational books – on the sums received (or 'net receipts') by publishers after discounts to booksellers or retailers. There is no such thing as a 'normal' royalty rate, although many publishers use 10 per cent as a reasonable benchmark.

Royalty rates can vary widely, and with some titles (particularly those with very high start-up and origination costs), a sliding scale is sometimes paid, for example: 5 per cent of 'net receipts' up to a sales level of 3,000, 7.5 per cent up to 6,000, and 10 per cent thereafter. The argument here is that early in a book's lifecycle, the publisher is still trying to recoup its start-up costs and has less margin to share with the author, but once sales have passed a certain level, the rate can increase.

Basis of royalty

Authors of consumer titles, particularly those whose agents negotiate the contract, may demand that royalties are paid on the selling price of their book, or 'recommended retail price'. The problem for publishers is that some sales channels can be serviced only by way of very deep discounts. A chain bookstore that takes large quantities of a lead title, holding stock as well as promoting the book in-store, will demand a discount of well over 50 per cent. Supermarkets and online bookstores demand even deeper discounts.

Advances

Authors who write for a living will expect to be paid a sum upfront for the work they have been contracted to do. An advance is a portion of the royalties that the book will 'earn' for the author, once it is published. This money on account serves two purposes: it is a statement of commitment from the publisher, and it allows authors to cover some of their living costs while they are writing the book.

Many authors of academic and educational books do not write for a living. The books (or contributions to publications such as journal articles) represent an important part of their individual (or their institution's) reputation – even their career advancement – but their main source of income comes from their work as teachers or researchers. Publishers of books for these sectors may have very high start-up or origination costs in the form of artwork and illustrations, and so may not be in a position to pay substantial advances. Advances represent a considerable drain on cash for publishers, particularly if a work takes two to three years to write, trial and publish. As a rule of thumb, it is unwise to pay an advance that amounts to more than half what would be paid in royalties when the first printing has been sold (see example below).

Advances are usually paid in stages – say, 25 per cent on signature of the contract, 25 per cent on delivery of an acceptable and publishable manuscript, and the balance on publication. Authors (or their agents) may demand a larger share upfront, while publishers will try to conserve their cash by paying the largest portion of the advance nearest to the date when revenue starts to come in to cover that advance. A compromise could be a division into equal shares – a third on signature, a third on acceptance, and a third on publication.

Unless forced to by the promise of substantial other income (from broadcasting rights or film options), publishers should resist pressures to pay large advances that run the risk of never being earned. In business terms, this is like locking up sums of money – cash – that could turn out to have no value. Unearned advances will need to be written down in the accounts, and will constitute a loss on the profit and loss account.

Author costs and charges

If a work contains a large number of third-party items for which copyright clearance must be sought and paid for, it is normal for authors to share in both the work of identifying and clearing those permissions, and paying for part of them. Sometimes the publisher and author will agree a budget for text extracts (an anthology of articles or stories, for example). Up to the level of this budget, the publisher may pay for permissions. For extracts that exceed the budget, the author will carry the charge – normally in the form of deductions from his or her royalty earnings. The same principle can apply to photographs: the author may provide some that belong to him or her (at their own expense), but if pictures are licensed from a photographic library, the costs of these may be partly borne by the author.

Most contracts also stipulate that if authors make editorial changes to their work when it is in proof form (as opposed to merely correcting printer's errors) then a ceiling is placed on the cost of those changes – usually 10 per cent of the total typesetting costs. An author who makes changes that cost more than this will be charged, once again by having excesses deducted from royalties.

Shares of subsidiary income

Most licensing agreements between publishers and authors allow the publisher to develop other works based on the original typescript, or to exploit the value of the asset in other ways. These can take the form of adaptations (such as a translation into another language), the re-publishing of an extract in a magazine or periodical (a so-called serial right), or an exploitation in another medium – dramatization, a film or TV option, or the creation of a software product derived from or based on the original work.

The contract will specify the shares of income from these other rights that are to be paid to the author. The split is often 50:50, although in the case of exploitation by way of a broadcast on radio or television, or an option to make a film, a higher proportion – sometimes as much as 90 per cent – is paid to the author. Money received in the form of subsidiary rights income, is remitted at the next accounting period, in addition to royalties owed to the author, and is set against any remaining advance or any expenses the author may have incurred.

Model workings

Table 7.2 contains two examples of a four-year sequence showing an author's royalty payment and shares of other income. Publication takes place at the beginning of Year 2. The book is published at a price of £20 and initially 3,000 copies are printed. In the first example the author is paid a royalty of 10 per cent based on the net sums received by the publisher. The book sells at an average discount of 25 per cent. In the second example, the royalty is based on the recommended retail price.

Permissions

Permissions need to be sought and cleared, and any fees paid, before publication. These costs can be borne entirely by the author, or absorbed into the production cost of the publisher, or shared in some way by author and publisher. Permissions (and fees) may apply to text extracts (prose or poetry); artwork, diagrams and drawings reproduced from an existing source (not necessarily published); photographs (whether commissioned or licensed from a picture library); and web material (whether textual, consisting of images, or a composite mixture).

In the following narrative sequence, the author and publisher are working together to produce an illustrated anthology of literature and non-fiction from a particular region.

Text material

This comprises 20 third-party owned prose extracts of 500–1,000 words and 10 third-party owned poems or poetry extracts of 50–100 lines. For

TABLE 7.2

	Year 1	Year 2	Year 3	Year 4 (reprint 1,500)
1. Royalty based on net receipts				
Sales (unit)	-	2,000	1,000	600
(value)	-	30,000	15,000	9000
Royalty	(10% receipts)	3,000	1,500	900
Advance	(£2,000)	*Earned out*	-	-
Author costs (permissions)	(£1500)	(£500) *still owed*	-	-
Share of other income	-	750 *(serial rights)*	500 *(translation)*	-
Net payment	**(£3,500)**	**250**	**2,000**	**900**
2. Royalty based on selling price				
Sales (units)	-	2,000	1,000	600
(value)	-	30,000	15,000	9,000
Royalty (10% of selling price)	-	4,000	2,000	1,200
Advance	(£2,000)	*(earned out)*	-	-
Author costs (permissions)	(£1,500)	*(covered)*	-	-
Share of other income	-	750 *(serial rights)*	500 *(translation)*	-
Net payment	**(£3,500)**	**1,250**	**2,500**	**1,200**

the prose extracts, permission is granted for five of them at no charge. Of the remaining 15, the breakdown is as follows:

8 @ £100 each	£800.00
5 @ £200 each	£1,000.00
1 @ £500	£500.00
1 @ £750	£750.00
Total	£3,050.00

For the poems and poetry extracts, two are cleared with no fees being charged. Of the remaining eight, the breakdown is as follows:

5 @ £100 each	£500.00
2 @ £200 each	£400.00
1 @ £800	£800.00
Total	£1,700.00
Total extracts	£4,750.00

A budget of £3,000 for all the text extracts has been set by the publisher. However, the author is unwilling to fund the full additional £1,750, so the £750 prose extract is replaced by another piece costing £150 and the £800 poem is replaced by another also costing £150:

The prose budget now stands at	£3,050 - £750 + £150 = 2,450
The poetry budget now stands at	£1,700 - £800 + £150 = £1,050
Total:	£3,500

The author agrees to pay the extra £500 over the budget by having the sum deducted from his first royalty statement.

Artwork

Publishers normally pay for specially drawn artwork, and in our example only two third-party pieces are to be included, one on the back cover. The back cover illustration is charged at £1,000 and the other piece at £250. The publisher agrees to pay both these.

Photographs

The author supplies 100 of his own photographs, but they are of variable quality. The book is designed with space allocations for 50 photographs, and after some disagreements only 15 of the author's pictures are deemed to be of sufficient quality. A professional photographer is commissioned to produce 30 pictures to a specific brief, and is paid £300 for a day's shoot. This cost is borne by the publisher as part of the start-up costs.

The remaining five photographs must come from a picture library, and the rates for these are very high: a fee of £500 per photograph is quoted initially. After a lot of haggling, the library agrees to provide all five for a one-off fee of £1,500. When the picture library discovers that one of the photographs is planned to be used on the cover, they revise the figure back to £2,000. More negotiation follows, and a compromise is reached whereby the author and publisher agree to go halves on the picture library cost, each side paying £1,000 of the total bill.

So the author has agreed to pay £500 towards text extracts and £1,000 towards the cost of the photographs, a total of £1,500. He has been paid £1,000 of a £2,000 advance, so when the second half of the advance is due to be paid on publication, no more money is paid. Indeed, he still 'owes' £500, which will be set against royalties earned from the first year's sales.

Conclusion

The laws surrounding publishing are many and complex, and no one is expecting you to become an expert in them all. Rather, what we are suggesting is that an awareness of how copyright is applied to the business of publishing, the importance of agreeing a clear and mutually acceptable contract, and careful compliance with the use of licences and third-party rights is an essential part of becoming a professional publisher.

When things go wrong and lawyers need to be employed, the likelihood of a calm and amicable settlement of a disagreement has probably disappeared altogether. Disputes can be acrimonious and expensive, and they can do serious damage to your company's reputation. So, our watchword is 'be prepared'. The publisher that uses common sense, takes precautions, asks advice over anything technical, and grasps the basic principles of this chapter should be protected from making expensive mistakes. Prevention is better (and cheaper!) than cure.

Further reading

Benson, C and Jones, H (2006) *Publishing Law*, 3rd edn, Routledge, Abingdon

Davies, G (2005) *Book Commissioning and Acquisition*, 2nd edn, Routledge, Abingdon

Owen, L (2007) *Clark's Publishing Agreements*, 7th edn, Tottel, Haywards Heath

Understanding how rights and permissions work

08

Introduction

Publishers need to discuss and agree with potential authors the way the various rights in the work are going to be dealt with, and whether or not the author is prepared to grant a licence to the publisher to deal only with the volume published right. Each side also needs to agree on how the various secondary or subsidiary rights are to be handled. Many authors are happy to grant all these rights to the publisher – this agreement is sometimes known as an 'all territories, all languages, all media' agreement.

But often the author, or more often his or her agent, will reserve some of these rights because they feel they can exploit these rights more effectively (and perhaps for more money). Perhaps they have better contacts in the world of music, film and the web. They may feel that by leaving them with the publisher, nothing is going to happen. In the end, as with many dealings over rights, it is a question of negotiation. Either way, both parties must agree how (and how much) the author is going to be rewarded and paid, and how any revenue is going to be shared.

Authors and publishers often want to include material in their books whose rights belong to someone else – a third party. The author may want to include extracts from other published works. The publisher may want to include pictures or photographs from other publications, or maps whose copyright may be owned by the Ordnance Survey or another government body. These third-party rights will generally need to be cleared, and permission sought from the relevant rights owners. Some will be hard to track down, and others may demand a fee. The process is not difficult but it can be time-consuming, and is normally best done by someone with time and patience, and a sharp eye for detail.

Selling rights and permissions can bring valuable additional revenue to a publication that might not otherwise survive. Acquiring rights and negotiating third-party permissions can be costly, but may provide long-term benefits to a project. The way these transactions are conducted needs all the skills of a negotiator – one with a good grasp of production practicalities and a sound knowledge and awareness of what the law says. An essential part of this knowledge can be acquired from the first-rate standard work on the subject, *Selling Rights* by Lynette Owen, published by Routledge and currently in its fifth edition.

This chapter has been organized into four sections:

1 the way secondary or subsidiary rights are managed and exploited;
2 the principles behind permissions clearance when it has been agreed to include third-party owned material;
3 how a publisher should protect copyright in the works it publishes, and how permissions granted to third parties are managed and paid for;
4 collective licensing of reprographic rights.

At the end we include examples of calculations covering grouping reprints with rights sales to reduce cost, subsidiary rights payments, permission budgets and pricing, and how advances are earned out.

Subsidiary rights

In some sectors of publishing, subsidiary or secondary rights are rarely sold simply because the work in question does not lend itself to exploitation beyond its original publication in complete volume form. In other sectors, sales of printed copies of the book will not on their own generate enough margin to make the publication viable, so editors and rights managers must try to secure agreed secondary rights deals to contribute to the revenue stream and convince everyone that publication is feasible. An experienced rights manager will be able to visualize what opportunities a new book presents. Editors meanwhile can maximize those opportunities by bearing in mind some simple principles, many of which involve making a book less parochial and thus appealing to a wider more international market.

Territorial and format rights

What kinds of rights are typically sold to generate subsidiary income? The most obvious right is a territorial right. This means selling the rights to a local publisher who will produce and publish the work in its territory, usually exclusively. There are several reasons why this may be better than exporting large quantities of a work from the originating publisher's country. Local publishers will probably be better placed to sell and market the book through their own retail outlets. Customers may recognize and welcome a book published locally, but could be turned off by one that appears to be 'foreign'. Moreover, the price of an imported book (once freight costs have been included) may be much higher than if a local publisher had bought rights and manufactured locally.

In some countries there may be punitively high taxes placed on imported books, or other protective legislation in place. Until recently British (and other publishers of books in the English language) were prevented by law from exporting more than 2,000 copies of any book for sale into the United States. This so-called 'manufacturing clause' of US federal law was a blatant protectionist measure designed to force publishers to do rights deals so that local printers got the work of manufacturing local editions. Its abolition in 1986 was widely welcomed, not only outside the United States.

The importing publisher may welcome the opportunity of adding to its list without any editorial or much production overhead; this may make the deal more lucrative. Meanwhile, the selling publisher may also in the end make more money from a rights deal than from margins on export sales, where books will normally be heavily discounted. We explain the way these calculations work (and how the author receives his or her money) in the worked examples at the end of this chapter.

Territoriality

More recently, trading conditions and terms have changed. European Union law now states that anything available for sale in one territory of the EU (or the European Economic Area) must be equally freely available in any other territory. For example, a Dutch wholesaler importing from the United States a US edition of a book first published in the UK would, in theory, be entitled to sell that edition not only in Holland, but in any EU territory, including back into Britain, thus undermining the integrity of the whole territorial rights system. Publishers have tried to overcome this problem by acquiring licences from authors (or their agents) that make the UK and Europe an exclusive 'home' market. Then, if the author/agent sells the rights independently to a US publisher, that US company is not permitted to sell its edition anywhere in Europe.

For a while Australia introduced a rule that a work not published locally in Australia within 30 days of its being published somewhere else in the world (eg, in the UK or the United States) would not be protected by copyright. The regulation was partly intended to encourage works to be published locally (rather than imported), and also to give book buyers freedom of choice as to where they could buy books. Similar 'parallel importation' rules were introduced in New Zealand, allowing book buyers freedom to buy any edition they liked of a work, without being limited by restrictions that only allowed, say, the British edition of a work in English to be available locally.

Buying books online (at Amazon, for example), also makes the strict preservation of publishers' territorial rights difficult, if not impossible, to apply. In theory, the British Amazon (Amazon.co.uk) is not allowed to supply a US book from a publisher that does not have the rights to sell the work in the UK. Even supposing such a precise interpretation of those rights were made, the buyer could easily go onto the US Amazon site (Amazon.com) and get hold of the book there.

What does all this mean – and does it matter very much? The two conflicting arguments are those of the rights owner (or the licensee, the publisher) and those of the customer. It is clear that customers' expectations have increased thanks to the web: they have become used to getting things quickly, simply and cheaply – even for free. They see territorial restrictions on availability as petty and obstructive. Meanwhile, the publisher sees the integrity and exclusivity of its trading arrangements being undermined and even disappearing altogether. Publishers would argue that these freedoms may make it very difficult for them to recoup the cost of their investment in a new book. Authors may mind less, so long as their books are made as widely available as possible.

Export or rights sales?

British publishers sell large quantities of books direct to English-speaking parts of the world. Some markets will accept copies of a work in its original edition, or the territory may be too small for a local edition to be economically viable. Even in Europe there is a strong market for books in English, especially in Holland and Scandinavia. Here it is a matter of judgement as to whether or not selling stock of the work published in Britain in English will yield more revenue and margin than securing a translation rights deal and having a local publisher produce the book in the local language.

Paperback rights

What other opportunities exist for selling secondary or subsidiary rights in a work? First, we need to consider versions of the whole text produced in facsimile format – in other words, without change. This can cover other editions, the most important one of which is the paperback version. Here there may be two or three formats. A new jacketed hardback of a novel or biography may be seen as expensive (and geared principally to the needs of the library), so publishing new books for the first time in a large paperback format (known as 'C Format') has become a popular (and cheaper) alternative to the hardback. The 'B Format' is the one used for literary fiction or special interest non-fiction versions of an original hardback, and is preferred by up-market imprints such as Vintage and Picador. This is mainly to distinguish titles (and to set a difference in price) from the 'A format' mass-market paperback – the crime thriller or fat romance you buy at the airport for a long flight or for holiday reading.

Originally, paperback publishers such as Penguin and Pan were separate and independent from the established hardback publishers, which in the early days resisted allowing paperback editions to be produced at all for fear that they would undermine their own more lucrative sales. Now what is known as 'vertical grouping' is generally the order of the day.

Publishers such as Random House own a wide variety of imprints, both hardback and paperback, and tend to restrict sales of paperback rights to 'within the family'. This means that a hardback version of a book may be published initially under an imprint such as Jonathan Cape, and a year or so later the same book will appear as a 'B Format' paperback under the Vintage name. For some fiction (such as crime thrillers), the work will go straight from hardback into 'A Format' as a mass-market paperback. Occasionally works will be published simultaneously in both hardback and paperback formats, although publishers will usually leave a gap between editions. This is so that markets (at the higher price) can be fully exploited before the gates are opened to a wider market, one where customers would never spend £20 on a book, but may be happy to part with £6.99.

E-book rights

As we write, the whole issue of e-books and the right to publish them is in the melting pot. Digitized versions of books have been available for at least 10 years, but the machines to read these electronic versions have been crude, clunky and relatively expensive. The Rocket E-book Reader came already loaded with Dostoevsky's *Crime and Punishment*, a version of the Funk & Wagnall dictionary and Lewis Carroll's *Alice's Adventures in Wonderland*. At US$199, its size, weight and rather feeble battery made it unappealing. But now we have the Kindle, Sony's E-Book Reader, and Apple's latest offering, the I-Pad, all allowing us to acquire huge amounts of text and store them on a compact and elegant reader with an attractive screen, typeface and backlight.

Leaving aside the dire warnings that such machines spell the end of the book (no more likely, perhaps, than the advent of television spelling the end of films and cinemas), there are some difficult and still unresolved rights issues to be addressed. Some publishers assumed that selling an e-book was just another way of exploiting a subsidiary right, and that contracts from the 1980s or 1990s (where no mention was made of e-books) left them free to sell e-book rights as if they were an extension of the right they already had to sell audio or broadcasting rights. Recent lawsuits in the United States (in particular the Rosetta case) suggest that the courts regard e-books as a new primary right, not an extension or subsidiary right of the original licence to publish in volume form.

Problems also arise in assessing what to charge for e-book sales and how to calculate the correct share of income that authors should receive. This is especially true when e-books are sold as electronic downloads rather than as a disc in a cover, as if it were merely another version of a book. Some authors have been reluctant to grant these rights to publishers, believing that they may not be in the best position to exploit them. Agents sometimes argue that it would be better to go direct to another producer that will exploit this potential more quickly and more widely. Publishers meanwhile resist this, arguing that to lose the opportunity for selling e-book rights narrows and restricts their ability to recoup their original investment.

Educational and large print

Away from the fevered world of trade and consumer publishing, there are other rights opportunities for making a whole work available in other editions. Sometimes contemporary works of literature are prescribed as set books to be studied for an examination, or as part of a school curriculum. The text may have to be read and a student's understanding of it assessed as part of a qualification. An educational edition of this kind may have additional study notes with summaries of the story, assessments of the main characters or events, and analyses of the key issues. All this may be linked to an exam for which the work has been prescribed. Even though the work may already be available in hardback and paperback, the rights holders may agree that an educational edition constitutes an additional and quite separate market for the book.

For some years, specialist publishers have produced versions of popular books under licence in a large print format for the visually impaired. Visual disability takes many forms other than total blindness, and publishers have been willing over the years to allow editions to be produced in Braille, or other forms. However, these specialist tactile formats can be read by only a small proportion of those with visual impairment.

In 2003, a change in the UK law allowed the visually impaired access to copyright works as a statutory right. This did not mean that publishers were obliged to produce all their books in other formats. The ruling compelled them to allow *access* – which in reality meant making the books they produced available in digital formats such as HTML and XML. This has been relatively simple as far as new books are concerned, but scanning and digitizing extensive backlist titles has proved a lengthy and expensive process. Those championing the cause of the visually impaired have in some cases become impatient and frustrated at the lack of titles available. For all rights transactions directly with those providing for the visually impaired, it has long been an accepted tradition that no payments have to be made for Braille or other versioning technologies.

Translation and adaptation rights

There may be opportunities for translations (of the complete work) into other languages. For publishers that produce works in English, there are both advantages and disadvantages. English is the second most widely spoken and used language in the world (Chinese is number one, Spanish number three). So most British publishers think first in terms of *selling* translation rights. In the UK, the strongest markets for translation are in European territories, with Spanish, French, German and Italian leading the field. The strength of English as a dominant spoken language has made British publishers more reluctant than their European neighbours to *buy* translation rights, although in recent years the detective thrillers of Henning Mankel and Stieg Larsson have made acquiring English-language rights from Swedish authors and publishers a major priority.

Normally, the publisher buying the translation rights to publish the book in its territory in another language will organize and pay for the translation. An important aspect of this process is ensuring that the translation is done accurately, and for both the original author and publisher to be satisfied with it. Some authors will insist in their contract that all deals of this kind are passed for their approval before the deal can go ahead. It is quite common for authors to demand that they see and approve (or have someone check) the translation. A poor translation would probably be judged as an infringement of the author's moral right of integrity.

Simplifying by abridging or condensing

Translation is known as an 'adaptation right', but there are other adaptations that can be made to a work. Students learning a language in school may need a simplified version of a work whose language and grammar would otherwise be too difficult for them to understand. Over many years, the *Readers' Digest* has, as the name implies, issued abridged or condensed versions of literary classics. For those titles out of copyright, no permissions or rights terms need to be agreed, but in other cases the consent of both the publisher and the author (or the author's estate) will need to be granted. A number of authors object strongly to having their work adapted in this way, and refuse permission for their works to be abridged (made shorter by cutting sections but keeping to the original text) or condensed (made shorter by rewriting some parts and omitting or paraphrasing others).

Serial rights

Staying with the print format for the moment, the next opportunities lie in selling the rights to publish extracts from the full work. The most common type of deal will involve serialization of parts of the work in a magazine or newspaper. Sections of a diary by an eminent but notorious politician will probably be snapped up by a Sunday newspaper, usually before publication. This first serial right has the important advantage for the publisher of providing powerful promotion and marketing benefits, with people who have tasted and enjoyed the extracts then wanting perhaps to buy the whole book. Extracts may have a market after publication, too, and these second serial rights can bring in welcome extra revenue.

For publications well outside the publisher's main area of activity, a one-shot periodical right can yield a separate sale and income. A celebrity chef (or his or her agent) might succeed in selling serial rights of his or her new cookery book and autobiography to a Sunday newspaper, but another specialist magazine might include a different extract from the same book describing his or her passion for hang-gliding in detail.

Rights in other media

Audio and dramatization rights

For some trade and consumer titles, there may be audio opportunities to exploit. Straight readings (on CD or as downloads) by one voice of the full text are one market. Readings or dramatizations broadcast on the radio are another. As with print, there are additional rights to be considered for simplifying a work by producing abridged or condensed versions of it. These shorter editions may also be valuable for learners studying the language who need shorter texts or simplified levels of syntax and vocabulary, together with the added benefit of hearing a native speaker demonstrate how the language should be spoken.

Film and TV options

Some very popular books, perhaps with a strong central character, can attract the attention of film and television programme makers and producers. The procedure here is that interested companies bid for an option (often an exclusive one) so that they can spend enough time considering how they might make a film and where they are to get the necessary funds to do so. These options are time-limited, and can be renewed, though once more than one company has asked for an option, the publisher is then in a better place to negotiate and even auction the option. However, very few of these options actually lead into the making of a film or a TV development. The sheer cost of doing so is a major deterrent, as the large number of credits listed at the end of a film might suggest.

Character merchandising rights

For well-known characters (mainly in children's publishing) there are opportunities for selling merchandising rights. Sometimes a character may have been made familiar to children through a film or television series. But the character needs to be strong and well-known enough in the first place for merchandising opportunities to be worthwhile. Disney publications are an example, although that corporation does not license its characters outside its own company. A lot of revenue was made originally by Britt Alcroft when she acquired the merchandising rights to the Revd William Awdry's *Thomas the Tank Engine* series. Roger Hargreaves' *Mister Men* books are another good example.

The exploitation of merchandising rights can take many forms and bring in substantial revenue. Pens, pencils, stationery, brands of yogurt or drinks, gifts and clothing or sportswear – the list is as long as the imagination of the merchandiser will stretch. Private railway companies running heritage or tourist lines sometimes put on *Thomas* events that appeal to children travelling in the steam trains. Putting a replica of Thomas in the form of a larger than life-size face on the smoke box of the steam engine involves the payment of a substantial fee to the present owners.

Digital rights

Apart from e-books, where a whole work is made available in electronic form, a key group of rights that have developed strongly in the last few years have been digital rights, usually to make the work or parts of it available in electronic form. Initially the means of delivery was the cassette tape or, more recently, the CD tucked into a flap at the end of a book, but increasingly websites are offering content to download.

These e-versions of works often take the form of supplementary material to enhance or add on to the original print publication. Rights to exploit works in this way are still difficult to define precisely and even harder to give a commercial value. This is because there is no easy way of measuring the value of the use, and no easy method for 'counting' units of sale. Licences are usually negotiated through one (or more) of these criteria: measuring the number of people at a site and estimating the frequency with which they will access it; stipulating a time period such as a year or three years; or counting the number of hits (or downloads) that authorized users make on the site. Sometimes a combination of these charging mechanisms is used.

A further complication arises when there is no agreement on how much should be charged for this additional material – or whether in fact it should be free, as part of a promotion campaign, or because an evangelical or propaganda motive lies behind the publication. In this last example, Creative Commons principles or licences may apply (see page 223 in Chapter 7). Even when the process is meant to be commercial, tracking and charging for these activities has proved difficult, making it hard to apply any revenue collected to the relatively high development costs of digital or e-versions of printed books.

Shares of revenue from rights sales

The author's contract will specify the number and nature of the subsidiary rights granted to the publisher, and that will define the extent of the licence the author has granted to the publisher. A key part of this section of the agreement will specify what share of any revenues from subsidiary rights sales each party should get. It is unusual for an author to receive less than half the proceeds from a rights sale. For authors not concerned with these rights, or for books where the opportunity for rights exploitation is limited, this default position of an equal or 50:50 share will readily be accepted by both sides.

In many contracts, especially those for trade and consumer market books, the author will get a bigger proportion of the total, right up to 90 per cent of any revenue from a rights sale. A rate of 75 per cent to the author is common when a book is serialized in a magazine or newspaper. So, while £20,000 for a serialization deal in a Sunday paper sounds good, bear in mind that the publisher will get only £5,000 from this amount.

Often authors who are paid a large advance for their work will depend on lump sums from these subsidiary rights sales to 'earn out' the advance they have been paid. However, once new money is due to authors they will be anxious to receive prompt payment for these transactions. For publishers that settled royalty accounts only once a year, it was sometimes possible for authors to have their share of a rights sale credited to their account in mid-January of one year, and not to receive the money for it until March or April of the following year, some 15 months later. Many newer contracts specify that authors should have any lump sums of this kind over a particular amount remitted to them within 30 days.

Collective licensing of reprographic rights

Authors will not receive from the publisher their share of any money due to them under collective licensing schemes. This will normally be sent direct to authors from the agency or collecting society that acts on their behalf. In the UK, the Authors Licensing and Collecting Society distributes this money. Publishers receive their share of this revenue direct from a body such as the Publishers Licensing Society. The way collective licensing rights are managed and administered is explained more fully towards the end of this chapter.

Methods of making rights sales

To clarify the way we describe some of these methods for selling rights, we refer to two parties: the selling publisher, which normally initiates the process and has authority or a licence to sell the rights in question; and the buying publisher, which is looking to buy a licence (possibly an exclusive one) to exploit the right in its territory. The method chosen for completing a rights sale for a whole book will often be determined by the extent of illustrations in the work, and the opportunity each side has for buying cheap print services in its own market. Sometimes the method will be determined by the selling publisher's need to tie together a number of deals with a reprint for its local edition: this may make substantial savings in cost.

Licence deal

A common way of agreeing a rights deal is to offer a simple licence to publish. This will define the extent of territory being offered, possibly not beyond the publisher's own country boundaries; whether or not the book is to be translated and into which language(s); and details to specify how much is going to be paid, and when (and how often) the buying publisher must report on sales and remit payment, sometimes against an agreed advance.

Film deal

The selling publisher will often provide nothing physical to help the buying publisher manufacture the work. Sometimes raw production material, such as film or digital files, will be supplied at cost so that the buying publisher can use these files rather than creating new ones and adding to both time and expense. A film deal, as it is often called (even when digital files are supplied), allows the buying publisher to make changes to the text and to edit or even substitute photos or other pictures that may not be suitable for the market.

Once any changes have been made, the buying publisher arranges to have the work printed and copies delivered to its warehouse. The publisher will pay a royalty on receipts after discount from local sales, keep account of sales and royalties earned, and prepare accounts and make payments to the selling publisher once or twice a year. The selling publisher will then need to share this income with the author, with the split of revenues as set out in the contract.

Bound copies or sheets deal

For books that are heavily illustrated or which contain a lot of full-colour images, it may make more practical sense (and save money) if the selling publisher handles all stages of manufacture, and supplies the buying publisher with either bound copies of the book in its edition, or flat printed sheets of the work so that the local publisher can bind the books with materials or in a style that may be specific to the country in question, or required by its libraries. Manufacturing rights sales of this kind require some procedures that if not followed carefully would render the deal uneconomic.

Under this process, the selling publisher supplies a copy of its (and the author's) book, together with film (or digital files) of the printed text, normally translated into the local buying publisher's language. The selling publisher may be planning a reprint for its market, and it may have more than one foreign customer wanting to buy copies of the book. If the work in question contains a substantial number of four-colour illustrations, the printer will be asked to print the whole print run – the reprint and the foreign editions – together: but the printing will be in two stages, and at this first stage only the illustrations will be printed.

If you look at colour books that have been published in many editions and several languages, you will notice that, on the whole, the text and illustrations are kept apart – the black print of the text matter always appears on a plain white background, separate from the pictures. The designer may think that the original book would look better if the text were printed over the illustrations, or even 'reversed out', that is, appearing as white text against the darker background of the illustration. With books that have the potential to be published in several languages, the designer is likely to be over-ruled, or will know to avoid this in the first place. Changing text and putting in translated words that are an integral part of the colour artwork or photograph involves considerable extra expense, as the alterations have to be made to each of the four colour files separately.

Instead, publishers and printers work with what is known as the 'fifth black working'. All four colour elements of the illustrations are printed together: cyan, magenta, yellow and black. The black of the text, however, is printed separately – and this printing can be stopped so that the text of each of the languages in the composite print run can be put in at the right moment. The full-colour print run might be of 10,000 copies, and the sheets will then be put through the machine again to incorporate 3,500 copies in English, 2,500 copies in Spanish, 1,500 copies in French, 1,000 copies each for Danish and Norwegian, and 500 copies in Bahasa Malay. The way this works (and saves costs for all parties concerned) is shown at the end of this chapter.

Printing the 10,000 copies together will give a better unit cost than if each of the six language editions had been printed separately. The selling publisher will then mark up this cost (sometimes to double the basic cost), and add in provision for the author's royalty and the freight costs for shipping the books or sheets to the buying publisher's warehouse. This quoted price has to be acceptable to the buying publisher, which will know the highest acceptable retail price that the book can be sold at. Both parties – buying and selling – have to agree that there is enough margin for each of them to make the deal worthwhile.

Co-edition publishing

The same principle of printing different versions of a book at the same time applies in the world of co-editions. This is a complex and formerly lucrative market where the benefits of developing and printing several editions of essentially the same work for a world (or at least a developed world) audience brings substantial savings to the process and ends up with a price that seems affordable to a mass market, but still gives an acceptable margin to the participating publishers.

The origins of this market lie in the increasing availability in the 1960s of good cheap full-colour photolitho printing, particularly in what was then Eastern Europe. A pioneer in this field was Paul Hamlyn – both the man and the company – and he made a fortune by recycling the content of books and magazines, or reprinting old ones, in the well-established fields of cookery and gardening, finding an international range of customers for them, and ordering long print runs at rock-bottom cost. He also acquired rights to many of the images contained in the books, thus removing the need to clear permission for each new or recycled use of the content.

Publishers and their partner packagers have developed this market substantially in those fields that 'travel' – that is to say, that can appeal to a wide audience through not containing too many local or cultural elements that would make them unrecognizable or unattractive to readers in other countries. Food and wine, fine art, ancient history, natural history, planets and the universe, most scientific topics – these are the subjects that lend themselves well to co-edition publishing. Local customs, tourist destinations, orienteering and walking tend to be too specific to a location to have much appeal outside the country or region described. *Long Distance Trails in the Rockies* would have little co-edition appeal to publishers or their readers in Australia.

Children's publishing also benefits from the economies of simultaneously producing international co-editions. The re-telling of classic fairy stories, myths and legends is one aspect of this market. Some of the 'non-fiction' topics that work for adults – ancient history, space and wildlife – can also appeal to several international markets at the same time.

Let us consider an author who is commissioned to write a book with the title *My Best Book of Trains*, published by Kingfisher in a long series of 32-page books with the titles '*My Best Book of ...*'. The author starts by submitting outlines and artwork briefs for 15 agreed 'spreads' (double pages). These are discussed and refined with the book's designer and editor before the artist is commissioned. Once the page layout and design have been agreed, the author must then write an exact number of words to fit that overall design. After the main text has been written, captions for the pictures will be needed, and a glossary and an index composed.

Typically, an author with this commission will be paid a flat one-off fee, depending on the final length of the book. A figure of £1,500 is normal: £250 after the spreads have been approved, £1,000 on completion of the writing, and £250 once the captions, glossary and index have been finished. Now the publisher will try to sell rights in this book to as many other countries as possible, particularly if care has been taken to make it international in content. There should be editions in several European languages and perhaps later in Chinese, Thai or Tswana. The author will not be paid any more money for these various editions, and will not be consulted about them, or about any re-use of his or her original work.

Cultural issues in children's non-fiction

With children's co-editions, there can be problems in what is culturally acceptable to different audiences. A book for 10–12-year-old school pupils about life in present day Italy might include a section on family life. A British publisher or packager producing this title would recognize and probably want to include the portrayal of Sunday lunch in the home – several generations of the same family sitting round a large table outside, eating and drinking while protected from the sun by large umbrellas. Some of the men would probably be smoking cigarettes, and there would be a large bottle of wine on the table, with everyone drinking – certainly the women and possibly the children too. Such a depiction would be quite unacceptable to schools and libraries in many parts of the world where alcohol and tobacco are forbidden. Even in the southern United States, strict religious beliefs would mean teachers and librarians could strongly object to such a scene, and as a result forbid adoption of the book in schools.

Changing economic factors

The main difference between co-edition publishing and selling bound copies or sheets as part of a rights deal is that for co-editions, the editorial and development work is done in advance. It is usual for one partner in the process to take the lead and undertake the pre-press work, but costs may be shared from the outset, and agreeing on content can be the subject of lengthy debate. Technology has enormously helped the process of developing international co-editions now that very large digitized files of information (including colour artwork) can be sent back and forth with no time delay. On-screen editing and designing also mostly removes the need for 'wet proofs' – printed sheets of the pages produced to check content and quality. Printing often takes place now in the Far East – China, Singapore and Korea, for example – and shipping times to whichever market is buying the edition remain a factor: does losing time this way reduce or even remove the value of single-run printing?

The same technology that has benefited the co-edition market is also killing it. It is now possible to produce quite short print runs in full colour where both the quality and the cost are acceptable to the market. The costs and delay of shipping large quantities of books halfway round the world are beginning to look poor value when compared to doing the same job on a more modest scale at home – to say nothing of ethical issues to do with carbon footprints, global warming and the like. There are still significant savings to be made by concentrating the *development* of large-scale international projects in one place, if not the manufacturing, and companies like Toucan Books and Brown Partworks still make a good living from producing multi-volume encyclopaedias and other major reference works for both an adult and a children's audience.

Besides, the book is no longer necessarily either the starting or the finishing point for any rights sale. The digital file, produced electronically, stored in a secure database that is accessible to end readers as well as to customers, or partner-publishers, and requiring no storage space whatsoever, may be a pattern for the future in some markets. The idea of the virtual warehouse – no printed books, merely a catalogue of what is available digitally and on demand – has been discussed for about 10 years now. The death of the book may have been exaggerated by those dazzled by the capability of technology rather than its effectiveness, but printed sheets in bound covers must join a much broader range of media, or delivery platforms, and it is unlikely that manufacturing will form nearly as much a part of rights business in the future as it has in the recent past.

Trading in rights

Speed and ease of communication and the ability to send large amounts of data quickly and cheaply over the internet have revolutionized the way rights business can be conducted. Printing large quantities of co-editions in one place and shipping books round the world may be replaced in time by local short-run printing, once the economics of print-on-demand have been shown to work commercially for the parties involved.

In the meantime, how do international rights partners meet and establish their basis for trading partnerships? Surely the same technology that allows sending digital (or virtual) copies of publications anywhere in the world can be applied to the business of forming commercial relationships and setting up business deals?

Does this not mean the end of the book fair? The first great international book rights fair was established in Frankfurt in 1946. For many years, this European city played host to the biggest and most successful book fair in the world – bearing in mind that the 'world' of rights buying and selling was limited to what we might now call western (or 'northern') countries – Western Europe and North America. Eastern Europe and most of Asia, Africa and Latin America were excluded. The giant potential of India, Russia and above all China was largely ignored. Successful book fairs soon established themselves in Bologna (children's books), London, Guadalajara (Mexico and the whole of Latin America), and both Delhi and Beijing. Book Expo in Chicago or New York established an important base in North America.

Since the 1980s the situation has changed. With the end of the Soviet Union in 1989 and the unification of Germany in 1990, eastern Europe and central Asia have emerged as important markets for rights business, as has much of the rest of south and south-east Asia. Once China joined the Berne and Universal Copyright Conventions in 1992, European and US publishers began cautiously to undertake rights selling (and to a lesser extent buying) in China.

The truth is that while technology can speed and ease the process of bringing rights deals to fruition, there is nothing really to match the importance of meeting potential clients and partners face to face, getting to know them, and forming professional relationships based on mutual trust and shared experience. As with much of publishing, nothing can replace this human element – and book fairs thus continue to flourish, even though to a cynical outsider they sometimes seem to emphasize the social side of receptions and parties at which eating and drinking feature almost more than the business side of the occasion.

Besides, many fairs contain a cultural rather than just a commercial element, with authors reading their works or launching new titles, publishers showcasing their finest titles, booksellers trading in new and second-hand books, and members of the public visiting to see and marvel at the sheer number and range of new publications.

Book fairs in Paris and Buenos Aires are not predominantly rights fairs, while those in Cape Town and (in happier times) Harare, Zimbabwe, were showcases for new writers and illustrators, and almost a national statement of individual identity to try to redress the balance in international rights business – or rather, its essential imbalance. Very few rights sales are made from the developing to the developed world. The reasonable complaint from publishers in Africa, Latin America and South Asia is that rights traffic tends to be almost entirely in one direction.

Conducting business at book fairs

There are those who look with envy at the rights manager preparing to set off for an international book fair, but the reality is not so glamorous. The keynote to a successful fair is preparation. This first involves establishing a clear idea of which titles (new and backlist) have the potential for rights sales, and verifying carefully which rights and licences you have at your disposal to exploit – either from your authors or from other publishers.

Then comes the expensive task of booking a display stand before the deadline, and sending out sample copies for display, as well as ensuring that adequate publicity and promotional material has been dispatched, and being sure your company has been correctly and fully entered into the online or printed catalogue for exhibitors and visitors. Dummies of future titles made up as books or BLADs (brief layout and design booklets) also need to be prepared.

Next comes the important task of making appointments with key contacts in companies well in advance – who do you want to see? Will their schedules fit with yours? Should you go to their stand and see them, or invite them to come to your stand and see you? Should you leave time to explore the fair in order to find new contacts and get a feel for what publishers are doing in other parts of the world?

A rights manager's main task is to sell rights, and in larger companies he or she will be accompanied by a publishing or editorial colleague whose principal task is to buy rights or acquire licences. If the companies you are hoping to see offer both opportunities – for you to sell rights and for your colleague to buy them – further careful co-ordination of timetables and schedules will be needed.

For publishers in countries whose first language is English, and whose books are published mainly in English, the principal objective will be to sell translation rights to publishers in other countries. There may be opportunities to sell territorial rights to other English-speaking territories, and to offer digital as well as print rights, so long as these are at your disposal.

If you don't make adequate preparations, it can become a nightmare of time management – especially if you do not carefully establish what your main priorities are. First-time visitors to book fairs who go ill-prepared often come away reeling with a mass of vague impressions, punch-drunk with the sheer scale of the event, the huge number of exhibits and visitors and the overwhelming sense of there being too much to take in.

Experienced rights professionals try to make appointments every half hour from 9 till 6, with an hour for lunch. If every slot is filled during a three-day fair, that allows 48 appointments, but no time (apart from that hour at lunch) for exploring or – as any rights person will tell you – the happy chance of making a lucky encounter.

Selling rights involves three basic stages – first, offering a publisher that is really interested in a title an option: probably an exclusive opportunity to consider a title for a short fixed period of time. To reach a decision, the terms of the deal and costs of film or of bound copies need to be provided and, ideally, rights managers have these ready prepared.

For major or popular titles, it may be necessary to offer first, second and even third options. Clearly, it is essential to keep full details (electronically, ideally) of your meetings, plus the exact order and timing of any options. You may need to provide additional information or costings after the fair, and negotiate deals if you have more than one potential customer. It may even come to auctioning a title to a range of bidders.

The final stage of concluding a rights deal is to produce a contract, get the party to agree the terms and to sign it, and to issue an invoice for any initial down payment, usually in the form of the first stage of an advance. These three stages may take some time, and meeting a new client at a book fair will sometimes not lead to a concluded deal until the following year. Established clients may reach final agreement much more quickly.

With established rights relationships, maintaining the contacts, checking that accounts have been supplied and payments made, and constantly keeping alert for new opportunities makes the business of rights selling a continuous process – rewarding, if you have the mind for detail, but frustrating when deals do not come to fruition. For companies, it is worth remembering that most subsidiary rights income is net income – in other words, it is not subject to overhead costs, and can be added straight to the bottom line of contribution or operating profit.

Identifying and clearing permissions

Copyright in a novel or work of fiction that contains no references to or extracts from anything written or produced by someone else will lie entirely with the author of the novel. If the work really does contain no elements belonging to a third party, then the person or department with responsibility for identifying, clearing and paying for permission to use such items will have no work to do.

But what if the author has used as the title for his or her book some words from a famous song? And what would we think if a well-known catch phrase from a television comedy programme was placed on the dedication page, or epigraph, of the same book? This section of this chapter is designed to alert everyone – author, editor, publisher, web designer – to the importance of knowing which items may need the permission of the rights owner if they are to be included in your book.

Text permissions

If you or your author want to include a substantial extract from another publication, the chances are you will need to seek the rights owner's permission and you may have to pay a fee. There are many myths surrounding the need to clear permissions. Some people say it's all right to use fewer than 400 words or less than 25 per cent of the book. Others claim that using material for educational use or in scholarly research is acceptable. People use the phrases 'fair dealing' and 'fair use' as if they were interchangeable, and authors often assume things on the web are free, or even free of copyright.

The truth as we saw in the last chapter is that a rights owner has the exclusive right to authorize (or not) the use of any substantial part of his or her work. So if the work is still 'in copyright' (in other words, the author died less than 70 years ago), and the part you want to use is 'substantial', then it would be wise to seek the rights owner's permission. Publishers and others have tried over many years to define what a 'substantial' part of a work actually is, but it has proved difficult, as the judgement must be as much a qualitative one as a quantitative one.

Fair dealing and fair use

In the previous chapter we tried to define what is meant by fair dealing, and to show how what was initially a copyright exception found in academic and scholarly research has passed, in a limited way, into the realm of publishing. The main difference is that the single copy needed for a researcher has become the multiple copies of a published book or journal. The main similarity is that to be 'fair', use of other people's work must be for reference – for *criticism* and *review,* as it were – in support of the author's principal argument. The term 'fair use' is the one used in US law. Generally it offers a broader range of exceptions than 'fair dealing', especially if the extract is for educational use. Care needs to be taken that the wider range of exceptions available in the United States does not somehow cross to the UK with the assumption that the definitions are in some way equivalent.

So how do we judge when a piece that one of our authors wants to include in a book is or is not 'substantial'? Some guidelines were drawn up in 1981 by the Society of Authors and the Publishers Association. They suggest that up to 400 words of prose, or 40 lines of poetry, so long as these do not constitute more than 25 per cent of the whole work, can be quoted without permission or the need to pay a fee. However, there are major risks in using this numerical formula, mainly because an item that may be thought insubstantial in one context could easily be considered substantial in another. The best way to proceed is to make a judgement based on what constitutes the essence or substance of a piece of text.

One line of a poem by Philip Larkin (who died in 1985) may be deemed 'substantial', and the publisher (Faber & Faber) may ask for a high fee. The opening chord of the Beatles' 1964 hit 'A Hard Day's Night' would be instantly recognized by most people and could well also be considered 'substantial'. So what guidelines should a professional publisher work to?

The first thing to clarify is that we are normally talking only about text, as it is usually impossible to decide what an insubstantial part of a painting or a photograph could be – surely, cutting or cropping a photo would always involve taking a substantial part of it. To decide in which cases text extracts can be used under the fair dealing exception, we need to return to the words *criticism* or *review*. The most common accepted use of fair dealing is when a scholarly writer is building up an argument, and wants to illustrate or underline key points with reference to another published writer.

Examples of what is 'fair'

Imagine you were writing a book or journal article about the way countries are governed. The purpose of the book could be historical, political or social, or a combination of all those approaches. Let us assume that much of the piece will be devoted to the differences between democracy and autocracy, and the way republican rather than monarchist regimes have emerged, with royalty often becoming merely symbolic. Britain's move over many years from the rule of an all-powerful monarch to a democratically elected parliament would probably feature. You might want to cite something written by George Orwell (who died in 1950) given that he made quite a study of the ways countries are governed:

> England is the most class-ridden country under the sun. It is a land of snobbery and privilege, ruled largely by the old and silly.

These 24 words are taken from a three-part article called *The Lion and the Unicorn*. Orwell wrote this and Secker & Warburg published it in 1941. Prefaced by the words 'As Orwell wrote,' this is a perfect example of fair dealing, so long as the source is fully and properly acknowledged. Yet consider these rather better-known words:

> All animals are equal, but some animals are more equal than others.

This extract is of course from *Animal Farm*, also by George Orwell, published in 1945. It consists of only 12 words, exactly half the number of the first extract. Yet, it is a much more substantial part of *Animal Farm* than the lines about class and snobbery were of *The Lion and the Unicorn* – indeed, the phrase has passed into public mythology, and is the very essence of that book. Now imagine you are compiling a gift book of famous sayings from the 20th century, full of wise and witty statements of famous people, the kind of thing that makes the reader say, 'My word, that's clever (or funny); I wish I'd thought of that!'

For two reasons, if you were to include that short piece from *Animal Farm* in your book of famous sayings, it could never be considered as fair dealing. As we have seen, the words are the very essence of *Animal Farm*. The second reason is that the extract is not being used for *criticism* or *review*: the whole point of a book of famous sayings is that it will include substantial pieces which, taken together, constitute enough value in their own right for people to decide they want to buy the book. That 'value' belongs to the creative originality of George Orwell, and permission must be asked of the Estate of Eric Blair (Orwell's real name), and his publishers, Secker & Warburg (now part of Random House).

So, judging what is and is not fair dealing depends on a qualitative judgement of what is substantial, not just in percentage or numerical terms. The purpose (or value) of the publication in which the extract will appear is another crucial factor. So, too, is the position in which the extract is to appear: using words embedded in the main narrative of a book may be acceptable. Putting the same words on the cover or the dedication page may make the use more prominent and thus more 'valuable'. Care needs to be taken if you want to alter the wording of an extract, or cut sections out of it. Both these actions might infringe the moral right of integrity of the author. In most cases, the exact wording and position of a text permission should be approved by the rights owner.

Artwork and fine art permissions

If your author has found an image in a book or on a website that is drawn artwork, commissioned by the original publisher, it may not be immediately clear who the rights owner is. Often illustrators are required to assign copyright in the reprographic rights of their work to the publisher, in which case the publisher will need to grant permission. The same would not be true for a famous children's book illustrator who was also the book's author. In this case the agreement of both the artist and the publisher will be needed, although it is usually best to start by approaching the publisher. Even if it cannot speak for the rights of the author/artist, you should be able to contact that person through the publisher.

There are some exceptions to this need to seek permission. The International Association of Scientific, Technical and Medical publishers (STM) has drawn up a protocol that allows member publishers to use each other's basic factual or scientific drawings or diagrams without special permission (or paying a fee) – there are only so many ways of depicting the way the human eye works, or how the stamen of a flower grows.

If your author wants to include an example of contemporary fine art, care needs to be taken that all 'interested parties' in the rights chain have given their consent. For a painting or sculpture created by an artist whose works are still in copyright, it may be necessary to seek the consent of the artist (or his or her estate), the owner of the piece of art, who may have loaned it to the gallery where it is displayed, and the photographer whose picture you are using. Since 1989, photographers have had the same full rights protection as other creators; the position on earlier photographs is not so straightforward.

Permissions for photographs

The copyright position on photographs is not quite the same as for other creative works. In the UK at the time the 1956 Copyright Act became law, rights to reproduce a photograph were often controlled by the owner of the negative, bearing in mind that a long time ago those negatives were in the form of heavy glass plates, and difficult to move around. Between 1957 and 1989 (when the 1988 Copyright, Designs and Patents Act became law), the person who commissioned the photograph was usually the rights owner. It is only since 1 August 1989 that copyright in a photograph has belonged to the photographer. So it is quite important when clearing permission for use of photographs that you can establish *when* the photograph was actually taken.

If your author finds photographs in a book or on a website that he or she wants to include in a book, the same procedure for clearing permission applies as that described above for artwork, except that the rights owner may be the commissioner, not the photographer, depending on the date the picture was taken. Frequently, publishers source photographs from picture agencies or photo libraries that will make it clear what rights they are able to grant to the publisher. These will normally be in the form of a non-exclusive licence, specifying the extent of the use and restricting re-use to reprints based on total print-runs provided to the agency. You (or your authors) may be tempted by 'free' sites that appear to offer standard photos for use freely in publications. Although such sites do exist, many will allow 'free' use of their photographic images only for personal reference or private use – and those definitions would not cover the act of publishing. It is important that you check carefully the terms and conditions for using these images, even if they appear to be long and boring and printed in very small type.

Some publishers have found commercial picture libraries increasingly restrictive and expensive and have instead commissioned photographers to take pictures to their requirements, always ensuring that the reprographic right to publish the photographs has been assigned to the publisher. This may prove cheaper than paying repeat fees to agencies, assuming that the picture you want is not available on a genuinely free site.

Moral rights in photographs

Artists and photographers have moral rights in their work, just as authors do. You need to ensure their works are credited and their moral right of paternity asserted. Problems can arise if you decide to crop or minimize a picture, perhaps to fit it into an available space. Changing a colour picture into a black and white version, or providing a background colour tint to a black and white photograph – all these might constitute an infringement of the creator's moral right of integrity.

Sometimes publishers will want to commission an illustrator to draw artwork or a picture that is based on an existing illustration or photograph. Great care needs to be taken not to copy any distinctive detail too faithfully. The original owner of the copied artwork might argue that such direct and detectable copying was an infringement of copyright.

An educational publisher produced a book on how to play a particular sport, and an artist was commissioned to do the pictures. He used as a source another book about the sport that contained photographs of the various moves and actions. These were generic and approved by the sport's regulatory body; unfortunately, the artist copied a distinctive feature on one of the player's shorts – a thin white stripe between two black stripes. The rights owner of the original book noticed and sued – successfully – for breach of copyright. The moral of the story is that exact copying of a picture could be an infringement of copyright, so care needs to be taken to disguise or alter the source to avoid detection.

Permissions for film and TV extracts

As this section of the chapter progresses, we are getting into more and more difficult fields where it can be hard if not impossible for authors or publishers to get permission. If you wanted to use a still photograph on a book cover taken from a television soap opera, permission would almost certainly be refused. The reason would not be the intransigence of the television company; more likely the problem would lie in the fact that such a picture contained many images (and recognizable actors) all of which might be protected by copyright (in performing as well as creative rights).

Once a work has been presented in multimedia form – a television programme, a cinema movie or a DVD, for example – it is likely there will be many embedded copyrights within it. Classic films or episodes from a television serial will contain dozens of rights owned by a wide variety of 'interested parties', all of whom may have a separate claim to rights in the work: the author, writer of the screenplay, composer of the accompanying music, actors and musicians with performing rights, the television or film company that made the series, even the location where the programme was filmed. So the company cannot give blanket permission for all these rights as it may itself have been granted narrow or restrictive usage rights when it made the film.

Some producers of news programmes or factual features on television may be in a better position to grant permission, and may look favourably on requests for re-use of minimal parts of the original. If that re-use is for educational purposes, the chances of success improve still further. Similar exceptions may be granted by online newspapers as well. It is always worth exploring websites to see what is and is not possible, as there are wide variations in the attitude of rights owners in this field.

Permissions for music and software

The difficulties here are considerable because, as with film and TV permissions, there may be embedded rights and multiple rights owners. There are of course both creative and performing rights in music. Both the composer of the music and the writer of the lyrics will have creative rights in a work, and the performers – instrumentalists, singers, performers, conductors – may all have rights that need checking and clearing. Since the 1996 EU Software Directive, the coding of a software program as well as the output you see on the screen has been determined as a 'literary work', and thus protected as much by copyright as the game or activity you see when you download the software.

Clearing permissions in a digital age

The process of identifying and clearing permissions has been made easier in some ways by the speed and depth of digital search technology. It may have become easier to find things you want, but that does not mean finding rights owners and getting their permission is any more straightforward. Besides, just as it has become easier to find things, so it has become easier for others to find you if by mistake you use something for which permission has not been given. The internet is a great spy, so compliance with correct procedures has become even more important.

Some publishers delegate the whole job of third-party rights clearance to their authors, insisting that if they plan to include such items they must find the rights owner and get the necessary authority. There are risks in doing this, as inexperienced authors may not be rigorous enough in checking out rights owners and can even assume permission is not needed in cases where it is. A wiser method might be to get all authors to identify third-party material and for the publisher or a freelance permissions person to undertake the necessary work in contacting rights owners and negotiating permission. Either way, a proper record must be kept of each permission granted (an e-mail exchange will do) so that the rights trail is complete and an imaginary audit (or actual challenge) can be safely and fully answered.

For anthologies or collections there may be budgetary issues to deal with as well. A limit might be set on the cost of permissions, and expensive items might have to be dropped in favour of ones that stay within the budget. Sometimes the author or anthologizer will be given responsibility for this budget, and given freedom to choose pieces up to the set limit. If the author wants to go over that limit, the permission costs may be set against his or her royalty account, and paid off as and when the published book earns royalties.

Avoiding trouble

The same kind of warranties and indemnities that should be sought from authors when drawing up a contract for a new book should be in place for any third-party items you include in the book. Like a virus that can corrupt a whole software system on your computer, liability for mistakes, copyright infringement and misuse of personal data can all cause problems that will be tiresome and time-consuming to sort out, and may be expensive – both literally, to your budget and costs, and metaphorically to your reputation.

The most common areas of concern are those where copyright is infringed or material plagiarized from another copyright work, and issues to do with personal data. Permissions to use photographs of children can be very difficult, especially if you are not sure that you have the consent of the individuals involved or of their parents if the children are younger than 16. Sometimes the conflict is between people's human right to withhold facts and details about their private life and the public's right to know about those details.

If a businessman spends time with prostitutes and gets them to dress up in fascist uniforms – is he less able to do his job because of this pastime? And should a sports personality who has an affair with another player's wife be allowed to stop a newspaper from publishing the facts? It is this conflict between our wish to have a right of privacy, and what could be called 'fair comment on a matter of public interest'.

Publishers need to be on their guard against these sensitive issues, even though in a picture of a recognizable individual, whether a painting or a photograph, it is more likely that the rights of the painter or the photographer will prove to be the important ones. Bear in mind too that taking a photograph from or in private property may be illegal because the photographer has had to trespass in order to secure the picture.

Publishers wanting to make incidental use in artwork or a photo of a registered brand would not normally need specific permission from the owner. A street scene with shop fronts and advertising hoardings would be acceptable. Once the use becomes specific – just one product – or comparative (X is better than/more popular than Y), then you will find patent and brand owners become protective and may be reluctant to grant permission, or they will demand unreasonably large fees.

Making value judgements in text is dangerous too. Captions like 'Supermarkets are killing the livelihood of small shopkeepers' under a picture of a well-known supermarket brand, or 'Burgers contain a lot of fat and sugar' under a named brand of a burger outlet should be avoided. In the second example, 'a lot of' is a subjective imprecise phrase, while the words 'fat and sugar' these days bring with them the implication that these substances are bad for you. Generally, rights and patents experts will encourage you to 'pluralize' and 'generalize' by using lots of different examples of a product (incidental use) or avoiding actual brand names altogether – colas, crisps and chocolates rather than Pepsi, Walkers and a Mars bar.

Over the lifetime of a book, people may want to use even shorter extracts as quotes in another book, and these permissions can be another valuable source of revenue. However, the cost of administering dozens of very small permission licences can too often exceed any revenue generated.

Assessing risk in uncleared permissions

What happens when either the author or the publisher cannot make contact with the rights owner? There are some who believe that a couple of e-mails and a follow-up phone call should be enough, but the decision to include third-party material without permission needs more care than that. First, we need to distinguish between a rights owner who cannot be traced or whose identity is not known, and one who just does not reply to our repeated requests. In the second case, a court might rule that 'no reply' is tantamount to 'no' – a refusal, in other words, even though a silent one.

In the first example, it is important to keep a full record of how hard you have tried to find the rights owner. A journal record of e-mails sent, failed phone calls made, even keeping the envelopes of any letters returned with 'unknown' or 'gone away' written on them – all these would help in mitigation, should problems arise later. Some publishers even go so far as to put some money aside to pay rights owners should they reappear claiming their due. This 'money in escrow' is another good way of proving that you took all the steps you could to secure permission.

It is not a good idea to set a deadline for a reply and say you will go ahead even if you have not heard back. 'Unless we hear from you by 31 July 2011 we shall assume you have no objections and go ahead' is an example of an invitation to 'opt out' (say no) while most recent legislation insists that the rights owner 'opts in', and gives his or her informed consent, without which you cannot proceed. Placing a disclaimer in the front of your book is not much better. 'Every effort has been made to contact all rights owners but in the event of any omission the publishers will be glad to make the necessary amends at the earliest opportunity' has a fine ring to it, but no legal value at all.

In the end, incomplete permissions are a matter of assessing risk and making a decision. Not being able to find the owner of the rights in a photograph of an unidentified country house in the 1930s might constitute an 'acceptable risk' – in other words, only a very slight chance that the rights owner could appear and an even slighter chance of there being legal problems, beyond an apology and the payment of a belated fee. No one can make the judgement for you, but those experienced in the rights and permissions business will always say that you should err on the side of caution. 'If in doubt – ask!'

Protecting rights in your own publications

The implicit assumption so far in this chapter has been that a publisher sells rights in works to other publishers for gain, and seeks to acquire permission to use third-party rights, sometimes with the payment of a fee. In fact, the reverse in both cases can be just as common, and the money changing hands just as important. Acquiring rights to other works may be like acquiring primary rights from authors to publish their work – a question of understanding how the process works, and negotiating fair and acceptable terms for both parties. Granting permission to other publishers to use your own work involves setting up a clear policy, including charges, and having the time and the budget to administer what can be a fiddly and costly process.

In both cases, publishers should think of their publications as a set of valuable assets that need protection as well as being exploited. That value lies less in the cash worth of the printed stocks of titles sitting in your warehouse, and more in the copyrights you have either acquired or licensed from others, especially authors. If your company were to be sold tomorrow, an accountant or an auditor would look at the balance sheet to compare the value of those assets – your copyrights and licences – and set them against the liabilities you have to people who have invested in your company or lent you money. The ratio between the two sides will be a key part of how you value those assets and assess the strength of your company.

Acquiring rights to other publications by buying in licences or actual printed books can be a good way of growing your list without the delay and cost of relying solely on organic growth generated by your commissioning editors. A US schools publisher in the 1990s grew from a US$2.3 million to a US$8 million company in just three years by the simple process of buying in titles from elsewhere and 'versioning' them for the US market. This meant changes to up to 50 per cent of the text (all printed in black on a clear white background) and of about 15 per cent of the illustrations that were culturally specific to other countries (such as Australia and the UK) and unacceptable to US schools. Even with these changes, the speed of acquisition allowed for considerable growth at relatively low cost.

Digital re-purposing

A similar approach is taking place now as publishers move to create digitized files of all they produce so that the core material they own can be re-purposed in different formats or media for a wide variety of different markets. Databases of acquired rights or assets from earlier publications can form the basis of a whole range of additional publications, including web-based material that can be complementary to the original publishing programme. As time goes on, the origins of these databases will be less and less print-based, and a system for managing these digital rights must be devised.

Protecting works that have potential as digital components or arrangements of other works involves setting up a system that records metadata and information, and identifies both the part of the work, the status and personal details of the owner (if the publisher has it under licence), the identity of the user (and their authority to use material), and the kind of use that user intends to put the material to (read, store, distribute, adapt and store, etc). These identifiers can be attached to existing systems such as ISBNs and ISSNs, but a greater degree of granularity is required – smaller bits of the whole – and so digital object identifiers are increasingly being introduced to map the landscape and catalogue the offering for web searchers and browsers.

Protecting rights and exploiting assets were simpler when the partners were just authors and publishers. In the last few years, big companies that do not at first glance look like publishers have come on to the scene and fundamentally changed the relationship between the creator or author, the publisher as an intermediary who adds value, and the user or reader who pays for access to what the author and publisher provide. The basis for change is the way technology has allowed us all to be authors and publishers.

Publishing for the community is based on the notion that many people would like to break down the authoritarian structure of publishing by which the reader is provided with what the publisher has decided shall be 'the work'. If it's a book costing £20 then apart from discounts online or '3 for 2' in a bookshop, the reader has to buy the whole book – even if he or she only really wants Chapters 2 and 3. The web has created a culture whereby consumers can acquire only the bit that interests them, and they want it immediately, without restrictions or cumbersome access procedures, and ideally *free*.

Supplying 'bits of stuff', not whole works

Meeting this expectation has fallen to the likes of Amazon and Google, and they have encouraged the expectation that users should be able to search for and get hold of the part they need. The Google Library project has gone a long way to meeting this apparent need by digitizing huge numbers of titles and making them available to subscribers and others online. Many of the scanned titles are out of copyright, but the vast majority are out of *print* – what Google calls 'not commercially available'. The general view is that these are 'orphan works' – in other words, it is hard if not impossible to track down who the rights owner is, and therefore making that title available via Google is doing everyone a good turn.

This has led to a long-running dispute with the American Association of Publishers and the Authors Guild in the United States, both of which regard this process as a breach of copyright. A settlement has been proposed, and then revised, but the judge has not yet ruled if the terms of the settlement are fair or unfair. If they are judged fair, then Google will be entitled to continue scanning works and making them available to subscriber members. Google has to make some retrospective payment, and a Book Rights Registry will be set up – but the issues behind this dispute are worth looking at as a sign than rights ownership and management may change radically.

The reality is that Google is less interested in the content it is providing and more in the opportunities delivering such content gives it for what it calls 'complementary publishing'. This means, for example, placing advertising round online displays of works and charging advertisers whose products may have little or no relationship to the content being displayed. This trend has been called 'the case of the mustard and the sausage'. When you buy a hot dog, the sausage in its roll has a price, and the mustard you add to it is free. Google – and other search engines and service providers – would much rather let consumers have the hot dog (content) for free and charge premium rates for the mustard (the advertising).

Publishers need to look at this problem with close attention, because it seems to be demoting and diminishing their role as trusted and valued intermediaries. Instead of preserving their main role of ensuring quality and authenticity, and adding value by approving only the best material, that role has been taken by individuals going down a self-publishing route, and by the big search engines whose motive is advertising revenue and profits and to whom 'content' – once so highly prized by publishers – has diminished considerably in importance. These are tumultuous times, and you should follow their development on the many websites devoted to these issues: www.googlesettlement.com is a good place to start.

Collective licensing of reprographic rights

For some publishers, particularly in the educational and academic fields, additional income is received regularly from collective licensing. These revenues are paid by schools, universities and colleges, businesses and government departments that wish to copy parts of works, and whose copying goes beyond the limits set by the fair dealing exception, So, when a teacher in school wants to copy part of a textbook or a lecturer wants to copy a journal article, and distribute copies to pupils and students, the institution needs a licence to do so, and an annual fee must be paid. The process is similar to the way rights owners receive money from the PRS/MCPS alliance (Performing Right Society/Mechanical

Copyright Protection Society): if music is played in a restaurant, bar or hairdresser, a licence is required, and the composer and musicians eventually receive a small share of the licensing revenue.

For reprographic rights, how does it work? When the UK's Copyright Licensing Agency was set up in the 1980s, people at that time wanted to photocopy parts of works. In the last few years, the need has been to scan or digitize works and make them available on a secure institutional repository, such as a university intranet. One of the problems from the beginning has been gathering enough data about what has been copied to distribute the licence fees fairly, as keeping full records of all copying was never a practical option.

The Copyright Licensing Agency (CLA) has two constituent parts: the Publishers Licensing Society (PLS) and the Authors Licensing and Collecting Society (ALCS). PLS represents the interests of publisher rights owners, and ALCS acts for authors and other creators. Together they own and manage CLA, and some of the directors of PLS and ALCS are also directors of CLA. The interests of artists are also managed by CLA acting on behalf of the Design and Artists Copyright Society (DACS) which receives a share of the revenue from copying or scanning artwork and photographs that have appeared in books or periodicals.

Before CLA can offer any licences to users such as schools or businesses, it needs the authority of the rights owners, just as anyone acquiring or licensing a right needs to seek permission from the rights owner. In most books there are at least two rights owners – the author and the publisher – and they both need to mandate CLA to act on their behalf, issue licences to copy their works, and eventually to collect and distribute revenues back to them. These mandates are in effect non-exclusive licences, with CLA offering licensees a repertoire of works that can be copied.

In the early days it was difficult to persuade licensees such as schools to take out a licence because not all the rights owner publishers had mandated PLS to offer their works to potential users. Besides, institutions that had already been illegally copying extensively resented having to take out (and pay for) a licence to do it. Conversely, many publishers were reluctant to sign on to the scheme as they feared a licence to photocopy would merely encourage teachers in schools, for example, to do more of what they were convinced was already happening – indiscriminate and excessive copying without permission or payment. Gradually the points were taken on board and each side saw this compromise as acceptable. Now teachers and lecturers can copy legally under licence, and rights owners get some compensation for the copying that is done.

CLA licences

How do the licences actually work in the UK? It was clear from the start that the idea of full record keeping of everything copied would not be accepted. When the first licences (for primary and secondary schools) were being negotiated, teachers refused to do this, while policing illegal copying was also seen as impractical. Instead, a sample of schools keeps full records for a limited period. The sample takes in a variety of school types, and a spread of regions in the UK. The sample is changed regularly so that over time data are gathered from as wide a range of schools as possible. On the basis of data collected in this way, a full picture is extrapolated and numbers of copies adjusted to reflect the amount of actual copying.

Both state-maintained and independent schools are now part of the scheme (as are language schools), and they pay for the licence on the basis of the number of pupils in school – currently around 75p per pupil in primary and £1.25 in secondary. The costs are borne by each local education authority (or independent school) but they have mostly delegated payment to a representative schools body. Similar systems are in place for other licensees. In universities and colleges, the rate (now around £5) is based on the number of full-time (or equivalent) students on roll. In businesses, the number of management-level employees is used as the basis for the calculation, with levels of price determined by the size and nature of the business.

Once the licence fee revenue has been collected, it is distributed to the rights owner groups, after the deduction of costs. These net sums are on the whole divided equally between publishers and authors, with a smaller share being set aside for members of DACS. Although the scheme was derided in its early days, with cynics saying it was a case of 'spending pounds to chase pennies', CLA now regularly distributes well over £50 million a year. Individual publishers get annual payments running into five or six figures, and like all 'subsidiary rights' revenue, it is net income. The rights owners have had to spend no time or money collecting these sums.

This description of the educational and academic licences issued by CLA is a small part of the reprographic licensing that is offered internationally, and schemes in other countries vary widely from this model. In Germany, for example, the government charges a levy on photocopying and other machines, similar to a tax like VAT. An essential feature of the UK's scheme is that is voluntary – it was set up and has been run by the rights owners themselves, rather than imposed in the form of legislation by government. The terms of the licences have all been negotiated by the parties concerned, not handed down by law. This means that those most interested in the scheme's success – the rights owners themselves – have a huge incentive to make it acceptable and successful, and this they have largely achieved.

International RROs

UK rights owners receive money from other reproduction rights organizations (RROs) around the world. CLA has reciprocal agreements with over 20 similar bodies, mostly in Europe and North America. The way these bodies work together is overseen by IFRRO, the International Federation of Reproduction Rights Organizations. Money is sometimes received by CLA without any data about what has been copied, and in these instances the income is distributed in accordance with shares established through the last six UK distributions.

The way money is collected and distributed is not calculated in a precise way: it couldn't be. The method has been described as a 'blunt instrument' but is also probably the 'least worst' way of doing it. In some countries, income is distributed on the basis of the size of the rights owner company; several RROs do not collect any data about what has been actually copied. But over the 30 years in which collective reprographic licensing has been established, most parties accept, somewhat reluctantly, that the system, though flawed, is better than a situation where no licensing of any kind was available.

Now licences include the right to scan print works, and even to copy digital works. Scanning or digitizing a print publication has generally been accepted by rights owners as a logical extension of the old photocopying model. Instead of distributing paper copies of a few pages from a book, the copied article or chapter is posted on a secure network, available only to the registered users (students and teachers). It is harder to see if the copying of works that are 'born digital' will form part of an RRO's licence in the future. Some companies believe that collective licensing of digital works (or bits of works) needs to remain under their control. It is possible that RROs in the next 10 years will decline and even disappear as individual rights owners set up systems to manage those rights themselves.

Worked examples of subsidiary rights payments

We think of income from publishing deriving mainly from sales of copies of a published book. This primary revenue may be the only source of income for an author, often paid in the form of royalties based on a percentage of sales. However, there are many other secondary ways of exploiting the assets represented by a book, and substantial revenue can be generated by these other sources.

There are broadly three ways of defining the way publishers and authors can exploit what are usually known as subsidiary rights:

1 other editions or versions of the complete work;
2 selling rights to parts of the work (textual or illustrative) reproduced in facsimile ways;
3 adapting or exploiting the original material and producing it in different media.

1. Complete work

If another publisher buys the rights to produce an edition of the original work, this buyer will usually pay a royalty on sales of the local edition. It depends then who manufactures the local edition: the original publisher can manufacture and supply finished copies (bound or in sheets) of the buying publisher's edition. This finished copy is often printed at the same time as the original publisher's reprint, so that both parties can benefit from the longer print run. Alternatively, the selling publisher can provide film or digital files of the original work so that the buying publisher or publishers can print their own edition.

The first method is especially useful when books are in full colour, as the example below shows. This is because short print runs of books in full colour are still very expensive, even with print-on-demand technology.

Publisher prints
Look how the savings work to the benefit of everyone:

Seller A wants to reprint 1,000 copies.

Buyer B wants 800 copies for its market in its language.

Buyer C wants 700 copies for its market in its language.

Total: 2,500 copies.

Buyers B and C provide files of the text in their languages. The bulk of the book consists of illustrations in full colour. It is much more economical to print all 2,500 copies of the illustrations together, and then drop in each of the different text printings separately.

Cost for 800		
	Make ready	500
	Printing 800 @ **£1.50**	1,200
	Royalty of 50p	400
	Freight @ 50p	400
	Total	**£2,500**
		(unit cost £3.13)

Cost for 2,500		
	Make ready	500
	Printing 2,500 @ **80p**	2,000
	Royalty of 50p	1,250
	Freight @ 50p	£1,250
	Total	**£5,000**
		(unit cost £2)

With a unit cost of £2 to the publisher, it would try to sell on the special editions to buyers B and C at about twice the printing unit cost (including make ready), plus royalty and freight. For Buyer C (700 copies):

Total printing cost for 2,500 (make ready and PPB)	£2,500
Unit printing cost	£1
Charge to Buyer C	£2
Plus royalty and freight (50p + 50p)	£1
Total charge to Buyer C	£3
700 copies (royalty and freight inclusive)	£2,100

The selling publisher has to share the royalty element of this income with the author, according to the contract: 700 x 50p = £350.

Of this, 75 per cent goes to the author (£263) so the publisher is left with £87 – hardly a fortune after so much work. But note it has also made a margin of £700 on the cost of manufacturing C's copies.

Publisher supplies film or files

A Nigerian publisher reaches agreement with a South African publisher in Johannesburg to sell the Xhosa language rights of one of its illustrated titles, printed in four colours. The original book sold for $30.

The Nigerian publisher agrees to provide digital files at cost with a 10 per cent handling charge so that the South African publisher can make use of the four-colour illustrations unchanged. It translates, sets and produces a file of the black text in Xhosa. 'Cost plus 10 per cent' means the actual price paid for the digital files, plus a 10 per cent handling charge – the overhead cost of production staff ordering it and sending it. This mark-up is not shared with the author. Six months later the South African publisher produces and publishes its edition. It prints 2,000 copies. The local selling price is 195 Rand (a dollar is worth about R8.00). An 8 per cent royalty on the South African published price is agreed with the local publisher. When it sells out its edition the expected earnings will be:

8 per cent of R195 x 2000 = R31,200 ($3,900)

When the deal was concluded, an advance of R15,000 was agreed, about half the expected income. The South African publisher paid this advance as soon as the contract was signed, and the money was paid over in November. It converted to $1,875.

In December the following year, the South African publisher prepared accounts. To that point, it found it had sold 1,200 copies of the book. At 8 per cent royalty, R18,720 was due. But an advance had already been paid of R15,000 so, when the account was settled the following March, the balance of R3,720 (about $465) was received by the original publisher.

At the end of that year, 500 more copies had sold. The price of the book in South Africa had been increased to R225 from 1 January, so royalty earnings for the year were 8 per cent of R225 x 500 = R9,000 (about $1,125). The money was paid the following March.

The original publisher's contract with the author states that the share of income from translation rights shall be 75:25 (75 per cent going to the author, 25 per cent being kept by the publisher). Table 8.2 shows how it works.

It's a lot of work for quite small sums of money – but most of the work is done by the publisher to whom you have sold the rights.

TABLE 8.2

Date	Event	Income R	$ Equiv.	Author (75%)	Publisher (25%)
Oct 10	Xhosa Language rights sold	–	–	–	–
Nov 10	Advance received	15,000	$1,875		
Mar 11	Author's accounts for second half 10	–	–	$1,406	$469
Dec 11	South African accounts prepared for 11 (1,200 sold)	(18,720 less advance)	–	–	–
Mar 12	Account paid	3,720	$465	–	–
Sep 12	Author's accounts for first half 12 paid	–	–	$349	$116
Dec 12	South African accounts 12 prepared (500 sold)	(9,000)	–	–	–
Mar 13	Account paid	9,000	$1,125	–	–
Sep 13	Author's accounts for first half 13 paid	–	–	$844	$281
	Total income to end 2013			**$2,599**	**$866**

2. Parts of works

The permissions calculations at the end of the last chapter showed the kinds of items and possible rates charged when a publisher wishes to *acquire* rights to parts of an author's, a photographer's or another publisher's work. Reversing the process, it is appropriate for publishers to derive income from selling parts of the publications to which they hold rights. However, it can be a lot of work to achieve sales of many different small parts of dozens of works, so it is not normally a very profitable side of the overall business. Additionally, the publisher (even acting on the author's behalf and with his or her authority) will not always own all the rights in the parts of the work that other publishers may wish to acquire.

Text extracts

If you publish the works of a famous fiction writer or a poet, there will be a steady demand from other publishers wanting to include extracts, stories or single poems in anthologies, or collections of genres of work. Examination boards may want permission to include part of a work in literature papers. The big question – and one that's impossible to answer – is, 'How much should I charge'? Looked at purely from a commercial point of view, you might say, 'As much as you can get away with', but there are other factors to consider.

The issues under which you should reach a decision are *ethical, cultural, moral* – and, of course, *commercial*. The balance that has to be struck is one that gets a reasonable return for both the author and the publisher, but does not prevent legitimate third-party users from re-publishing a work (or part of it) by charging prohibitive or greedy prices. Besides, there can be a benefit in promoting and publicizing your author's work in other publications. A judgement also has to be made on how much of the whole work is being requested for re-use, how prominent the use is (will part of it be used on the cover of the book?), and how extensively the publisher's new work will be sold and distributed.

The greater the use (and prominence) and the wider its dissemination, the higher the fee that may be appropriate. Bear in mind too that under the terms of fair dealing (or fair use), publishers may use an insubstantial part of a work without seeking permission or paying a fee. Note too that the publisher and author will normally require the extract or the work to be reproduced exactly as in the original.

It is no longer possible to provide costs for a range of permissions, but some guidelines were published a few years ago by the UK's Society of Authors and Publishers Association for prose and poetry. These have been marked up for inflation, and are listed here as examples, not as industry guidelines:

Prose	£150 – £200 per 1000 words
Poetry	£100 – £150 for the first 10 lines
	£2.50 – £3 per line from 11–30 lines
	£1.75 – £2 per line for 31 lines and over.

These were for world rights, so lower fees would be in order for more limited use, or if the work was to be used in a low circulation specialist journal.

Illustrations

Artwork is normally commissioned, as are some photographs. Acquiring artwork that has already been published or using photographs from a picture library requires a licence and usually the payment of a fee. The cost will depend on two things: the size of the reproduced illustration on the page, and the extent to which the new work will be published and disseminated.

The British Association of Picture Libraries and Agencies (BAPLA) produced some guidelines a few years ago to show a range of prices, now also marked up and shown in Table 8.3. Again, these should be taken as examples only.

The rule of thumb, again, is that lower fees may be appropriate for publications with limited circulation, and higher fees for a prominent re-use, such as on the cover rather than in the main text.

Rights owners of photographs, for example, will almost always have given you limited rights in the form of a non-exclusive licence. So you cannot sell on rights to a work in one of your publications to a third party if you have only been granted limited rights. For instance, a page of a textbook may contain text, artwork, photographs, diagrams and even maps. You can only sell the rights to reproduce that page if you hold rights in *all* those components – which would be unlikely.

TABLE 8.3

Page size %	UK rights	Commonwealth rights	World, English language	World, all languages
25	£90	£110	£140	£170
50	£100	£130	£170	£205
75	£125	£150	£205	£230
100	£170	£205	£270	£295

Licensing terms

When selling rights you must ensure publishers reproducing or republishing material continue to respect your creators' moral rights. This will normally mean insisting that they reproduce things accurately and completely, so that there is no danger of infringing creators' moral rights in their work.

3. Adaptations and exploitations

Some works lend themselves to substantial further exploitation, in different forms and new media. A novel can be dramatized and performed; it could be read on the radio, either in a complete form or abridged or condensed; it could form the basis of a screenplay for a film or television programme to be made. Sections of the novel might be published in a newspaper or magazine. Before publication (first serial rights) such extracts can help publicize the book. After publication (second serial rights) it can extend the appeal or sale of the work to new or wider audiences.

For many educational and academic publications, such glamorous possibilities are very limited. However, a publisher might want to adapt a section of a textbook for a different audience (at a lower ability level, or in simplified language). This would come under the heading of adaptation or abridgement rights. So, often it is the *medium* in which the exploitation takes place that defines and limits the rights – audio, visual (still and moving images), audio-visual, digital/electronic, and so on.

For some popular children's works, the characters will become so familiar that merchandising rights can be sold, and the image of the famous character used on all sorts of goods and merchandise – from T-shirts to mouse mats, from yoghurt to beans. Licences to use these characters can be very lucrative, if the publisher has retained a share in the rights. However, most of the money in these examples goes to the author or creator.

Whatever the form or medium of exploitation, the author's share has to be agreed. It will normally not be less than 50 per cent of the income received from the rights sale and can be as high as 90 per cent for consumer books. A 75 per cent author/25 per cent publisher split is a reasonable midway point, while in education and academic publishing, a 50:50 split is much more common.

An income and royalty statement after the first year of publication has been prepared for Jackie Jones' novel, *One Night of Romance*. The book is priced at £15. To indicate how rights income can be generated and distributed, Table 8.4 shows a high profile mass-market work, which has commanded a large advance for the famous author.

TABLE 8.4

One Night of Romance	
Royalty advance	£200,000
25,000 copies at 10% of selling price	£37,500
Less returns reserve (20%)	(£7,500) = £30,000
25,000 copies at 10% of average receipt of £8	£20,000
First serial rights sold to Sunday newspaper for £100,000 (90% to author)	£90,000
Option for TV serialization £50,000 (90% to Jackie)	£45,000
Advance on French and Spanish translation rights £10,000 each (Total £20,000) (75% to author)	£15,000
Total royalty and rights share income generated	**£200,000**
Less advance already paid	*£200,000*
New royalty and rights income now due to author	**£0.00**

Conclusion

Subsidiary rights come in all shapes and sizes, and many publications will offer no opportunities for exploitation, except perhaps translation. Generally, finding and securing deals that generate rights income can be expensive and hard work, though much of the revenue is free of overhead, as the work of generating the income has largely been undertaken by the buying publisher.

From a business point of view, this revenue is often a welcome (and sometimes unexpected) extra. Agreeing how that income is to be split with the author is the key issue to negotiate and resolve.

Further reading

Owen, L (2006) *Selling Rights*, 5th edn, Routledge, Abingdon

The worked examples of subsidiary rights payments on pages 271–74, and on this page, are derived from material first published in 2001 in Copyright and Contracts, a resourced-based learning programme *by the Oxford International Centre for Publishing Studies. The adaptations are reproduced with the kind permission of Oxford Brookes University.*

Careers in publishing

09

Introduction

We now turn to the question of what job you might take up in publishing. If you are already in publishing, you might be thinking about whether the job you have is the right one for you. But at least you are in! But for both parties, you need to think carefully about the publishing function in which you might flourish and also what sector of publishing might suit you best.

There are two opinions about where and how to start out. The first view is that it is more important to get your foot in the door and into publishing than be concerned about whether that entry point will be right for you in the long run. The second view is the opposite, proposing that you will save time, and possibly grief, if you go for what you think will be best for you. There are arguments to support both sides, and it is possible to cross over from one functional area to another. In the past, if you entered editorial, you stayed in editorial; if it was production, you stayed in production. You were defined by the point at which you entered. These days, publishing management can see advantages to be gained by allowing people to cross functional boundaries. A marketer can certainly bring additional insights and experiences into the work of the editorial department, for example. An editor moving into production can bring some understanding to that department of why and how authors are so hard to manage, and why schedules are so difficult to keep. This will not stop production staff tearing their hair out sometimes, but if you can somehow anticipate and accept occasional mayhem, when it happens, it is not so shocking.

Crossing from one publishing sector to another is much more unusual. There are distinct differences between specialist publishing and consumer publishing, and even between different sorts of specialist publishing and consumer publishing, but the gap between specialist and consumer is the Great Divide. If you have learnt everything in one of those sectors and developed the skills needed for them, when you attempt to cross over it is a bit like starting again. But it has been known to happen, usually when there are exceptional individuals involved.

So what are the arguments for and against what we might call 'opportunistic' entries into publishing, and 'considered' ones?

Opportunistic

Pro

- You get a job, any job, but the point is, you are now *in* publishing.
- You might discover that you are better suited to this kind of job and this kind of publishing than you realized.
- You learn to get on with the job, even if you know this kind of work is ultimately not for you – it's character building!
- You now have something real on your CV.
- If you do move to another function and sector, you know exactly why you want to move: uncertainties have become clarified.

Con

- You find yourself fundamentally uncomfortable and unhappy in the function or in the publishing sector.
- Because you are not happy, you do not work at your best.
- You might even question whether publishing is the right career for you.
- You 'serve time' doing the job, just waiting for a respectable moment to leave, and that respectable period is going to be anywhere between one year and 18 months, because employers take a dim view of people who move around too quickly and too often.
- When you try to move into another function or sector, you have got to provide the recruiters with very good reasons for changing track, otherwise they might think that you have no sense of direction or commitment.

Considered

Pro

- Having thought through very carefully what kind of job, and the sector, in which you want to work, you choose something in which you are likely to flourish.
- In spending time thinking about what suits you best, you probably have a better understanding of your own character, your temperament and your strengths and weaknesses. This is a sign of maturity.
- If you are happy in your job, you will get more satisfaction from it, your work will be good, and you are likely to advance up the career ladder.
- Having made the right decision, you are now able to bring that enthusiasm to your job that is so necessary for working in publishing.

Con

- In waiting and looking for the 'right job', you could become fixated on something quite precise, which you think is what you need and want.
- Hanging on for something that is 'exactly right' for you can lead to inhibition about applying for jobs. Applying for jobs (even if you don't get them) is actually good practice for that interview where you do get the job!
- Putting all your eggs in one basket is a high-risk strategy. Everything stands or falls on getting the 'right job'. You may be missing other opportunities.
- By focusing so intensely on this one thing, you fail to discover that, in fact, you could be better suited to something else.

It is up to you to decide where to plunge in for there is no perfect advice that anyone can give you. But measure up the pros and cons carefully: at your entry-level job you are not well paid, so you need to be able to compensate for that by truly feeling that you are getting some benefit out of the job.

Sector characteristics

In some senses, we are on dangerous ground here trying to sum up what sort of people work in each sector, because there are many examples of people one would expect to find in specialist publishing, but in fact are consumer publishers, and vice versa. You can find flamboyant people working in specialist publishing and mild mannered, quiet people in consumer publishing. The most important thing to ask of any of them is, 'How good are they at their jobs?' That is all that matters. Nevertheless, having said that, it is possible, and tentatively, to make some broad statements about what kind of publishing attracts what kinds of people.

Consumer publishing

This sector handles the big names of the author world. Not all its authors are famous, but many of them will be known to the general public, and some will be veritable stars. To handle such authors you need confidence. Some people might even call it brashness, but there is no point in trying to work with these authors if you are too shy to talk to them. Editors in particular have to overcome their shyness, or even their sense of awe, if they are to work successfully with these authors. Occasionally they might have to handle an author who is phenomenally famous, such as a big star of the cinema who has written his or her autobiography. It is probably best to remain in that person's shadow, yet nevertheless still try to be an effective editor.

Marketers have to present their marketing plans to these authors and their agents, and possibly defend them. Again, confidence is vital – confidence not just in what you are proposing, but generating your own self-confidence in what you propose because that will get people on your side. Be prepared, however, to take criticism on the chin. Big authors have high expectations! The sales staff out in the marketplace have to sell these authors' books to maximum effect, and that requires performance.

The production staff in a consumer house are less likely to be directly affected by these issues, with the exception of designers whose work, like that of the editor and the marketer, will be highly scrutinized by the consumer author.

Consumer publishing is more visible – it represents the books we are most likely to see in the shops – requires bigger investment (the books have large print runs), is highly competitive, and only succeeds if it makes a fairly immediate impact. The sort of people required to work in this sector are not those that dislike parties, hate being the centre of attention and prefer a quiet evening at home with a good book. To sum up, they are more likely to lie towards the extravert end of the continuum from pathologically shy to Type A personality.

Specialist publishing

There are many working for specialist publishers who are the 'life-and-soul-of-the-party' type, but even those who are not are still as sociable and gregarious as those working for consumer publishers. However, specialist publishing operates in a different way to consumer, and the type of people who are happy and comfortable in it will reflect those differences.

For a start, specialist publishing is rarely opportunistic. It is almost always planned ahead, using information gleaned by editors, and sometimes marketers, which can provide fairly detailed market knowledge of what specialist book buyers want. Fundamentally, these book buyers need books that will help them enlarge their subject knowledge, and help them pass examinations or write better essays, for example. These markets change slowly, allowing time to plan ahead and adjust to changes that are coming up. What changes might these be? Perhaps a change in the national curriculum for schools; or a change in university funding that will bring more students into certain subjects; or its opposite – less funding at higher education level for other subjects, which will certainly mean fewer students studying them. These changes do not come out of the blue. They fall into the public policy area, and tend to be discussed in the public arena, so publishers in these areas get early warning, which allows them to plan. The lesson to learn from this, of course, is that you must take an active interest in what is going on in your area.

Specialist books, therefore, are constructed and designed with this in mind. People working for specialist publishers are unlikely to be the type who just grabs at any book offered. On the contrary, this person is judging what is on offer quite precisely in line with what market needs are. People who work in this kind of publishing like to analyse and plan, and more often than not, they are working two to three years ahead, preparing what they want to publish to take advantage of, for example, a change in the way in which a subject may be taught. Risk is not absent in the lives of these publishers, because specialist publishing is still competitive. It is not a guaranteed piece of safe ground. Even the great university presses, such as Oxford and Cambridge, are not free from the competitive threats posed by mainstream academic publishers. But overall, typical specialist publishers are more likely to pause and think before diving into the next project.

Similarly, the marketers for these books are going to plan all promotion and selling activities on the basis of what they precisely know about their market and where they find it. Just think of the difference in the marketing plans we outlined for a consumer book and a specialist book in our marketing chapter. A specialist marketer cannot promote simply on the back of enthusiasm. It is sometimes said of consumer publishing that you do not know if there is a market for a book until you have published it. The specialist publisher never moves without knowing there is a market for it, and how to 'speak' to it.

People working in specialist publishing, like those in consumer publishing, will regard a quiet night in with a good book as something to partake of every now and then, but are less likely to worry about missing out on something if they do stay at home. They will also actively enjoy planning and thinking ahead and, in all likelihood, think it unintelligent not to do so. All we can conclude is, 'Horses for courses'. And what do you think would suit you best?

We now turn to the kinds of job you might take up when you first enter publishing.

Editorial

The typical entry job is that of *editorial assistant*. Your job will be to support the work of anyone on the editorial continuum, from editor, to senior editor, up to editorial director, often these days also called 'publisher'. These editors need to concentrate on big issues such as content and list development, their relationship with their authors, and team-working with members of other departments. The job of the editorial assistant, therefore, is to take on a lot of the administrative load contained in an editor's job. Essentially this means:

- printing up documents (often manuscripts) for the editor;
- arranging meetings for them, including taking authors out to lunch;
- planning and organizing their travel;

- sending synopses or manuscripts to advisers for evaluation;
- making phone calls or sending e-mails on behalf of the editor, who will of course convey to you what needs to be said or written.

All these jobs are relatively straightforward, but there are others that you will be asked to do once you have begun to develop experience and have a better idea of how things function.

Copywriting is something that editorial assistants are often asked to do. You will be given the author's description of the book and asked to turn it into copy that is suitable for jackets or covers. Your editor will check what you have written and give you tips for improving it. You might even be sent on a copywriting course. Eventually the editor will give you more of a free hand, although it is good practice for all editors to check what someone else has written.

Contracts are often handled by editorial assistants. Nobody should be asked to work on a contract without some training. Most large publishing corporations will have contracts departments that draw up a contract based on the information supplied by editorial, in which case, following some experience and training, you might instruct the contracts department on the main points to appear in the document. Consumer publishers, working in a very competitive world, will have a greater variation in terms and conditions, which is why consumer publishers tend to have contracts departments. In other companies, editors work with 'model' contracts, which they will hold as digital files on their computers. Model contracts are only useful if the company does not provide much variation in the terms and conditions offered to its authors. Specialist publishers are most likely to fall into this category. The editorial assistant, therefore, will be asked to fill in the blanks, meaning the advance on offer, if any, and the royalties, plus the delivery date and the length of the book and number of illustrations.

The *bureaucracy* of a publishing house is something an editor would prefer to avoid, because it mostly means filling in forms. When a book goes into production it is accompanied by many forms, including those for production stating the number of copies to be printed, the formats, suggested prices and, when appropriate, instructions on layouts and jacket design. Other forms to be filled in will contain information for the marketing and rights departments. As you would expect, that information covers markets, readerships and levels, not just for the domestic market but also for overseas. If your company has a distribution relationship with an overseas company, there will be a form that provides information relevant to that company's needs. Again, this form-filling is not something you would be expected to do immediately after starting your job. You will be trained by the editor until you reach the point where you can fill them in on your own. The wise editor, however, should always check them before they are handed on.

These are the main items that an editorial assistant is expected to work on before progressing upwards. The editorial chapter (Chapter 3) provides further insights and information on the work of an editor.

There is one further level between editorial assistant and editor, and that is *development editing*. In some houses, the person who does this might be called an *assistant editor*, although there are some distinctions to be drawn. A development editor usually works in a house that publishes textbooks. Such houses take an active part in ensuring that the written material is in textbook style, and the relationship between the development editor and the author can become quite close. An assistant editor might equally become involved with the author, although perhaps not so much in the writing if the book is not a textbook. An editor who has an assistant editor would require him or her to keep in close touch with the authors, to find out how things are progressing, and to deal with concerns they might have. Both these jobs, therefore, are excellent ways of learning more about working with authors and are further steps along the way to becoming an editor.

The strengths and weakness of this entry-level job

The strengths are:

- You will not get closer to the job of being an editor without being one yourself. The job allows you a front-row seat. Inevitably, the editor is going to talk to you every day about what is happening with hopeful authors and existing authors, and about teamwork with other departments. You will learn about the highs and the lows, and through listening to the editor you will learn how the job is done.

- Whether the editor intends it or not, you might pick up information that is not public, about authors, colleagues and management. This happens simply because the editorial assistant is the natural *confidant* of an editor. You must use what you hear with discretion!

- Learning about contracts is really important. This knowledge will stay with you for the rest of your editorial career.

- Because the work of the editor is at the core of the publishing function, the editor reaches out right across the house. You will learn more quickly about other departments.

The weaknesses are:

- You might not like working constantly in someone else's shadow. The chances of getting a job immediately as an editor are fairly unlikely. Serving as an assistant to someone is something you may not be able to avoid.

- Your boss, being an editor, will be utterly involved in the job to the extent of not always being entirely sensitive to your needs. Remember that, because when you become an editor you will need to be considerate of your editorial assistant.

- You might have to work in this job for quite some time. We've already mentioned the inadvisability of switching jobs too often, but that apart, no one gets promoted from editorial assistant to editor unless there is a job for him or her to fill. Publishers do not, by and large, create special jobs to meet the development needs of editorial assistants.

- Even if an editor's job comes up, there will be no automatic succession for you. Editorial assistants only get promoted if there is enough confidence around that they will be good at this job.

- Some people are good at assisting but not so good at the risk taking, evaluation and judgement that are required of an editor. Just because you are good at assisting, don't assume that you will become an editor.

One final point on editorial: many editorial assistants have prayed for and craved the position of editor. Then they become an editor and immediately have a crisis. As you will have gathered from Chapter 3 on the work of an editor, this is a very tough job and one that is also very exposed. For some people, this is the equivalent of finally being called on stage, and then freezing through sheer fright. If you can get through that immediate sense of being overwhelmed by what is expected of you, the job has tremendous compensations. But do not think that because you have been made an editor, everything will now be wonderful. The job will present you with another set of even more difficult challenges.

Marketing

The entry-level job here is *promotion assistant*. Like the editorial assistant, you will essentially work under the guidance and direction of the person next up on the line of management – a promotion manager. Marketing is about strategizing and planning; promotion carries out the practical activities that develop from that.

Here the job is likely to entail *writing copy* for leaflets, catalogues, websites or advertisements. It is unlikely that you will be creating copy from scratch. You will be using the copy provided by editorial, which is the copy written for a book's jacket or cover, and adapting it to suit the different uses you will have for it. Like the editorial assistant, you will be trained to write this copy. If you are working on the company's website, you would most certainly be trained to provide the kind of copy that this medium requires.

As well as writing copy, you might also be *designing* rudimentary leaflets, perhaps for use at conferences or fairs. To have some experience of design software is an advantage, and you should make that clear when interviewing for a promotion job. You may also be asked to provide *support work with conferences or fairs,* making bookings and other arrangements.

Another set of tasks could be *coordinating information to be sent to an author:* for example, rounding up reviews that have been published, or providing a complete checklist of all promotional activities that have taken place, which someone more senior (the promotion manager or the marketing manager) will send to the author.

The strengths and weaknesses of an entry-level marketing job

Strengths are:

- Seeing at first hand how strategies and plans turn into real actions that will help support the book in the marketplace. This is all part of the kind of valuable experience that turns good ideas into good ideas that work.
- It will give a very good grounding in understanding that marketing is not all fluff.

- As with those in editorial, you learn the craft from the ground up and your everyday contact is with more experienced people who will provide insights and much role modelling.
- If you work in a small or medium-sized house, you are likely to be involved in promotion meetings and will be exposed to colleagues further up the ladder, whose discussions will teach you a lot about the relative value of various promotion activities.
- Inevitably you will have contact with authors, which may or may not be a blessing (depending on whether they are making demands on you), but this is always invaluable experience as you will soon discover that marketing is as important to authors as the design on their books' jackets.
- You will also have frequent contact with the sales department, bringing you closer to the reality of the retail world outside your office.

Weaknesses are:

- It can sometimes seem boring to be working on fairly rudimentary tasks. Leaflet design at this level, for example, is difficult to see as a real design challenge.
- If you do send information to authors, you can find yourself at the wrong end of their complaints about the marketing their books have received.
- As with editorial, just because you prove capable of acting as a promotion assistant, this does not guarantee promotion. You will need to be lucky to find an opening, and you will need to have demonstrated that you have both the creative instincts and the organizational capability for running complex promotion and marketing campaigns.

The next step up from this entry-level job will be to *marketing executive*, where you will expected to:

- draw up promotional plans;
- place advertisements;
- have more direct involvement in author support;
- brief the sales reps at the sales conference;
- take responsibility for part of the website.

Other marketing-related jobs

These can include being a *sales assistant*, where you might arrange appointments for reps, organize their sales tools such as AIs and jacket covers, or point-of-sale materials. Chapter 5 gives more information on sales work and the kind of people needed in a sales team.

Some of the larger publishing houses will have their own *public relations* departments. If you start as an assistant in the PR department, you will send out review copies and press releases, which someone more senior than you will write. You might help organize a launch event, sending out the invitations and organizing the wine and food. There will definitely be a budget for this and the choice of venue and refreshments will be decided by your manager. There are many things occupying a PR manager, so your help will be needed in organizing press campaigns and media interviews.

Both the jobs of sales assistant and PR assistant are excellent training for anyone who has decided that sales or PR are where their interests lie in career terms. However, both are equally good training grounds for a job in editorial and, of course, in marketing. The connection with marketing is obvious, but not everyone realizes that exposure to the 'sharp end' of selling books and raising public interest and awareness in books is equally valuable for editorial work.

Rights

Chapter 8 on rights covers what this work is really about. The rights department exploits any capability that a book has to create extra income, whether it is through translations, serializations, electronic packages, or radio, film and television versions. To be a good *rights executive* you have to be partly editorial and partly sales and marketing. You need to understand the book, its readers, and the reputation of the author (that's the editorial side) and you also need to know how to sell your product to an interested party. Like all good sales and marketing people, you have a sense of what the buyer might be interested in, and why. This might entail talking to a rights buyer at the Frankfurt Book Fair and drawing his or her attention to a new book on self-help, for example, which you know will be of interest to an overseas company that is strong in this area; or selling serialization of a non-fiction book to a newspaper whose readers like to read about celebrities. Rights executives also draw up contracts for licensees, so attention to detail and a full understanding of publishing law is very important.

If you start as a *rights assistant*, again you will be working with and supporting someone at a higher level. It could mean sending out copies of books, arranging travel, and possibly attending book fairs. The rights executive is likely to take personal responsibility for the contracts – although you might be asked to draw them up under his or her supervision – and contacting rights licensees to ask for sales figures and to check on the progress of their editions. Rights executives tend to foster good and long-lasting relationships with their counterparts in licensee companies, which is why they will not always hand over responsibility to assistants for key areas such as sales, contracts and progress chasing.

Rights departments have become even more important in recent years because of digital technology, which can provide for much more flexible treatment of content than a book ever could. With the possibility of seemingly endless treatments of content, the rights executive has to be fully aware of the ramifications of certain rights deals, whether they will make money for the author and the publisher, whether such a deal could actually damage the sales of the books, and so on. Will you allow your book to be published online by another company, perhaps through an e-library? The potential may look good, but it could kill off the sales of the book – you need to exercise some shrewd judgement.

There is an equally strong reason for rights emerging as a vitally important department. As more and more publishers in previous 'closed' economies, such as the countries of the former USSR and China, enter the world economy and wish to translate English books into their own languages, rights departments have become the front line in protecting copyright. In every deal they make, they have to ensure that the book will be properly protected in respect of copyright. There have been many examples of foreign publishers changing the text in the course of translation, not accounting properly for sales, and sub-licensing other versions of the book in their territories, when the contract they signed did not provide for this. Working in rights these days can be very interesting indeed!

Production

The production department can sometimes be known as the 'boiler room'. We don't go into it very much, yet what it does is essential.

Without doubt, most production departments are perceived as being full of rather helpful, practical people, which is why editors are often seen rushing into production departments crying, 'This book is really late. Can you put it on fast track please!' Production is, more than any other department, dealing with practical reality. It gets the books made. It deals with other practical people, called typesetters, printers and binders; editorial and sales and marketing deal with hopes, guesses and prayers, and plenty of luck!

From this you might assume that apart from the intrusion of those anxious editors, the production department is a haven of calm. Compared to the other departments it is, but that is not to say it is without pressure. Production departments need people who can project-manage on a grand scale, for each will be personally responsible for the design, pre-press work and eventual manufacture of dozens of books. It is not only the scale of demand but the detail that will go into it. Each book is, as we say, different, which in practice means that we seldom publish books whose appearance is identical to all the others. For production staff this means dealing with very different kinds of design, layouts, paper and bindings, all of which are appropriate to each individual book. There is also a small army of freelancers to manage: the copy-editors, proofreaders, indexers and designers. They have to be found, and their schedules proposed and managed. Freelancers who are new to the house have also got to be 'tested'. No publisher takes on, for example, a copy-editor without finding out whether he or she is competent or not. Then there is the interface between production and the typesetters, printers and binders. All that has to be planned and managed. These companies on the manufacturing side do not work in a haphazard way. They are schedule-driven.

Before we look at an entry-level job, we can say clearly that production staff have to be organized, calm, efficient, schedule-driven and very resourceful. If your personality does not include these attributes, you are not suited to production.

A typical entry-level job would be as a *production editor* or *production controller*. It is possible to start work as an assistant to a production editor or production controller, but this role really is an administrative one, and for career and progression reasons you should start as a production editor or controller. You will be trained on the job, starting with the more easily learned functions and gradually moving up. Your job will eventually entail:

- organizing pre-press and manufacturing work;
- establishing schedules for copy-editing, proofreading, printing and binding of individual books;
- contacting and engaging freelance copy-editors, proofreaders and indexers who are available to work within the established schedules;
- contracting companies that will typeset, print, machine and bind the books, and agreeing schedules with them for each individual book;
- contacting and engaging designers to work on the inside and jacket design of individual books;
- arranging for designers to be briefed either by marketing or editorial, depending on the design policy of the publishing house;
- informing authors of dates for their input on copy-editing and proofreading;
- providing the same information for editorial if it is editorial's responsibility to give this to the authors (practice differs between publishing houses);
- arranging for indexes to be compiled (by a freelancer) if the authors have elected not to compile them themselves;
- providing regular updates for editorial about a book's progress through pre-press and manufacture;
- presenting accurate production costs for editorial that will feed into the decisions on book prices.

In some houses, production editors or controllers might design book jackets, using design software. This is most likely to happen in houses publishing books that do not need high design values on their jackets – typically highly specialist books. Obviously it is desirable that production staff have some design ability!

Further up the ladder you could become a *production manager*. Your job then will be to manage the production controllers and editors and negotiate terms with the manufacturing suppliers. Some managers will also get involved in the detail of special, more complex projects, but the day-to-day responsibility of the individual books will lie with the production editors and controllers.

Strengths of the entry-level job

If you think you like being organized, planning work flows, dealing with complex project management that will include individuals and companies outside the publishing house, getting a sense of satisfaction from holding the finished product in your hands, then you are probably well suited to this job. Both craft and organization are involved. By and large, you are able to avoid some of the more irritating and egotistical behaviours witnessed by editorial and marketing, whether this is on the part of authors or staff!

Weaknesses

Your contact with the business side of publishing is not acute. You are unlikely to be involved in the investment issues of choosing what is published and how it is sold. Away from the 'sharp end' of publishing, some production staff feel that not only are they not involved, but they are overlooked. This might be a strength of the job rather than a weakness if you would like to concentrate on the design and making of books.

Applying for jobs

Getting your first job in publishing is seldom easy, but if you try hard and prepare yourself, you will succeed. We cannot tell you how to bring magic to your application, or to yourself if you are called for interview. However, here are a few tips.

Contrary to what we said earlier about the pros of getting *any job* in publishing, never think about that in a casual way. If you approach the application and the interview thinking, 'Well, I'll try this one today', it will shine through. Convince yourself that you do want to have a particular job, otherwise you will come across as indifferent, as a sausage machine rolling out applications.

Prepare by researching the lists of the houses to which you apply. Get to know what they publish. During interviews, questions will certainly be asked about what you know or feel about their publications and why you want to work on them. A shrug of the shoulders or a 'Don't know', is a disaster. Having done your research, think carefully about what you feel you can offer their publishing – particular skills, experiences or knowledge that you think will be useful to them.

Arrive on time for your interview. People who arrive very early are as much a nuisance as those who arrive late.

Dress respectably – no jeans, T-shirts or hats. If you have an exotic style of dressing, tone it down for the interview. Publishing is not a profession filled with people who like to dress very formally but there is a line between looking 'good casual' and 'Hey, I just threw this on when I got out of bed!'

Do look interested! Be prepared to talk. 'Yes' or 'no' answers are of no help to you here. Be friendly without being pushy, and alert without looking as though you are hyperactive. Remember these people are wondering what you might be like to have around every day.

You will also be asked if you have any questions to put to them. Make sure you have some. Telling the interviewers you have no questions tends to make you seem a bit passive. The only exception to this is if you have had a very extensive exchange with them, in which case, you can say, 'Well, I did have some questions but I think they've been covered in our conversation.'

When they indicate that the interview is at an end, make sure you say something along the lines of, 'Thank you. I very much enjoyed coming here, and wish to emphasize how much I would like to have this job.' The interviewers will have heard this before, but it is always worth saying.

Finally, your CV needs not to exceed two pages in length and should never have any spelling, punctuation or grammatical errors in it. Be wary of personal statements in which exaggerated claims are made. They never fail to come across as boastful or unrealistic. We've seen CVs where individuals have claimed to be 'perfectionists', 'first-class organizers', 'truly creative', and 'outstanding project managers', and all this before they have even got their first proper job! Remember that whatever you claim for yourself in your personal statement, you must have examples of things you have done to back them up.

Publishing *is* a people business

One of the pleasures of working in this profession is that it is able to recognize individuality, which is only possible if you see the workforce as being made up of people who are different, one from the other. You do not have to go and work in the army or in a factory to find situations in which everyone has to be, somehow, roughly the same, or can 'fit in', which is another way of expressing conformity. As a result of authors being at the centre of our business, we celebrate and approve of individuality, because it is of great professional value to us. This attitude can be lived out in the career paths of individuals. If you can grab opportunities that come your way, and if you realize that your strengths are there to be used, then you might end up, very happily, in a very different place than the one you envisaged when you were thinking about your career path.

There is the example of the young woman who, on interviewing for a place on a postgraduate degree course in publishing, said that her ambition was to be a poetry editor. However, when she sat through her lectures on publishing law, she fell in love with it. When she graduated, she went into the contracts department of a consumer publishing house where she eventually became contracts director. This seems to represent a large leap from poetry editing to drawing up contracts, but is it? After all, contracts are precision itself, yet behind that precision lies the real meaning, the anticipated enactment of many possibilities that might arise in the publication of a book: precision and interpretation.

On the whole, we would counsel you to avoid having a career firmly mapped out in your mind. We are not suggesting you should not have ambition, but our experience has shown that many of the most successful people we know in publishing have not remained on a determined path – or conveyor belt. Yes, they have moved around, both in function and in publishing houses, but on each occasion, they were playing to their strengths. This is far more enjoyable than taking a job that might offer status and more pay, but requires that you constantly have to hide your weaknesses – in other words, working out of your depth! Being driven by ambition is all very well when it works. The first time things do not happen as planned, you are likely to be knocked sideways, because you have not prepared for failure. In fact, it might not be so big a failure, but as a result of your assuming that your conveyor belt would keep moving forward, you become unstuck.

Remain open to possibilities and avoid rigid thinking and attitudes. This is the best human response to working in a very human business, and it is also the best response to working in an entrepreneurial environment. Successful entrepreneurs are seldom rigid. They are flexible, responsive and always looking for ways to improve what they bring to the marketplace. They always feel they can and must do better!

Conclusion

These, then, are the employment opportunities available to someone starting out in publishing. We have not mentioned warehouse and distribution work, or areas such as administration, human resources, or finance, since these jobs are often done by specialists who happen to have chosen publishing as an agreeable area in which to work. What unites all these entry-level jobs, whatever the function or the sector, is that there is a lot of competition for them, and you need to prepare yourself for this. Anyone who gets the first job they apply for is very fortunate indeed. Being disappointed but then having the courage to pull oneself together and press on to the next opportunity is essential. As we mentioned earlier, going through several interviews is not wasted time. You get better at being interviewed, and as you visit various publishing houses and meet the staff there, you can sort out uncertainties in your mind about where you want to work, and why.

Further reading

Baverstock, A, Bowen, S and Carey, S (2008) *How to Get a Job in Publishing*, A & C Black, London

Glossary

advance   Lump sum payment made (usually to authors) on account, set against royalties that will be payable in accordance with sales of the book, but only after the advance has earned out *(see also* **unearned advance**).

assert   Process by which rights owners state their entitlement to ownership of **moral rights,** such as **paternity** and **integrity** *(see also* **waive**).

assignment of copyright   Transfer (often in the form of a signed agreement) whereby the copyright in a work moves from one party (eg an author) to another (eg a publisher).

bad debt   A sum of money that cannot be collected relating to an invoice issued to a customer who does not or cannot pay, either because the business has failed or the debtor has disappeared. This **provision** allows for a (small) proportion of unpaid invoices that count as sales, but are never settled or turned into cash.

BLAD   The letters stand for 'brief layout and design', and the booklet typically takes the form of an 8- or 16-page mock-up of a highly illustrated colour book with text and pictures in position; generally used to generate interest in rights and co-edition sales.

breach   Failure to keep to the terms of, for example, an author's contract; a **material breach** can be sufficiently serious for the contract to be terminated.

budget   A financial plan (either income or expenditure) set and agreed in advance of an accounting period *(see also* **forecast**).

cash flow   An important measure of liquidity in a publishing business, often felt most strongly in the gap of time between spending money on costs and receiving payment for sale of finished goods.

cast off   An estimate of how many printed pages in a book will be made from the number of sheets in an author's typescript.

cease and desist   Refers to an injunction against publication of a printed work containing a legal infringement; the publisher must stop publication (and may be required to recall copies of the book and deliver infringing copies to an agreed place) *(see also* **notice and takedown**).

collective licensing   Grant of rights by one body to another allowing, for example, multiple copying under licence and for payment of a copyright work; revenues collected are then shared amongst rights holders.

commissioning editor   Editor in publishing company responsible for finding projects and authors in order to commission works and build the company's publishing programme.

community A word increasingly used to denote a group of people (customers or stakeholders) who may receive, create or interact with digital publishing initiatives, and contribute to their dissemination.

competitive advantage A marketing strategy or position that can place you ahead of a competitor and thus make your offer distinctive and more attractive.

contingency An extra allowance of time or money to cushion a project from unexpected delay or expenditure.

Creative Commons Licensing protocol that allows rights owners to determine the extent to which they wish to grant or reserve rights; takes the form of a suite of licences with symbols that authorize or prevent use of rights by others, almost always for non-commercial purposes.

critical path Scheduling process by which projects passing simultaneously through a production process can be plotted and timed so that potential clashes or work overloads can be anticipated and avoided (eg when one person or department is working on too many projects at the same time).

data protection Legal controls on the use, storage and dissemination of personal data, based on the principle that people should know in advance how details about them are going to be used. Based also on the requirement for people to be allowed to opt in (by saying 'yes' beforehand) rather than to opt out (by withdrawing their consent after the event).

defamation A written libel that makes right-thinking people regard the defamed person (who must be an identifiable individual) with less respect; for the defamed person to be successful in an action, the libel or defamation made against them must be untrue (*see* **libel**).

e-marketing Using the web and the internet to promote new publications or to make contact with new and existing customers; advantages include speed, cheapness, and the ability to reach large numbers of people instantly.

exclusive licence A grant of rights made to only one party, and typically that granted by an author to a publisher for the first publication of a book (*see* **non-exclusive licence**).

fair dealing An exception under UK law whereby an insubstantial part of a work may be copied, generally only for the purposes of criticism and review, or for private study and non-commercial research; can cause permissions departments problems and it is often difficult to decide what constitutes a 'substantial part'.

fair use A provision of US copyright law similar to fair dealing by which parts of works may be copied; generally the exceptions are broader, both under 'freedom of information' legislation, and for educational purposes.

false attribution A **moral right** which protects rights owners from having a work falsely attributed to them, thus endangering their reputation or standing in the eyes of others.

first serial right A subsidiary right granted to a magazine or newspaper to publish an extract from a book or other whole work *before* publication (*see also* **second serial right**).

forecast Strictly, an adjustment or revision to a **budget** in the light of information gained during the budget period; known in some companies as RF (revised forecast), it gives periodic (often quarterly) updates to the way a budget is performing, and adjusts the likely year-end result accordingly.

gatekeeper An editor or other person responsible for deciding (usually not alone) what will be published, and how a company's **list** will develop. A customer or fundholder who determines what will be authorized for adoption or expenditure, typically in an educational institution.

grant of rights   Key clause in a contract that determines the extent or range of rights granted (or assigned) by the author to a publisher, and which rights (if any) are thus reserved.

gross margin   The amount of money left after cost of sale (**pre-press** and manufacturing costs of books sold), royalties and **provisions** (adjustment for returns, principally) are deducted from sales revenue. The sum can be expressed as a percentage of sales revenue (or turnover) and is a key ratio for editors to assess in advance if a project is going to profitable (or not). It is sometimes referred to, less accurately, as 'gross profit'.

inalienable   Moral rights can only be claimed by an individual person, and these rights remain personal to him or her; the rights cannot be assigned or transferred to someone else – they are, in effect, inalienable.

inspection copy   Sample copy of a new publication supplied to someone who is in a position to recommend or order quantities of it (often a textbook) for use by pupils or students; it was once customary for these copies to be paid for or returned, and only kept as a free copy if quantities were ordered – the cost of administering this system was shown to exceed the cost of treating an inspection copy as a free sample.

integrity   A **moral right** that protects the wholeness or integrity of a work, such that if a rights holder or creator feels this right has been infringed, they can claim that their reputation has been harmed by their work being subjected to 'derogatory treatment'.

intermediary   A person or organization that links two parties, such as an author and a reader. Typically, this described a publisher's role: adding value to a creator's work, and bringing it to market. The unattractive word 'disintermediation' describes the process and denotes the view that this role may be redundant, and that going direct from author to reader is the new digitally enabled route to take.

interoperability   The key way that different elements of a (digital) publication can be created, archived and distributed to an unlimited number of partners thanks to standard systems of expression or identification.

legal term   The period of time for which copyright remains in force. In Europe and North America, this term or period lasts for 70 years from the end of the year in which the creator died. In much of the rest of the world, the period is 50 years p.m.a. (*post mortem auctoris* – after the death of the author).

libel   Defamatory statement made against an identifiable individual that causes people to think less of him or her. For an action against libel to be successful, the allegation must be untrue. *(see **defamation**)*.

list   A group of publications that create a distinct part of a publishing company's output. Smaller than a division or an imprint, and larger than a series, a list may be organized by theme or subject area or by age/ability level, and is often taken as a whole when calculating publicity budgets or assessing performance and profitability *(see **list-building**)*.

list-building   The main role of a commissioning or acquisitions editor is to increase the turnover and margin of a group of publications as a whole. Building a list may be achieved through extending the appeal and life of existing publications by producing new editions or ordering new covers, devising spin-offs or deriving new works from existing material – rather than just commissioning new books *(see **list**)*.

mandate   Authority given by rights holders to, for example, a reprographic rights organization, to allow their works to be included in a collective licensing scheme; it is, in effect, a **non-exclusive licence.**

merchandising rights   Sometimes referred to as *character* merchandising, these rights govern the production of artefacts on which a well-known children's character is prominently displayed, and one that will be instantly recognized by buyers. Characters that lend themselves to this process are people, animals or other creations whose fame has often been established by links to film and television. Walt Disney cartoon characters, the Mister Men and Thomas the Tank Engine are international examples.

milestone schedule   An outline schedule that establishes the dates by when certain stages in the production process have to be reached in order to achieve a certain launch or publication date.

moral rights   Rights owned by individuals that relate to and may affect their reputation and standing in the eyes of others. In the UK, the main ones are the right of **paternity** and the right of **integrity.**

niche   Used to refer to small or specialist markets where competition may be small or absent altogether. The dilemma for publishers can be deciding whether it's better to have 1 per cent of a huge market or 100 per cent of a niche market.

non-exclusive licence   An agreement between rights holders where one grants a licence to another, but reserves the right to grant the same licence to any number of others *(see* **exclusive licence**).

notice and takedown   The process whereby infringing material must by law be removed from a website or digital platform. Rights holders whose works have been posted or used illegally now have to right to give notice and insist that their material is taken down within a short and strictly applied time limit *(see also* **cease and desist**).

open access   A movement whose origins lie in the academic and research communities of US universities, and whose proponents argue that the publication process for research findings appearing in journals is too slow and expensive. They argue that posting research immediately and speeding up the review process would mean people could share in new information more quickly, and at less cost – even with authors of papers paying for their work to be published.

overheads   The indirect costs of running any business. In publishing companies, the direct costs of producing publications (pre-press and **PPB**), plus author royalties, are used to calculate **gross margin**, while overhead costs cover the people (salaries and expenses), the buildings they work in, and general expenses such as finance and administration.

patent law   A close relation to copyright law, patents generally protect inventions, names, brands, marques, logos, straplines, even typefaces – or (usually) a combination of these things. Unlike copyright, a patent must be registered and can be renewed.

paternity   One of a range of **moral rights** that grants to the rights owner the right to be identified as the author of a work. In the UK, this right must be asserted in writing and normally appears on the copyright page (title page verso) in most books published since 1989.

plagiarism   The deliberate copying of substantial parts of the arrangement of someone else's work. To be proven, the actual words of the plagiarized work have to have been copied – you cannot plagiarize ideas or plots.

pre-press   Stages of production that take place up to the point of manufacturing, or printing. The costs incurred at pre-press are generally only paid once, leading to the possibility that reprints will be much more profitable.

privacy The **moral right** of privacy prevents photographers who take pictures privately of people (with their permission) from exploiting those photos commercially. More general issues of privacy are increasingly governed in Europe by human rights legislation, while in the US there are much stricter laws governing privacy.

profit and loss account A standard accounting measure in which income and expenditure is broken down and listed, and the balance calculated, whether a profit or a loss. The P & L (as it is sometimes known) can be applied to an individual book, to a series or list, or of course to a division or company, and is both a historic summary of performance and a budget looking to the future – usually both.

promotion Budgeted expense set aside for marketing a publication. The cost is sometimes calculated as a percentage (ratio) of the expected sales revenue. In **P & L** accounts, the sums are sometimes referred to as 'A and P' (advertising and promotion). Note, the cost is usually listed separately from general marketing **overheads.**

provision Allowance in budgets for unexpected extra expenditure, and used both historically as a penalty and in future forecasts as an insurance policy against the possibility of the need recurring. Common provisions relate to stock **write down** (printing too many books), **returns**, an **unearned advance** and **bad debt.**

public domain Works whose legal term of copyright has expired. Material produced by public or governmental bodies may or may not be protected by copyright and, although publicly available at no cost, may not be in the public domain.

push/pull marketing Push marketing describes the efforts and expense of telling people about a new publication, while pull marketing covers the devices used for drawing the customer to a place where they can buy your product.

reserved Used to describe a right that has been kept by a rights owner, such as an author. Creators can grant all or some rights to a third party like a publisher, while reserving others. The phrase 'all rights reserved' is a general notice appearing in some books as a warning to others that permission or a licence must be sought before exercising any protected rights.

return A financial term denoting the money recouped from a business investment. Whether a bet placed on a horse, or a stake placed into the development of a publication, an important measure of its success (or otherwise) will be this return on investment, often expressed in accounts as ROI.

returns Books returned unsold from retailers who generally buy on consignment, or on a 'sale-or-return' basis. This curious but well-established arrangement is sometimes allowed for in a profit and loss account and an author's contract as a returns **provision.**

second serial right A subsidiary right granted to a magazine or newspaper to publish an extract from a book or other whole work *after* publication *(see also* **first serial right**).

segmentation Divisions or sub-divisions of markets that may appear homogenous. For example, children read books in school and books at home, and sometimes it's the same book. From a market point of view, however, the teachers who buy school books and the parents who buy books for reading at home are different segments of the market.

slippage Term used to denote lateness in a schedule, when a date 'slips' because a partner in the production process (such as an external supplier, like an author), has not kept to the agreed dates and delivered on time.

social media Publishing on the web has created a whole new range of communities – those who contribute to blogs, wikis, or Facebook, or who twitter and tweet.

Useful for marketing and **promotion**, publishers are still struggling to commercialize such essentially personal and often ephemeral activities; moreover, ones that most participants expect to be free.

substantial part   Wording from the UK's Copyright Act denoting the amount of a work that merits protection by copyright, and in contrast to those items or parts that can be used under the **fair dealing** exception.

synopsis   An essential early stage in assessing a project, usually submitted by an author interested in attracting a publisher to his or her work, or an editor evaluating a new author's potential for the company's **list.**

trade and consumer   Well-established shorthand for the publishing genre that (a) takes the largest share of any book market (b) always proves most attractive to new and student recruits to the industry, and (c) is probably the hardest from which to make sustained and substantial profits.

treating and dealing   Phrase to be found in new legislation following the European copyright directive, and referring to online activities such as distributing or adapting a rights owner's material. This process might not be undertaken for commercial gain, but could still be protected by copyright, and thus is not considered as an exception to copyright.

unearned advance   That portion of an advance on royalty paid to an author not covered by revenue from sales of the book, plus any subsidiary rights income. In other words, if the book does not sell enough copies for the royalties those sales would earn to cover and exceed the advance already paid, any unearned sums will be subject to **write down** and may form part of the future **provisions** in a **P & L** account.

versioning   A term generally found in the United States where publications potentially attractive to the local market need to be adapted to suit those domestic needs, whether in cases of spelling and grammar, or in the familiarity of buildings, clothing and street scenery.

vertical publishing   The policy of keeping the potential for different versions of a publication in the same group. As companies merged and larger publishers absorbed smaller ones, the various imprints in a big group became able to cover all the different iterations of a publication, whether hardback to paperback, or educational edition to e-book.

viral marketing   Placing promotional information in a system (like a community or on a database) where those who read the information pass it on to others, thus themselves contributing to the marketing process.

waive   The opportunity for a rights owner not to exercise his or her **moral rights.** Such rights cannot be assigned, but they can be waived. Many authors choose instead to **assert** their moral rights.

warranty and indemnity   Standard term of most contracts whereby one party (eg the author) guarantees certain things to the other party (eg the publisher). Such warranties can cover the fact that the work belongs to the author, that he or she is free to agree to the terms of the contract, and that the material he or she submits will not pose any legal problems, or contain third-party 'trouble'. The author further agrees to indemnify the publisher against any costs arising from failure to uphold any of these warranties – a circumstance, in reality, that is rarely met and difficult to apply.

write down   A process whereby cash expended and accounted for as an asset on a balance sheet is revalued. Such value – of stocks, royalty advances and debtors – may be partially written down in value, or can be entirely written off.

Some publishing acronyms

AI	Advance Information (sheet)
ALCS	Authors Licensing and Collecting Society
AQ	Author's questionnaire
A&P	Advertising and promotion (budget)
CLA	Copyright Licensing Agency
CTA	Copyright transfer agreement
DACS	Design and Artists Copyright Society
IFRRO	International Federation of Reproduction Rights Organizations
MCPS	Mechanical Copyright Protection Society
MTA	Minimum Terms Agreement
PDF	Portable document file
PLR	Public Lending Right
PLS	Publishers Licensing Society
PPB	Paper, print and binding
PR	Public relations (budget)
PRS	Performing Right Society
RAE	Research assessment exercise
XML	Extensible markup language

INDEX

NB: page numbers in *italic* indicate figures or tables